C-1060   CAREER EXAMINATION SERIES

This is your
PASSBOOK for...

Special Agent FBI

Test Preparation Study Guide
Questions & Answers

NATIONAL LEARNING CORPORATION®

COPYRIGHT NOTICE

This book is SOLELY intended for, is sold ONLY to, and its use is RESTRICTED to individual, bona fide applicants or candidates who qualify by virtue of having seriously filed applications for appropriate license, certificate, professional and/or promotional advancement, higher school matriculation, scholarship, or other legitimate requirements of education and/or governmental authorities.

This book is NOT intended for use, class instruction, tutoring, training, duplication, copying, reprinting, excerption, or adaptation, etc., by:

1) Other publishers
2) Proprietors and/or Instructors of "Coaching" and/or Preparatory Courses
3) Personnel and/or Training Divisions of commercial, industrial, and governmental organizations
4) Schools, colleges, or universities and/or their departments and staffs, including teachers and other personnel
5) Testing Agencies or Bureaus
6) Study groups which seek by the purchase of a single volume to copy and/or duplicate and/or adapt this material for use by the group as a whole without having purchased individual volumes for each of the members of the group
7) Et al.

Such persons would be in violation of appropriate Federal and State statutes.

PROVISION OF LICENSING AGREEMENTS – Recognized educational, commercial, industrial, and governmental institutions and organizations, and others legitimately engaged in educational pursuits, including training, testing, and measurement activities, may address request for a licensing agreement to the copyright owners, who will determine whether, and under what conditions, including fees and charges, the materials in this book may be used them. In other words, a licensing facility exists for the legitimate use of the material in this book on other than an individual basis. However, it is asseverated and affirmed here that the material in this book CANNOT be used without the receipt of the express permission of such a licensing agreement from the Publishers. Inquiries re licensing should be addressed to the company, attention rights and permissions department.

All rights reserved, including the right of reproduction in whole or in part, in any form or by any means, electronic or mechanical, including photocopying, recording, or by any information storage and retrieval system, without permission in writing from the Publisher.

Copyright © 2024 by
National Learning Corporation

212 Michael Drive, Syosset, NY 11791
(516) 921-8888 • www.passbooks.com
E-mail: info@passbooks.com

PASSBOOK® SERIES

THE *PASSBOOK® SERIES* has been created to prepare applicants and candidates for the ultimate academic battlefield – the examination room.

At some time in our lives, each and every one of us may be required to take an examination – for validation, matriculation, admission, qualification, registration, certification, or licensure.

Based on the assumption that every applicant or candidate has met the basic formal educational standards, has taken the required number of courses, and read the necessary texts, the *PASSBOOK® SERIES* furnishes the one special preparation which may assure passing with confidence, instead of failing with insecurity. Examination questions – together with answers – are furnished as the basic vehicle for study so that the mysteries of the examination and its compounding difficulties may be eliminated or diminished by a sure method.

This book is meant to help you pass your examination provided that you qualify and are serious in your objective.

The entire field is reviewed through the huge store of content information which is succinctly presented through a provocative and challenging approach – the question-and-answer method.

A climate of success is established by furnishing the correct answers at the end of each test.

You soon learn to recognize types of questions, forms of questions, and patterns of questioning. You may even begin to anticipate expected outcomes.

You perceive that many questions are repeated or adapted so that you can gain acute insights, which may enable you to score many sure points.

You learn how to confront new questions, or types of questions, and to attack them confidently and work out the correct answers.

You note objectives and emphases, and recognize pitfalls and dangers, so that you may make positive educational adjustments.

Moreover, you are kept fully informed in relation to new concepts, methods, practices, and directions in the field.

You discover that you are actually taking the examination all the time: you are preparing for the examination by "taking" an examination, not by reading extraneous and/or supererogatory textbooks.

In short, this PASSBOOK®, used directedly, should be an important factor in helping you to pass your test.

SPECIAL AGENT FBI

DUTIES AND RESPONSIBILITIES
As the primary investigative arm of the federal government, the FBI is responsible for protecting the United States by preventing future terrorist attacks, conducting sensitive national security investigations, and enforcing over 260 federal statutes.

The FBI's top ten investigative priorities are:
1. Protect the United States from terrorist attack
2. Protect the United States against foreign intelligence operations and espionage
3. Protect the United States against cyber-based attacks and high-technology crimes
4. Combat public corruption at all levels
5. Protect civil rights
6. Combat transnational and national criminal organizations and enterprises
7. Combat major white-collar crime
8. Combat significant violent crime
9. Support federal, state, county, municipal and international partners
10. Upgrade technology to successfully perform the FBI's mission

While the FBI remains committed to other important national security and law enforcement responsibilities, the prevention of terrorism takes precedence in investigations.

The FBI also works with other federal, state and local law enforcement agencies in investigating matters of joint interest and in training law enforcement officers from around the world.

When you join the FBI, you join a united effort against crime. It's a rewarding career for anyone who has the ability and desire to contribute to the proud history and bright future of today's FBI.

To ensure that FBI Special Agents (SA) are fully prepared to meet their responsibilities as leaders in the law enforcement community, applicants must pass a standardized Physical Fitness Test (PFT). The test consists of the following four mandatory events: 1) one minute sit-ups; 2) a 300-meter sprint; 3) maximum push-ups; and 4) a 1.5-mile run. SA Applicants must pass the PFT in order to be eligible for admission into a New Agent Training (NAT) class.

The FBI Academy at Quantico, VA

Each new Agent serves a two-year probationary period upon entering on duty with the FBI. However, preference eligible veterans serve a one year probationary period. At the FBI Academy, you will join a class of Special Agent trainees for slightly over 18 weeks of intensive training at one of the world's finest law enforcement training facilities.

Your classroom hours will be spent studying a wide variety of academic and investigative subjects. The FBI Academy curriculum also includes intensive training in physical fitness, defensive tactics, practical application exercises, and the use of firearms. Several tests will be administered in all of these areas to monitor your progress.

Upon successful completion of Academy training, you will graduate and receive the credentials of an FBI Special Agent.

Your First Assignment

As a newly appointed Special Agent, you will be assigned to one of the FBI's field offices based on the current staffing and/or critical specialty needs. New Agents are permitted to make known their preference for assignment and consideration is given to your desires; however, assignment will be based upon the staffing needs of the FBI.

Your first months will be guided by a veteran Special Agent who will help you apply the lessons learned at the FBI Academy.

Advancement

Throughout your career with the FBI, you can qualify for additional training and promotion to a variety of administrative and supervisory positions.

Special Agents enter as GS 10 employees on the law enforcement government pay scale and can advance to the GS 13 grade level in field non-supervisory assignments. Promotions to supervisory, management, and executive positions are available in grades GS 14 and GS 15 as well as in the Senior Executive Service. All Special Agents may qualify for availability pay, which is an additional premium compensation for unscheduled duty equaling 25 percent of the Agent's base salary.

As an FBI employee, you will be entitled to a variety of benefits, including group health and life insurance programs, vacation and sick pay, and a full retirement plan.

QUALIFICATION REQUIREMENTS

Entry Requirements

To carry out its mission, the FBI needs men and women who can fill a variety of demanding positions. To qualify as an FBI Special Agent, you must be a U.S. citizen, or a citizen of the Northern Mariana Islands, at least age 23 and not have reached your 37th birthday on appointment. Candidates must be completely available for assignment anywhere in the FBI's jurisdiction. Candidates need to have at least 20/20 vision in one eye and not worse than 20/40 vision in the other eye. If an individual has a satisfactory history of soft contact lens wear and is able to meet correction to 20/20 in one eye and no worse than 20/40 in the other eye, safety concerns are considered mitigated and applicant processing may continue. In addition, policy for color vision allows continuation of applicant processing if those who fail initial color vision screening are able to successfully complete the Farnsworth D-15 color vision test.

If an applicant has had laser eye corrective surgery, a six month waiting period is required with evidence of complete healing by ophthalmology clinical evaluation.

Special Agent applicants also must meet hearing standards by audiometer test. No applicant will be considered who exceeds the following: a) average hearing loss of 25 decibels (ANSI) at 1000, 2000, and 3000 Hertz; b) single reading of 35 decibels at 1000, 2000, and 3000 Hertz; c) single reading of 35 decibels at 500 Hertz; and d) single reading of 45 decibels at 4000 Hertz.

Candidates must possess a valid driver's license, and be in excellent physical condition with no defects which would interfere in firearm use, raids, or defensive tactics.

Applicants must possess a four-year degree from a college or university accredited by one of the regional or national institutional associations recognized by the United States Secretary of Education.

Critical Skill Needs

Candidates who otherwise meet entry requirements and possess one or more of the following critical skills are currently deemed essential to address our increasingly complex responsibilities and will be prioritized in the hiring process.

1. Accounting
2. Computer Science and other Information Technology specialties
3. Engineering
4. Foreign Language proficiency (Arabic, Farsi, Pashtu, Urdu, Chinese [all dialects], Japanese, Korean, Russian, Spanish and Vietnamese)
5. Intelligence Experience
6. Law Experience
7. Law Enforcement or other Investigative Experience
8. Military Experience
9. Physical Sciences (Physics, Chemistry, Biology, etc.)

Although the above listing includes the most critical investigative skill needs, the FBI continues to be a diverse agency with employees possessing various experiences. Candidates who possess skills and experience such as accounting, law, business, education, and health care are also encouraged to apply.

Entry Programs

LAW

To qualify under the Law Program, you must have a JD degree from a resident law school.

ACCOUNTING/FINANCE

Any applicant who wishes to be considered for the Accounting Program may qualify when he/she either: 1) Has been certified as a CPA; OR 2) Possesses a four-year business degree with a major in accounting, or related business degree that included or was supplemented by 24 hours of accounting courses and an additional six semester hours of business law or other elective business courses, and two years of progressively responsible accounting work in a professional accounting firm or comparable public setting, such as a state comptroller or the General Accounting Office, the last which would be in a management, team leader or other type of position which would provide experiences in a variety of areas (banking, insurance, problem solving, etc.) and allow for exposure and experiences dealing with higher level organizational entities, i.e., partners and directors.

LANGUAGE

To qualify under the Language Program, you must have a BS or BA degree in any discipline and be proficient in a language that meets the needs of the FBI. Candidates will be expected to pass a Language Proficiency Test.

COMPUTER SCIENCE/INFORMATION TECHNOLOGY (CS/IT)

To qualify under the CS/IT Special Entry Program, the applicant must have a computer- or information technology-related degree, a degree in Electrical Engineering, a Cisco Certified Network Professional (CCNP) certification, or a Cisco Certified Internetworking Expert (CCIE) certification.

DIVERSIFIED

To qualify under the Diversified Program, you must have a BS or BA degree in any discipline, plus three years of full-time work experience, or an advanced degree accompanied by two years of full-time work experience.

Competitive candidates will complete a battery of written tests and, in some cases, specialized testing in your field of expertise. If you pass these tests, you may be eligible for an interview based upon your overall qualifications, your competitiveness among other candidates, and the needs of the FBI.

Successful completion of the written test and an interview will be followed by a thorough background investigation that will include: credit and arrest checks; interviews of associates; contacts with personal and business references, past employers and neighbors; and verification of educational achievements.

Just as some things can qualify you for a career as a Special Agent, some things can disqualify you. These may include: conviction of a felony or major misdemeanor; use of illegal drugs; or failure to pass a drug-screening test. All candidates will be given a polygraph examination to determine the veracity of information provided in the application for employment to include the extent of any illegal drug usage and issues surrounding security concerns.

Applicants must be U.S. citizens and consent to a complete background investigation, urinalysis, and polygraph. Only those candidates determined to be best qualified will be contacted to proceed in the selection process.

The FBI welcomes and encourages applications from persons with physical and mental disabilities and will reasonably accommodate the needs of those persons. The decision on granting reasonable accommodation will be on a case-by-case basis. The FBI is firmly committed to satisfying its affirmative obligations under the Rehabilitation Act of 1973, to ensure that persons with disabilities have every opportunity to be hired and advanced on the basis of merit within the FBI. The Federal Bureau of Investigation is an Equal Opportunity Employer. All qualified applicants will receive consideration for this vacancy. Except where otherwise provided by law, selection will be made without regard to, and there will be no discrimination because of race, religion, color, national origin, sex, political affiliations, marital status, non-disqualifying physical or mental disability, age, sexual orientation, membership or non-membership in an employee organization, or on the basis of personal favoritism or other non-merit factors.

SPECIAL AGENT FBI

APPLICANT INFORMATION
FBI SPECIAL AGENT SELECTION PROCESS

TABLE OF CONTENTS

Page

SECTION 1: FBI Special Agent Application and Selection Process

General Information	1
Qualifications for the Special Agent Position	1
FBI Employment Drug Policy	2
Special Agent Transfer Policy	3
Special Agent Firearms Policy	3
Special Agent Application and Selection Components	4
Retesting	5

SECTION II: Testing Process

Logistics and Procedures	5
Rules	6

SECTION III: Phase 1 Tests

Introduction to the Phase 1 Tests	7
Tips for Taking the Phase 1 Tests	8
Scoring	8
Biodata Inventory	8
Logical Reasoning Test	10
Situational Judgment Test	14

SECTION IV: Phase 2 Tests

Introduction to the Phase 2 Tests	15
Tips for Taking the Phase 2 Tests	15
Scoring	15
Structured Interview	15
Written Exercise	16

SPECIAL AGENT FBI

SECTION I: FBI SPECIAL AGENT APPLICATION AND SELECTION PROCESS

General Information

The Special Agent Selection Process consists of a variety of steps, and two sets of tests: Phase 1 and Phase 2 tests. The tests that will be administered as part of the selection process were developed to provide an assessment of critical skills and abilities that are required upon entry to the FBI Special Agent position. These critical skills and abilities on which Special Agent applicants will be assessed include:

A. Ability to Write Effectively
B. Ability to Communicate Orally
C. Ability to Organize, Plan, and Prioritize
D. Ability to Relate Effectively with Others
E. Ability to Maintain a Positive Image
F. Ability to Attend to Detail
G. Ability to Evaluate Information and Make Judgment Decisions
H. Initiative and Motivation
I. Ability to Adapt to Changing Situations
J. Physical Requirements

This section presents information on qualifications for the Special Agent position and describes general information about the application and selection process. Section II presents general information about the testing process. Then, Section III describes the tests included in Phase 1, while Section IV describes the tests included in Phase 2.

Qualifications for the Special Agent Position

Special Agent candidates must:
1. be a United States citizen or a citizen of the Northern Mariana Islands

2. be completely available for assignment anywhere in the Bureau's jurisdiction

3. have reached his/her 23rd but not his/her 37th birthday

4. have uncorrected vision not less than 20/200 (Snellen) and corrected 20/20 in one eye and at least 20/40 in the other eye. All applicants must pass a color vision test.

5. meet following hearing standards by audiometer test. No applicant will be considered who exceeds the following: (a) average hearing loss of 25 decibels (ANSI) at 1000, 2000, and 3000 Hertz; (b) single reading of 35 decibels at 1000, 2000, or 3000 Hertz; (c) single reading of 35 decibels at 500 Hertz; (d) single reading of 45 decibels at 4000 Hertz.

6. possess a valid driver's license

7. be physically able to engage in firearm use, raids, or defensive tactics

8. all candidates must possess a four-year degree from a resident college or university which is certified by one of the six Regional Accreditation Associations

Special Agent candidates must qualify under one or more of the following entrance programs:

LAW - law school graduates with two years of undergraduate work.

ACCOUNTING - graduate of a four-year college or university with a degree in accounting or degree in another discipline, preferably economics, business or finance, with a major in accounting. An applicant must also have passed the Uniform Certified Public Accountant examination or provide certification from the school at which the accounting degree or major was earned that he/she is academically eligible to sit for the above examination.

LANGUAGE - four-year college degree plus fluency in a foreign language(s) for which the Bureau has a current need.

DIVERSIFIED - four-year college degree plus three years of fulltit.1e work experience. Those individuals possessing an advanced degree need only two years work experience.

The following are automatic disqualifiers for the Special Agent position:

1. felony conviction

2. student loan in default (insured by U.S. Government)

FBI Employment Drug Policy

The Federal Bureau of Investigation is firmly committed to a drug-free society and workplace. Therefore, the unlawful use of drugs by FBI employees will not be tolerated. Furthermore, applicants for employment with the FBI who currently are using illegal drugs will be found unsuitable for employment. The FBI does not condone any prior unlawful drug use by applicants. The FBI realizes, however, some otherwise qualified applicants may have used drugs at some point in their past. The following policy sets forth the criteria for determining whether an applicant's prior use makes her/him unsuitable for employment, balancing the needs of the FBI to maintain a drug-free workplace and the public integrity necessary to accomplish its law enforcement mission, with the desirability of affording the opportunity of employment to the broadest segment of society consistent with those needs.

CRITERIA

1. An applicant who has illegally used any drug while employed in any law enforcement or prosecutorial position, or while employed in a position which carries with it a high level of responsibility or public trust, will be found unsuitable for employment.

2. An applicant who is discovered to have deliberately misrepresented her/his drug history in connection with her/his application will be found unsuitable for employment.

3. An applicant who has sold any illegal drug will be found unsuitable for employment.

4. An applicant who has illegally used any drug, other than experimental use of cannabis, within the past ten years will be found unsuitable for employment, absent compelling mitigating circumstances. Experimental use of drugs other than cannabis, which occurred more than ten years prior to the application for employment will be evaluated based upon the general factors specified below.

5. An applicant who has used cannabis within the past three years will be found unsuitable for employment. Experimental use of cannabis which occurred more than three years prior to the application for employment will be evaluated based upon the general factors specified below.

GENERAL FACTORS

1. The kind of position for which the person is applying, including the degree of public trust or risk in the position;
2. The nature and seriousness of the conduct;
3. The circumstances surrounding the conduct;
4. The decency of the conduct;
5. The age of the applicant at the time of the conduct;
6. Contributing societal conditions; and
7. The absence or presence of rehabilitation or efforts toward rehabilitation.

Special Agent Transfer Policy

The Director of the FBI maintains the authority to transfer any FBI employee when it is in the best interest of the United States Government. All Special Agents are subject to transfer at any time to meet the organizational and program needs of the FBI. FBI Special Agents accept the possibility of transfer as a condition of their employment. Special Agents may be transferred where and when the needs of the FBI may dictate. In this regard the overall needs of the Bureau, to include the assurance that investigatory experience levels are appropriately represented in all field offices, along with budgetary considerations, take precedence. The personal needs and preferences of the Agents are considered wherever possible in carrying out the transfer policy.

Special Agent Firearms Policy

In 1934, Congress authorized Special Agents of the Federal Bureau of Investigation to carry firearms under Title 18, USC, Section 3052. Special Agents are initially trained at the FBI Academy, Quantico, Virginia, for all aspects of the use and maintenance of firearms and related equipment under their control.

Special Agents must be armed or have immediate access to a firearm at all times when on official duty unless good judgment dictates otherwise. Special Agents may be required to utilize deadly force should circumstances dictate.

Special Agent Application and Selection Components

There are five main components to the selection process:

- INITIAL APPLICATION. All applicants will be required to complete a short form application titled, PRELIMINARY APPLICATION FOR SPECIAL AGENT POSITION (FD-646) and the Applicant Background Survey (FD-804). When complete, the initial application and Applicant Background Survey should be sent to the Applicant Coordinator at the FBI Field Office nearest to where you live.

  Applicants will be screened using this Initial Application to determine whether or not they meet the minimum qualifications outlined above. All applicants will be informed of their standing upon review of their applications. Those who are selected for further processing will be notified of this in advance by the Applicant Coordinator from the FBI Field Office nearest to them. They will be scheduled at a particular date, time, and location to take the Phase 1 tests.

- PHASE 1 TESTS. The first phase testing process consists of a battery of three tests, including: Biodata Inventory, Cognitive Ability Test, and Situational Judgment Test. These are all paper-and-pencil tests, and they are described in more detail in Section III. Individuals will be notified in writing whether they have passed or failed the first phase tests within 30 days. Those passing the first phase tests will be invited to submit the more lengthy application described next

- SUBMISSION OF APPLICATION FOR EMPLOYMENT (FD-140). Applicants who pass the Phase 1 tests will be notified by letter and asked to submit this application by a specific date. This application is titled, APPLICATION FOR EMPLOYMENT (FD-140). Applicants will again be informed of their standing at this point in the selection process. Those positively reviewed will be scheduled for the Phase 2 tests described below. Individuals will be notified of this by the Applicant Coordinator at the nearest FBI Field Office to them. They will be scheduled at a particular date, time, and location to take the Phase 2 tests.

- PHASE 2 TESTS. The second phase testing process consists of a Structured Selection Interview and a written exercise. Performance on these tests will be evaluated by FBI Special Agents, who will serve as assessors. Those who pass the second phase of tests will be sent a conditional offer of employment letter. However, final employment will be contingent on successful completion of the steps listed belowcation described next.

- FINAL APPLICANT SCREENING PROCESS. The final applicant screening process is comprised of several steps, including polygraph examination, full background investigation, drug test and pre employment physical examination. Each of these is described briefly.

- POLYGRAPH EXAMINATION. All applicants will be given a polygraph examination to determine the veracity of information contained in the APPLICATION FOR EMPLOYMENT (FD-140) to include the extent of any illegal drug usage and any issues regarding security concerns.

- **BACKGROUND INVESTIGATION.** All applicants will be afforded a full field background investigation that includes credit and criminal checks; interviews of associates; contacts with personal and business references; interviews of past employers and neighbors; and verification of educational achievements.

- **DRUG TESTING.** All applicants will be given a urine analysis to screen for drug usage.

- **PREEMPLOYMENT PHYSICAL EXAMINATION.** All applicants will be afforded a physical examination to determine physical suitability for the Special Agent position.

Retesting

All applicants who fail the Special Agent Written Test (Phase 1) are eligible to retest one year after the date of taking the test for the first time. Those applicants who pass the Special Agent Written Test (Phase 1) are eligible to proceed to the Structured Interview and writing sample (Phase 2); these applicants will only be allowed to take Phase 2 tests once.

SECTION II: TESTING PROCESS

Logistics and Procedures

When and Where. Phase 1 and Phase 2 tests will be administered at various locations throughout the United States. Applicant Coordinators at each FBI Field Office will coordinate the testing and inform applicants of the date, time, and location of their testing sessions.

How Long. It will take each candidate four hours to complete the Phase 1 tests and approximately three hours to complete the Phase 2 tests.

Travel Arrangements. Candidates will be required to make their own arrangements to travel to the testing location.

Scheduling. Applicants will generally be given a 30 day notice of their scheduled testing date, time, and location.

Only under exceptional circumstances will testing appointments be rescheduled. Since applicants will be notified of their scheduled date in advance, every effort should be made to be available at the scheduled time. If applicants have an important conflict with their scheduled appointment, they should notify the FBI Applicant Coordinator whose name will be provided on correspondence immediately to schedule an alternative date.

Tardiness. It is an applicant's responsibility to arrive on time for the scheduled appointment. If candidates are tardy, they will not be permitted to participate in the testing process, since the testing will be run on a strict time schedule.

What To Bring. Candidates must bring a driver's license to Phase 1 and Phase 2 testing. Applicants will not be permitted to participate in the testing process without proper identification. Applicants who have prior military service may also bring their Form DD 214, Certificate of Release or Discharge from Active Duty, to Phase 1 testing, if applicable. Applicants who carry firearms (i.e., who are in law enforcement positions) must NOT bring their firearm into FBI space or the testing facility.

Do not bring any of the following:
- This book
- Reference materials (dictionaries, textbooks, etc.)
- Pens or pencils (These will be provided)
- Reading materials (books, magazines, newspapers)
- Work-related materials
- Beepers/pagers (alarms on watches must be turned off)
- Papers (notification letter, notes, blank paper)
- Tape-recorder, cassette, or compact disc player, radio, calculator, camera
- Cellular telephones

What to Wear.

- Phase 1 Testing. Candidates are encouraged to dress in comfortable clothing.
- Phase 2 Testing. Candidates should dress in a professional manner. Business attire would be appropriate.

Rules

Restroom Use. Applicants may use the restrooms during breaks and not during administration of the tests.

Eating/Drinking. Eating and drinking will not be permitted during the testing, but will be allowed during breaks. Chewing gum or tobacco is discouraged during the interview, since oral communication skills will be evaluated as part of this exercise.

Phone Use. Candidates will not be permitted to use the telephone during the testing process. Do not bring beepers.

Leaving the Premises. Candidates will not be permitted to leave the testing premises during the testing. All breaks will be relatively short.

Talking. Once the orientation period has begun, applicants will not be permitted to talk with other applicants at any time during testing.

Discussing the Tests. Applicants should not discuss the examinations with anyone during or after the testing process. Discussing the tests may give others unfair advantages or disadvantages in the selection process.

Smoking. Smoking will not be permitted during the testing.

Time Limits. The time limits which have been set for the various tests will be strictly enforced. When time is called, applicants must immediately stop what they are doing and await further instructions.

FAILURE TO COMPLY WITH THESE RULES MAY RESULT IN DISQUALIFICATION.

SECTION III: PHASE 1 TESTS

Introduction to the Phase 1 Tests

When applicants arrive for the testing process, they will be checked in and asked to provide their driver's license. The license will be held by the Test Administrator until the testing is complete. A trained FBI employee will run the testing session. Three paper and-pencil multiple choice tests comprise the Phase 1 testing process. These are:

- Biodata (Biographical Data) Inventory
- Logical Reasoning Test
- Situational Judgment Test

When the testing process begins, applicants will be given one machine scan able answer sheet on which responses to all of the tests will be recorded. Different sections of the answer sheet are labeled for recording responses to each of the different tests.

On the answer sheet, applicants will be asked to print their last names, first names, and middle initials and then sign the form in a signature block. Applicants will also be asked to record their complete street address, city, state, and zip code on the answer sheet. The date and each applicant's Social Security Number will also be recorded on the answer form.

All information on the machine scan able forms must be filled in accurately, using only a #2 pencil that will be provided. Scratch paper will also be provided by test administrators. The answer ovals on the form must be filled in completely with dark, black marks. Any mistakes or stray marks must be completely erased. Failure to fill out the machine scan able forms properly may preclude the tests from being scored properly.

Once the general information on the answer form has been completed, each test will be administered in turn. The Test Administrator will distribute numbered test booklets, read instructions for the test, and answer any questions. Each test will begin when the Test Administrator indicates that timing for the test has started. When the time limit for the test has been reached, the administrator will call time. All applicants must cease working on their tests at that time and close their test booklets.

On the following pages, more information is provided about each test. Specifically, we provide a copy of the directions for each test and also the critical skills and abilities being measured. A manual has been prepared by the FBI to help applicants prepare for taking the Logical Reasoning Test. This Special Agent Exam Preparation Manual is free of charge and available through the FBI Applicant Coordinators.

Note: There are different versions of each test, only one of which you will receive. The tests look similar on the surface but are not. Therefore, any information regarding the tests that you obtain from others may be misleading and could harm your performance.

Tips for Taking the Phase 1 Tests:

- Read each question carefully.
- The time limits established for the Bidet Inventory and Situational Judgment Test should allow applicants to finish those tests without being rushed. However, you should work through the items efficiently.
- Work as quickly and as accurately as you can to complete as many items as possible. You should not spend too much time on anyone item.
- You will not be penalized for guessing answers on any of the tests.
- For the Biodata Inventory, it is very important that you answer the questions honestly. Do not choose what you think are the best answers; just describe yourself accurately. Doing otherwise will distort your test score and negatively affect your performance.

Scoring

Scoring. Scores on the Logical Reasoning Test, Biodata Inventory, and Situational Judgment Test will be combined to arrive at a final test score. The Biodata and Situational Judgment Test will be weighted twice as much as the Logical Reasoning Test in arriving at the final Phase 1 score. This is because the Biodata and Situational Judgment Test provide an assessment of a greater number of critical job skills than does the Logical Reasoning Test. A passing score has been established that will be applied uniformly to all applicants taking the test. There is one passing score that is based on the combination of all three tests rather than individual passing scores for each test. Thus, a very high score on one test can compensate for a lower score on another test.

Each applicant will be notified about his/her pass or fail status within 30 days of taking the tests. The actual test scores will not be disseminated. Those who pass the tests will be instructed regarding the next steps.

BIODATA INVENTORY

Directions for the Biodata Inventory are as follows:

This inventory contains 47 questions about yourself.

You are to read each question and select the answer that BEST describes you from the choices provided. Answer the questions honestly; doing otherwise will negatively affect your score.

Look at the example question below.

S1. In connection with your work, in which of the following have you taken the most pride?

    A. Having been able to avoid any major controversies.
    B. Having gotten where you are on your own.
    C. Having been able to work smoothly with people.
    D. Having provided a lot of new ideas, good or bad.
    E. Having been able to do well whatever management has requested.

In this example, you would select the answer that BEST describes what YOU honestly take pride in with regard to your work. You would completely blacken the oval corresponding to your answer selection (A, B, C, D, or E).

You will have 45 minutes to complete this inventory.

You will record your answer to each question on the separate machine readable answer sheet in the section marked Biodata Inventory. Be sure to fill in the ovals you select completely with dark marks. As you are completing this inventory, please DO NOT write in the test booklet.

Two example biodata items are:

In connection with your work, in which of the following have you taken the most pride?

- A. Having been able to avoid any major controversies.
- B. Having gotten where you are on your own.
- C. Having been able to work smoothly with people.
- D. Having provided a lot of new ideas, good or bad.
- E. Having been able to do well whatever management has requested.

When in a position at work or school which necessitated making decisions that affected others, how would others describe you?

- A. As someone who appeared to weigh all logical alternatives before making a decision in a timely manner.
- B. As someone who weighed all alternatives, but may have taken a long time to come to a decision.
- C. As someone who makes decisions quickly without weighing the alternatives.
- D. I have never been in this type of position

This test measures the following critical skills and abilities:
- Ability to Organize, Plan, and Prioritize
- Ability to Maintain a Positive Image
- Ability to Evaluate Information and Make Judgment Decisions
- Initiative and Motivation
- Ability to Adapt to Changing Situations
- Physical Requirements

LOGICAL REASONING TEST

General directions for the Logical Reasoning Test are as follows:

Each of the questions in the Logical Reasoning Test contains a reading passage followed by a lead-in phrase that introduces five response choices.

The Reading Passage

Questions in the Logical Reasoning Test are based on subject matter relevant to the Special Agent occupation but do not require job knowledge and do not always reflect true-to-fact job procedures. Therefore, in selecting your response, it is important that you accept every fact in the reading passage as true and that you use *only* the information given in the passage. Remember that you will not be judged on your knowledge of facts but rather on your ability to reason on the basis of given facts.

The Lead-In Phrase and the Response Choices

A lead-in phrase will follow every reading passage. This lead-in phrase will ask you to complete a sentence by selecting one among five response choices.

The lead-in phrase can be affirmative or negative:

- *From the information given above, it can be validly concluded that*
  OR
- *From the information given above, it CANNOT be validly concluded that*

It is important that you focus on the lead-in phrase in order to determine whether the question is affirmative or negative.

Affirmative lead-in phrases are followed by four invalid conclusions and one valid conclusion. Your task is to identify the valid conclusion. Negative lead-in phrases, on the contrary, are followed by four valid conclusions and one invalid conclusion, which will be your task to identify.

The lead-in phrase may also affect the response choices by circumscribing the inference to a certain set or situation. For example, the lead-in phrase *From the information given above it can be validly concluded that official court leave is granted to agents when* circumscribes the response choices to the context of circumstances in which official court leave is granted to agents.

LOGICAL REASONING TEST DIRECTIONS

To answer each question on the logic-based reasoning test, select the answer representing the only valid statement that can be made from the information contained in the paragraph. To identify the correct conclusion, it is essential that you use ONLY the information provided in the content paragraph.

Record your answer to each question on the machine-readable answer sheet. Make sure to completely fill in the circle that corresponds with your answer. You should provide only one answer for each question. Please do not write in the test booklet.

You have 90 minutes to read the questions and provide your responses. Do not start until I have instructed you to do so. I will give you a warning when you have one hour, 30 minutes, and 5 minutes remaining to complete the logical based reasoning test questions.

SAMPLE QUESTIONS

Question 1
Eventually, most citizens are summoned to serve on jury duty. If a government employee is asked to serve on a jury, official court leave is authorized with no charge to leave or loss of pay. Also, official court leave is always granted if the employee is summoned to appear as a witness in a judicial proceeding in which the government is a party. No fees rendered for service can be retained by the employee. Rather, they must be turned in to the agency in which he or she is employed. However, some payments designated as expenses by the courts, such as travel reimbursements, may be kept.

From the information given above, it can be validly concluded that official court leave

- A) is not granted to individuals other than government employees who are summoned to serve as jurors or to appear as witnesses in judicial proceedings in which the government is a party
- B) sometimes entails retention by government employees of fees received from the court for services rendered as jurors
- C) is never accompanied by reimbursement for expenses incurred by government employees while serving as witnesses in judicial proceedings in which the government is a party
- D) never entails loss of pay by government employees who are summoned to serve as jurors or to appear as witnesses in judicial proceedings in which the government is a party
- E) is not always granted to government employees who are summoned to appear as witnesses in judicial proceedings in which the government is a party

The correct response is D. The information in the passage establishes two conditions under which court leave is authorized for government employees without charge to leave or loss of pay: (1) if the employee is asked to serve on a jury and (2) if the employee is summoned to appear as a witness in a judicial proceeding in which the government is a party. Response D reiterates this statement in negative form: *Official court leave never entails loss of pay by government employees who are summoned to serve as jurors or to appear as witnesses in judicial proceedings in which the government is a party.*

Response A is incorrect because the passage gives no information about court leave policies for non-government employees.

Response B is incorrect because it contradicts the information in the passage, which states that no fees rendered for service as a juror can be retained by a government employee.

Response C is incorrect because it contradicts the information in the passage, which states that some payments designated as expenses by the courts, such as travel reimbursements, may be kept by a government employee.

Response E is incorrect because it is contrary to the information in the passage, which establishes that official court leave is always granted to government employees if they are asked to serve on a jury or if they are summoned as a witness in a judicial proceeding in which the government is a party.

Question # 1 is an example of an easy question in which three of the incorrect response choices contradict the information in the passage, while one incorrect response (response A) is based on unwarranted assumptions about a set of individuals that is not discussed in the passage. More difficult errors of reasoning are illustrated in the next two sample questions.

Question 2
Whenever an investigator is involved in an intelligence operation, he or she is required to examine multiple hypotheses, thus avoiding the quick pursuit of only one path, which could turn out to be incorrect. In a recent terrorism case, which thus far has proved to be exceptionally complex and remains unresolved, several hypotheses were initially generated about the suspects, conspirators, motives, and implementation of the terrorist act. Most of these hypotheses have been disproved.

From the information given above, it can be validly concluded that

- A) in any intelligence operation, an investigator who generates more than one hypothesis is more likely than not to succeed
- B) at least one of the hypotheses generated for the terrorism case mentioned above is not likely to be disproved
- C) if an investigator is not required to examine multiple hypotheses about a case, then he or she is not involved in an intelligence operation
- D) whenever an investigator fails to solve a case, it can be assumed that, most probably, he/she failed to generate more than one hypothesis about the case
- E) there are at least some investigative operations, other than those concerned with intelligence, that do not require the investigator to form more than one hypothesis

This question presents two aspects. One is the mandate to generate multiple hypotheses whenever an investigator conducts an intelligence operation. The second aspect is the interplay of possibilities and probabilities relative to the forming of hypotheses. The correct response, C, deals with the first aspect, while three of the four incorrect response choices deal with the second aspect. In the correct response, C, the inference (formally called a contra positive inference) represents a negative equivalent of the mandate found in the first sentence of the passage. The first sentence states an antecedent condition ("whenever an investigator is involved in an intelligence operation") from which follows a consequent condition ("he or she is required to examine multiple hypotheses"). If we transpose and negate these two conditions, as is done in C, we obtain an equivalent statement, in which the truth value of the original statement is retained.

Responses A, B, and D are based on unwarranted probabilistic inferences about (1) the likelihood that an investigator who generates more than one hypothesis will succeed (response A), the likelihood that at least one hypothesis will not be disproved in the terrorism case (response B), and the likelihood that an investigator who fails to solve a case will have failed to generate more than one hypothesis about it (response D). The passage provides no quantifying information from which such probabilistic inferences can be made. It only alludes to the *possibility* that a single hypothesis may be incorrect, which cannot be extrapolated into probabilities. In the context of probabilities, you should note that this test will not contain quantitative problems. You need to be alert only to verbal quantifying expressions such as "more likely than not," "unlikely," "most probably," etc.

Finally, in the case of response E, it is incorrect because the passage provides no information at all about investigative operations that may fall outside the set of intelligence operations.

Question 3
All forensic soil examiners compare the color, texture, and composition of two or more soils to determine if they share a common origin. Suppose, for example, that the suspect in a murder claims that soil recovered from her shovel-which actually came from a grave that she dug-was from her garden. The garden will be eliminated as the source of the soil on the shovel if and only if this soil is found to be dissimilar to soil samples taken from the garden.

From the information given above, it CANNOT be validly concluded that

- A) upon analysis and comparison, the soil samples taken from the shovel and the garden of the above-mentioned suspect will be dissimilar if the grave was not dug in the garden
- B) analysts who are not involved in the comparison of soil samples are not forensic soil examiners
- C) if, as a result of analysis and comparison, the suspect's garden is confirmed as the source of the soil on the shovel, then the soil samples taken from the garden and the shovel were found to be similar
- D) if an analyst is involved in the comparison of soil samples, then he or she will be classified as a forensic soil examiner
- E) if the soil samples taken from the shovel and the garden of the above-mentioned suspect are similar, then it can be assumed that the grave was dug in the garden

This question is an example of a difficult question. In the first place, it asks you to identify the only response choice that *does not* follow from the given information, which in and of itself makes the question slightly more difficult to analyze. Nonetheless, the difficulty of the question stems primarily from the logical complexity of its response choices. (If you are asking yourself why such complex reasoning must be included in the test, please bear in mind that the reason is, exclusively, relevance to the job. The information you will have to analyze on the job, including that found in legal manuals, will be generally as complex as this question, and frequently more so.)

The correct response is D. It represents the only fallacy found among the response choices. The fallacy is formally called a converse fallacy. The passage states that *all forensic soil examiners compare the color, texture, and composition of two or more soils*. From this information nothing can be concluded about whether or not there are analysts other than forensic soil examiners who carry out such comparisons. The information in the passage tells us only that the set of *forensic soil examiners* is entirely included in the set of *analysts who carry out soil comparisons* but tells us nothing about the composition or extension of the second set.

Response A is not a fallacy. The passage states (1) that the suspect's garden will be eliminated as the source of soil on the shovel if and only if this soil is found to be dissimilar to soil samples taken from the garden and (2) that the soil on the shovel came from a grave that the suspect dug. It follows that the soil samples will be dissimilar if the grave was not dug in the garden.

In the context of this question and this response, it is pertinent to note the use of the biconditional *if and only if*. A biconditional statement is defined as one in which the conditions included in the statement are interchangeable without affecting the truth value of the statement. Thus, to say that *the suspect's garden will be eliminated as the source of soil on the shovel if and only if this soil is found to be dissimilar to soil samples taken from the garden* is the same as saying that *the soil on the shovel will be found to be dissimilar to soil samples taken from the garden if and only if the garden is eliminated as the source of soil on the shovel*. This interchangeability of conditions permits the inference in response C: The statement in the passage establishes that *the suspect's garden will be eliminated as the source of soil on the shovel if and only if this soil is found to be dissimilar to soil samples taken from the garden*. It follows that *if the garden is confirmed as the source of the soil on the shovel, then this soil must be similar to soil samples taken from the garden*. In symbols, when we say *p if and only if q*, we are saying both that *if p then q and if q then p*. Hence, if we negate *p*, the negation of *q* must follow.

Both response B and response E illustrate the same type of inference that was illustrated before in question # 2 (Response C) except that, in question # 3, response B illustrates the inference (formally called a contra positive) in the context of sets, while response E illustrates it in the context of a conditional statement. These are discussed immediately below.

Relative to response B, the passage states that all forensic soil examiners analyze and compare soil samples. The transposed negative equivalent of this statement follows necessarily: analysts who are not involved in the comparison of soil samples are not forensic soil examiners.

Relative to response E, it represents the transposed negative equivalent of the statement in response A and hence retains the same truth value. Response A states that *if the grave was not dug in the garden then the soil samples taken from the shovel and the garden will be dissimilar*. Response E transposes and negates these conditions: *if the soil samples taken from the shovel and the garden are similar, then it can be assumed that the grave was dug in the garden*.

SITUATIONAL JUDGMENT TEST

General directions for the Situational Judgment Test are as follows:

This booklet contains 33 descriptions of problem situations. Each problem situation has between three and five alternative actions that might be taken to deal with the problem. You are to make two judgments for each problem.

First, decide which alternative you would MOST LIKELY choose in response to the problem. It might not be exactly what you would do in that situation, but it should be the alternative that comes closest to what you would actually do. Record your answers on the answer sheet by blackening the appropriate letter in the column labeled MOST LIKELY.

Second, decide which alternative you would be LEAST LIKELY to choose in that situation. Blacken the letter of that alternative in the column labeled LEAST LIKELY.

As you are taking the test, please DO NOT write in the test booklet. All of your responses will be recorded on the separate answer sheet in the section marked Situational Judgment Test. Be sure to fill in the ovals you select completely with dark black marks. You will have 1 hour and 30 minutes to complete this test.

Here is an example item:

You are shopping when you notice a man robbing the store. What would you do?

A. Leave the store as quickly as possible and call the police.
B. Try to apprehend the robber yourself.
C. Follow the man and call the police as soon as he appears settled somewhere.
D. Nothing, as you do not wish to get involved in the matter.

As shown in the example below, the respondent thought alternative B was the action that she would most likely take in the situation and thus, blackened the B for item 1 in the MOST LIKELY column. The respondent thought alternative D was the least likely thing she would do. Thus, the D was filled in for item 1 in the LEAST LIKELY column.

This test measures the following critical skills and abilities:

- Ability to Organize, Plan, and Prioritize
- Ability to Relate Effectively with Others
- Ability to Maintain a Positive Image
- Ability to Evaluate Information and Make Judgment Decisions Initiative and Motivation
- Ability to Adapt to Changing Situations

SECTION IV: PHASE 2 TESTS

Introduction to the Phase 2 Tests

Only applicants who pass the Phase 1 tests and are informed that they are still being considered in the selection process will take the Phase 2 tests. When applicants arrive for the testing process, they will be checked in and asked to provide their driver's license. This license will be held by the Test Administrator until the testing is complete. A trained FBI employee will run the testing session. Two tests comprise the Phase 2 testing process. These are:

- Structured Interview
- Written Exercise

On the following pages, more information is provided about each test, including the critical skills and abilities being measured by the tests.

Tips for Taking the Phase 2 Tests

- Be yourself.
- The evaluators will be taking notes during the interview to assist them in documenting the exercises. Do not let this distract you.
- Do not make assumptions about what the evaluators are looking for. The interview instructions are straight forward. There are no trick questions.
- Read the written exercise instructions carefully. Make sure you understand what the exercise requires. Do not go beyond the material which is provided; that is, do not make up facts.
- You may write on the written exercise materials.
- You should ask the administrator any questions you have regarding instructions for the tests.

Scoring

Scores on the Structured Interview and written exercise will be combined to arrive at a final score. The Interview will be weighted three times as much as the written exercise, which is a relatively narrow test measuring only a few critical skills and abilities required for the job. A passing score has been established that will be applied uniformly to all applicants taking the test. There is one passing score that is based on combined interview and written simulation performance rather than individual passing scores for each test.

STRUCTURED INTERVIEW
TIME LIMIT: 1 HOUR

The structured interview consists of 16 standard questions that will be asked of applicants. The interview will be administered by a panel of three evaluators. The interview will take one hour to administer and an additional 20 minutes to score. The evaluators will be FBI Special Agents who have been trained thoroughly how to rate the applicant's performance on the interview using standardized scoring criteria. After the Structured Interview is complete, the three evaluators will provide independent ratings of each applicant's performance. After the independent ratings have been made, the three evaluators will compare their ratings and resolve any discrepancies. The final consensus ratings will serve as the applicant's score.

When the applicant enters the room with the three member panel, the following directions will be read:

"We'd like to spend the next hour getting to know more about you. During the interview, we will ask you to tell us how you've dealt with various different kinds of situations in the past. In answering our questions, you can describe family, work, school, or social situations and how you handled them. We'd like you to tell us what you did in the situation, even if it was a team effort. We will be asking you 16 questions. Feel free to take a few moments to think about the answer you would like to give for each question. You'll be doing most of the talking during the interview.

One final instruction before we start. In response to each question, please be as specific and detailed as possible in describing the situation, your actions, and the outcome of your actions."

The interview will then commence. The panel members will rotate in asking questions of the interviewee, in turn. If an applicant cannot think of an answer to a question, the interviewer will suggest that they move onto the next question and return to the question that could not be answered at the end of the interview. As long as the interviewee provides an answer at some point, she/he will not be penalized. If, however, the interviewee fails to answer one or more questions prior to the end of the interview, this will adversely affect his or her scores.

The interview measures the following critical skills and abilities:

- Ability to Communicate Orally
- Ability to Organize, Plan, and Prioritize
- Ability to Relate Effectively with Others
- Ability to Maintain a Positive Image
- Ability to Evaluate Information and Make Judgment Decisions
- Initiative and Motivation
- Ability to Adapt to Changing Situations
- Physical Requirements

WRITTEN EXERCISE
TIME LIMIT: 90 MINUTES

At the start of this exercise, the following materials will be distributed to each applicant:

- Written exercise instructions
- Summaries of interviews
- List of Approved Reimbursements
- List of Approved Charges
- Summary of Expenses Submitted

A checklist will accompany these materials describing the contents. Applicants will record their Social Security Number on the checklist and then compare this listing against the actual materials. If any materials are missing, you should raise your hand for assistance. Applicants will be asked to initial the checklist to verify that all of the materials were provided.

In this exercise, the applicant is to assume that she/he is an investigative reporter working for a large metropolitan newspaper. Recently, a tip was received from a person who believed that a company was being overcharged for services. The materials provided to applicants are reports of several interviews and records relevant to this case. Convinced that there is clear evidence of overcharging, the applicant's job is to write a memorandum to convince the editor of the newspaper to allow him/her to write an article on the case.

In preparing the response, be sure to write legibly. Responses cannot be evaluated if they cannot be read.

This exercise measures the following skills and abilities:

- Ability to Communicate in Writing
- Ability to Attend to Detail
- Ability to Evaluate and Make Judgment Decisions

QUESTIONS & ANSWERS ON THE FBI

1. When was the FBI founded?
    In 1908, Attorney General Charles Bonaparte directed that Department of Justice investigations be handled by a small group of special investigators. This group was formed as the Bureau of Investigation and, in 1935, the present name of Federal Bureau of Investigation was designed by Congress.

2. Who is the head of the FBI?
    The head of the FBI is the Director.

3. How is the Director of the FBI appointed to his office?
    Legislation enacted in June 1968 provides that the Director of the FBI shall be appointed by the President with the advice and consent of the Senate.

4. What guidelines were used in setting up the FBI as a career service?
    FBI positions are filled on the basis of ability and character without political interference, and performance and achievement are the requirements for promotion within the organization.

5. What safeguards are there against abuses of authority by the FBI and its Director?
    The FBI's activities and operations are under constant scrutiny and review by the Attorney General, committees of Congress, the Office of Management and Budget, the courts, and the Nation's press.

ADMINISTRATIVE MATTERS

6. What kind of training do FBI Agents receive?
    All FBI Agents initially must graduate from a 15-week course at the FBI Academy located on the U.S. Marine Corps Base at Quantico, Virginia. It is a tough and demanding course in which the new Agent receives intensified training in such diverse subjects as Constitutional law, Federal criminal procedure, collection and preservation of evidence, investigative techniques, scientific crime detection, firearms, and defensive tactics. Periodically throughout an Agent's career he or she will receive refresher training designed to keep him or her up to date on the latest procedures and techniques of their profession.

7. Why is law a desirable educational qualification for the Special Agent position?
    In addition to having a knowledge of a suspect's rights and the applicability of Federal law to a given situation, FBI Agents must, during the course of a criminal investigation, collect evidence which is legally admissible to prove the guilt of the criminal. A legal education provides training in analyzing a set of facts and applying laws and regulations to them.

8. Why is accounting an alternate educational qualification for the Special Agent position?

Accounting is an alternative educational requirement because investigations of many matters under the jurisdiction of the FBI, such as bank embezzlements, frauds against the government, tort claims, Renegotiation Act cases, and other white-collar crimes require expert knowledge of accounting practices and procedures.

9. Does the FBI investigate domestic terrorism that originates in foreign countries?

Yes.

10. How often are Special Agents rotated in their assignments?

There are no specific tours of duty. Special Agent assignments are based upon the needs of the Bureau, and Agents must be available at any time for general or special assignment anywhere in the United States or its territories.

FBI JURISDICTION

11. What are the primary functions of the FBI and its Agents?

The FBI investigates violations of certain Federal statutes, collects evidence in cases in which the United States is or may be an interested party, and performs other duties specifically imposed by law or Presidential directive.

12. Then the FBI does not investigate all violations of Federal and Constitutional law?

True. The FBI can investigate a matter only when it has authority to do so under a law passed by Congress or on instructions of the President or the Attorney General.

13. What is the FBI's jurisdiction in the field of organized crime?

Most of the Federal statutes enacted to combat organized crime are aimed at eradicating interstate gambling, large-scale intrastate gambling, hoodlum loan-sharking, gangland infiltration of legitimate business, and interstate travel in aid of racketeering. Other statutes often utilized are those dealing with interstate transportation of stolen property, fraudulent bankruptcies and bank loans, extortion, thefts from interstate shipments, and labor racketeering.

14. What does the FBI do with facts and evidence gathered during an investigation?

If a possible violation of Federal law under the jurisdiction of the FBI has occurred, the FBI will conduct an investigation and thereafter present the facts of the case to the appropriate United States Attorney or Department of Justice official who will determine whether or not prosecution or further action is warranted. The FBI does not give an opinion or decide whether an individual will be prosecuted.

15. Are the CIA and the Secret Service part of the FBI?

No. The FBI is the investigative arm of the Department of Justice. The Secret Service is an agency of the Treasury Department, while the Central Intelligence Agency is an independent member of the Executive branch of the government.

16. Does an FBI Agent have powers of arrest or any authority outside the United States and its territories?
    No.

17. Does the FBI investigate matters involving narcotics or income tax violations?
    No. Narcotics are under the jurisdiction of the Drug Enforcement Administration in the Justice Department, while the Treasury Department handles tax matters. As a matter of cooperation, however, information developed by the FBI during the course of its investigations that relates to matters handled by other Federal, state, or local agencies is promptly disseminated to the agency having primary investigative responsibility.

18. Isn't the FBI a type of national police force?
    Definitely not. The FBI is a fact-finding organization investigating violations of Federal laws and its authority is strictly limited to matters within its jurisdiction.

19. Wouldn't a national police agency be the most effective force against crime?
    No. The same objective can be accomplished through cooperation of the various law enforcement agencies without surrendering to the democratically repugnant concept of a centralized, powerful police force.

20. What authority do FBI Agents have to make arrests?
    FBI Agents may make arrests without a warrant for any Federal offense committed in their presence, or when they have reasonable grounds to believe that the person to be arrested has committed or is attempting to commit a felony violation of United States laws. Agents may also make arrests by warrant.

21. What is the general policy of the FBI regarding arrests by Agents?
    Agents do not make arrests for *investigation* or *on suspicion.* Before arrests are made, if at all possible, the facts of each case are presented to the United States Attorney who decides whether or not a Federal violation has occurred and, if so, he may authorize Agents to file a complaint which serves as the basis of the arrest warrant.

22. How can I get a FBI security clearance?
    The FBI does not issue security clearances. It does conduct applicant-type investigations in certain cases at the request of other government agencies concerning individuals requiring security clearances. The results of these investigations are furnished to the requesting agency which then decides whether or not to grant the individual a security clearance.

23. Does the FBI propose passage of new laws it feels are necessary to fight crime?
    No. Proposing new legislation such as this is the responsibility of the Department of Justice; however, on the basis of investigative experience, the FBI may furnish comments or observations on legislative matters to the Department of Justice for its consideration.

24. Can the FBI be *called in* to investigate a serious crime, such as murder, when the local police are unable to solve the case?

No. The FBI has no authority to investigate local crimes that are not within FBI jurisdiction. The FBI will, however, render all possible assistance to the local police through the FBI Laboratory and Identification Division.

25. Briefly, what is the function of the FBI in the field of civil rights?

It is to objectively investigate alleged violations of the civil rights statutes within FBI jurisdiction and furnish the results of these investigations to the Department of Justice for a determination of whether further action or prosecution is desired.

26. If a crime is committed that is a violation of both local and federal laws, does the FBI *take over* the investigation?

No. State and local law enforcement agencies are not subordinate to the FBI and the FBI has no authority over them. Through cooperation, the investigative resources of the FBI and the local agency are pooled in a common effort to solve the case.

27. Are not FBI informants employees of the Bureau, much the same as Special Agents, except that they conduct only undercover investigations?

No. Informants are not hired or trained employees of the FBI, although they may receive compensation in some instances for their expenses and information. Informants are simply individuals who furnish information to the FBI on a confidential basis.

CRIMINAL INVESTIGATIONS

28. If a crime is committed on a military reservation, what is the jurisdiction of the FBI?

Generally, if only military personnel are involved, the matter will be handled by military authorities, unless the crime concerns government property or funds, in which case the FBI has jurisdiction. The FBI also has responsibility when only civilians not subject to military law are involved.

29. Does the FBI investigate ALL bank robberies?

The FBI has jurisdiction over robberies of financial institutions which are (1) members of the Federal Reserve System; (2) insured by the Federal Deposit Insurance Corporation or Federal Savings and Loan Insurance Corporation; **(3)** organized under the laws of the United States; or **(4)** federally insured credit unions.

30. If a child is missing under circumstances indicating that a kidnapping has occurred, but no interstate transportation is known, will the FBI begin an investigation?

Yes. The law provides that unless the victim is located or released within 24 hours, it is presumed that he has been transported interstate.

31. Isn't it true that the criminal work of the FBI is concerned with only serious Federal crimes such as bank robbery, kidnapping, and extortion?

No. The FBI's jurisdiction includes a wide range of responsibilities in both the criminal and security fields.

32. Does the FBI advocate payment of money that may be demanded by a criminal in an extortion or kidnapping case?

This is a decision that must be made by the family or person from whom the ransom is being demanded.

33. Does the FBI have any authority to investigate crimes involving thefts of large sums of money, jewelry or property?

Under the Interstate Transportation of Stolen Property Statute, the FBI investigates cases wherein stolen property valued at more than $5,000 is transported across state lines.

34. What is the basis for the FBI's jurisdiction in bombing cases?

Bombing investigations conducted by the FBI are handled primarily under the provisions of the Organized Crime Control Act of 1970. This Act, among other provisions, prohibits the use of explosives or incendiary devices against property used by the Federal government, federally funded activities, or activities which affect interstate commerce.

35. On what basis does the FBI select its *ten most wanted fugitives*?

This selection is based on several items, including the fugitive's past criminal record, the threat posed to the community, the seriousness of the crime for which the fugitive is sought, and whether nationwide publicity is likely to assist in apprehension.

36. Why does the FBI conduct investigations to locate some criminals under the Unlawful Flight Statute and not others?

The fugitive must be wanted by local authorities for prosecution, or confinement after conviction, for a crime which is a felony. Local authorities must have information that the individual has fled interstate, request FBI assistance to locate him, and agree to extradite and prosecute upon apprehension.

37. Does the FBI investigate graft and corruption in local government and in state and local police departments?

In certain instances, the FBI does investigate graft and corruption in local government and in state and local police departments under the Hobbs Act of the Anti-Racketeering Statute, the Interstate Transportation in Aid of Racketeering Statute, and the Organized Crime Control Act of 1970.

38. Are civil rights investigations a significant part of FBI caseload?
Yes.

39. How many people are convicted of crimes each year in cases investigated by the FBI?

Each year approximately 50,000 individuals are convicted of crimes in FBI cases.

40. When the FBI recovers stolen property, why is it not returned immediately in all instances to the owner?

Such property is often used as evidence in the trial of the thief. The disposition of recovered property is controlled by the United States Attorney or the federal court.

41. Will the FBI investigate the murder or suspected murder of a Federal employee who is killed while performing his official duties?
   Yes, but only if the employee is in one of the categories covered by the statute governing assaults and killings of Federal officers or if there is evidence of a violation of the statute governing conspiracies to impede or injure Federal officers.

42. If a citizen furnishes facts to the FBI and there is a question as to whether the facts constitute a Federal violation, who decides the question?
   The FBI will present the facts to the United States Attorney who then determines whether a Federal violation has occurred and whether the facts warrant prosecutive action.

43. What is the policy of the FBI concerning the use of firearms?
   An FBI Agent is trained to use firearms only in self-defense or to safeguard the lives of other persons.

44. If FBI Agents have authority only in the United States and its possessions and FBI jurisdiction is generally based on interstate transactions, how can the FBI investigate crimes on the high seas?
   The United States Constitution specifically grants Congress authority to pass laws governing crimes on the high seas. The FBI has jurisdiction over many of these crimes pursuant to Congressional enactment.

SECURITY MATTERS

45. To whom should I report information about espionage, sabotage and subversive activities?
   Information of this type should be reported immediately to the FBI.

46. Does the FBI compile a list of organizations it has designated as subversive?
   No. The FBI is strictly a fact-finding agency and does not designate or label organizations.

47. What internal security matters does the FBI investigate?
   The FBI has investigative jurisdiction of matters relating to sabotage, espionage, counterespionage, treason, insurrection and rebellion, seditious conspiracy advocating overthrow of the government, and other matters affecting the national security.

48. What are the primary sources of FBI authority to investigate subversive groups?
   The FBI's authority in this area is based on Congressional enactments and orders of the Attorney General.

49. Does the FBI investigate white hate groups as well as revolutionary groups?
   Yes. The FBI is charged with internal security responsibilities and any group which follows a policy of violation, and in any way violates laws over which the FBI has jurisdiction, will be thoroughly and impartially investigated.

50. Does the FBI investigate crimes against foreign diplomatic officials in this country?

Under the Act for the Protection of Foreign Officials and Official Guests of the United States, the FBI investigates murders, kidnappings and assaults against such individuals as well as damage to property of foreign governments in the United States. Jurisdiction under this Act is held concurrently with local authorities and the FBI investigates when the crimes committed would adversely affect the conduct of United States foreign affairs.

51. Does the FBI investigate foreign-inspired terrorist acts?

Yes. The FBI investigates such acts when and if directed against targets in the United States. These investigations cover terrorist hijackings, kidnappings, bombings and assaults when against foreign officials.

52. Does the FBI have representatives abroad? If so, what is their function?

Yes. The FBI has representatives in a few of the large foreign capitals for the purpose of effecting liaison with foreign police agencies in matters of mutual interest.

FBI COOPERATIVE SERVICES

53. Who has their fingerprints in FBI files?

The prints of criminals, aliens, government applicants and military personnel form the large part of FBI fingerprint records. In addition, many citizens voluntarily submit their fingerprints for personal identification reasons.

54. Does the FBI conduct fingerprint examinations for private individuals?

No. The FBI's Latent Fingerprint Section conducts latent fingerprint examinations only for law enforcement agencies and officials or for other Federal agencies.

55. If a person is arrested, fingerprinted, and the charge is later dismissed, how can the fingerprint record in the FBI be changed to reflect dismissal of the charge?

The FBI strongly urges all police agencies submitting arrest fingerprint cards to follow the case and submit a final disposition for the completion of the records maintained by the FBI. The information submitted, including dismissal of the charge if appropriate, will be placed on the fingerprint record.

56. Will the FBI furnish fingerprint records to private citizens?

Yes. Pursuant to Department of Justice Order 556-73, an individual may obtain a copy of his or her arrest record by submitting a written request directly to the FBI Identification Division, together with a set of rolled inked fingerprint impressions taken on a fingerprint card which indicates the individual's name and birth data. There is a required fee for this service.

57. Does the FBI exchange fingerprint information with foreign police agencies?

Yes. The FBI exchanges fingerprint information with 84 countries on a cooperative basis.

58. Will the FBI look for a missing person?

No. However, the FBI will post a stop notice in the files of the Identification Division at the request of relatives or law enforcement agencies and will notify the inquirer of any information received regarding the missing person's whereabouts.

59. What is the function of the FBI Disaster Squad?

The function of the FBI Disaster Squad is to identify, through fingerprints, the victims of disasters. The services of this specially trained group are available upon request of local law enforcement and governmental agencies or transportation companies following a catastrophe where identification of victims is a problem.

60. Does the FBI's Disaster Squad go automatically to a scene of ANY disaster to assist in identifying the victims?

No. The services of the FBI Disaster Squad are made available only at the request of a ranking law enforcement official or transportation agency involved. It can assist in identifying Americans in disasters abroad only at the specific invitation of the country involved.

61. What, if any, is the difference in training received by Special Agents at the FBI Academy and local police officers attending the FBI National Academy?

Special Agents of the FBI receive training specifically designed to enable them to handle investigative responsibilities of Federal offenses. The FBI National Academy curriculum is designed to enhance the administrative potential of local, county and state police. The emphasis is on local problems rather than Federal.

62. What other training assistance is afforded local law enforcement officers?

Approximately 25,000 local, county and state law enforcement officers receive specialized training at the FBI Academy located on the Marine Corps Base at Quantico, Virginia, each year. This training is determined by the needs of local law enforcement agencies. In addition, the FBI has more than 5,000 Special Agents qualified to instruct local law enforcement officers in various phases of their work. They are available on request to assist in training programs being conducted by these agencies in the United States.

63. Is the FBI National Academy available only to United States police officers?

No. Although the whole concept of the FBI National Academy is based upon the needs of law enforcement within our own nation, as a cooperation measure a limited number of officers from foreign countries are accepted in each session.

64. What is the National Crime Information Center?

The National Crime Information Center, popularly known as NCIC, is a computerized information system established by the FBI as a service to all criminal justice agencies – local, state and Federal. NCIC stores documented information on serialized stolen property, wanted persons for whom an arrest warrant is outstanding, and criminal histories on individuals arrested and fingerprinted for serious or significant offenses. This information can be instantly retrieved over a vast communications network through the use of telecommunications equipment located in criminal justice agencies in various locations in the United States, Canada, and Puerto Rico.

65. If an individual is being sought by local police for committing a crime, what assistance can be rendered by the FBI to locate the fugitive?

A stop will be placed against the fugitive's fingerprints in the FBI Identification Division and the local police will be immediately notified of the receipt of any additional fingerprints of the fugitive. The fugitive's name and identifying data will also be entered into the National Crime Information Center. Any criminal justice agency which subsequently inquires about this individual will be advised of his or her fugitive status. In addition, the FBI may conduct active investigation to locate the wanted person under Federal unlawful flight statutes.

66. Does the FBI furnish local police and other law enforcement agencies the identities of persons suspected of committing crimes?

Yes. Information coming to the attention of the FBI regarding local crimes is promptly furnished to the appropriate local law enforcement agency. Each year, approximately a million items of criminal intelligence-type information were disseminated to Federal, state and local agencies.

67. If an FBI informant furnishes information regarding a crime not within the jurisdiction of the FBI, does the FBI conduct investigations to verify the information or to prove the violation?

No. This information is expeditiously furnished to the agency having jurisdiction over the alleged violation, and the agency is advised that the information has not been verified by FBI investigation.

68. Does the FBI Laboratory conduct examinations of evidence for anyone other than the FBI?

Yes. The facilities and scientific expertise of the FBI Laboratory are available to all duly constituted law enforcement agencies in the United States in their investigation of criminal matters. Over 30 percent of the examinations conducted by the FBI Laboratory during the year are for outside agencies.

69. Does the FBI Laboratory charge other agencies for conducting scientific examinations of evidence?

As a cooperative measure, no charge is made for these examinations. In addition, FBI Laboratory experts will appear in court as required to testify to the results of their examinations at no cost to the local agency.

70. Does the FBI keep statistics on criminal offenses committed in the United States?

Yes. The FBI collects criminal data from police departments across the nation and compiles it into four quarterly reports as well as a comprehensive annual report. This statistical data is published by the Government Printing Office as the Uniform Crime Reports.

71. Are statistics maintained by the FBI on the number of persons confined to penal institutions and on divorces, liquor consumption, cigarette consumption, deaths and marriages?

No. These statistics are compiled by the Bureau of the Census and can be found in its annual publication entitled STATISTICAL ABSTRACT OF THE UNITED STATES.

72. Can FBI Agents or FBI Headquarters furnish legal advice?
    No.

73. Will the FBI recommend schools or courses to be taken by students?
    No. As a matter of policy, the FBI does not recommend specific schools to be attended or courses of study to be pursued.

74. Can the FBI send wanted posters and flyers on fugitives to individuals on request?
    No. Wanted posters and flyers relating to fugitives currently being sought by the FBI are sent primarily to law enforcement agencies and selected individuals and organizations which are likely to produce information regarding the fugitive's location.

75. How can I contact the FBI if I have information to report?
    The front page of most telephone directories lists the telephone number of the nearest FBI field office, all of which are open 24 hours a day, including Saturday, Sunday and holidays. Additional information concerning matters in this booklet can be obtained from any field office or by writing to: Federal Bureau of Investigation, United States Department of Justice, Washington, D.C. 20535.

76. Is the FBI an independent agency?
    No. It is a bureau of, and in, the United States Department of Justice, which is a cabinet department.

HOW TO TAKE A TEST

I. YOU MUST PASS AN EXAMINATION

A. *WHAT EVERY CANDIDATE SHOULD KNOW*

Examination applicants often ask us for help in preparing for the written test. What can I study in advance? What kinds of questions will be asked? How will the test be given? How will the papers be graded?

As an applicant for a civil service examination, you may be wondering about some of these things. Our purpose here is to suggest effective methods of advance study and to describe civil service examinations.

Your chances for success on this examination can be increased if you know how to prepare. Those "pre-examination jitters" can be reduced if you know what to expect. You can even experience an adventure in good citizenship if you know why civil service exams are given.

B. *WHY ARE CIVIL SERVICE EXAMINATIONS GIVEN?*

Civil service examinations are important to you in two ways. As a citizen, you want public jobs filled by employees who know how to do their work. As a job seeker, you want a fair chance to compete for that job on an equal footing with other candidates. The best-known means of accomplishing this two-fold goal is the competitive examination.

Exams are widely publicized throughout the nation. They may be administered for jobs in federal, state, city, municipal, town or village governments or agencies.

Any citizen may apply, with some limitations, such as the age or residence of applicants. Your experience and education may be reviewed to see whether you meet the requirements for the particular examination. When these requirements exist, they are reasonable and applied consistently to all applicants. Thus, a competitive examination may cause you some uneasiness now, but it is your privilege and safeguard.

C. *HOW ARE CIVIL SERVICE EXAMS DEVELOPED?*

Examinations are carefully written by trained technicians who are specialists in the field known as "psychological measurement," in consultation with recognized authorities in the field of work that the test will cover. These experts recommend the subject matter areas or skills to be tested; only those knowledges or skills important to your success on the job are included. The most reliable books and source materials available are used as references. Together, the experts and technicians judge the difficulty level of the questions.

Test technicians know how to phrase questions so that the problem is clearly stated. Their ethics do not permit "trick" or "catch" questions. Questions may have been tried out on sample groups, or subjected to statistical analysis, to determine their usefulness.

Written tests are often used in combination with performance tests, ratings of training and experience, and oral interviews. All of these measures combine to form the best-known means of finding the right person for the right job.

II. HOW TO PASS THE WRITTEN TEST

A. NATURE OF THE EXAMINATION

To prepare intelligently for civil service examinations, you should know how they differ from school examinations you have taken. In school you were assigned certain definite pages to read or subjects to cover. The examination questions were quite detailed and usually emphasized memory. Civil service exams, on the other hand, try to discover your present ability to perform the duties of a position, plus your potentiality to learn these duties. In other words, a civil service exam attempts to predict how successful you will be. Questions cover such a broad area that they cannot be as minute and detailed as school exam questions.

In the public service similar kinds of work, or positions, are grouped together in one "class." This process is known as *position-classification*. All the positions in a class are paid according to the salary range for that class. One class title covers all of these positions, and they are all tested by the same examination.

B. FOUR BASIC STEPS

1) Study the announcement

How, then, can you know what subjects to study? Our best answer is: "Learn as much as possible about the class of positions for which you've applied." The exam will test the knowledge, skills and abilities needed to do the work.

Your most valuable source of information about the position you want is the official exam announcement. This announcement lists the training and experience qualifications. Check these standards and apply only if you come reasonably close to meeting them.

The brief description of the position in the examination announcement offers some clues to the subjects which will be tested. Think about the job itself. Review the duties in your mind. Can you perform them, or are there some in which you are rusty? Fill in the blank spots in your preparation.

Many jurisdictions preview the written test in the exam announcement by including a section called "Knowledge and Abilities Required," "Scope of the Examination," or some similar heading. Here you will find out specifically what fields will be tested.

2) Review your own background

Once you learn in general what the position is all about, and what you need to know to do the work, ask yourself which subjects you already know fairly well and which need improvement. You may wonder whether to concentrate on improving your strong areas or on building some background in your fields of weakness. When the announcement has specified "some knowledge" or "considerable knowledge," or has used adjectives like "beginning principles of..." or "advanced ... methods," you can get a clue as to the number and difficulty of questions to be asked in any given field. More questions, and hence broader coverage, would be included for those subjects which are more important in the work. Now weigh your strengths and weaknesses against the job requirements and prepare accordingly.

3) Determine the level of the position

Another way to tell how intensively you should prepare is to understand the level of the job for which you are applying. Is it the entering level? In other words, is this the position in which beginners in a field of work are hired? Or is it an intermediate or advanced level? Sometimes this is indicated by such words as "Junior" or "Senior" in the class title. Other jurisdictions use Roman numerals to designate the level – Clerk I, Clerk II, for example. The word "Supervisor" sometimes appears in the title. If the level is not indicated by the title, check the description of duties. Will you be working under very close supervision, or will you have responsibility for independent decisions in this work?

4) Choose appropriate study materials

Now that you know the subjects to be examined and the relative amount of each subject to be covered, you can choose suitable study materials. For beginning level jobs, or even advanced ones, if you have a pronounced weakness in some aspect of your training, read a modern, standard textbook in that field. Be sure it is up to date and has general coverage. Such books are normally available at your library, and the librarian will be glad to help you locate one. For entry-level positions, questions of appropriate difficulty are chosen – neither highly advanced questions, nor those too simple. Such questions require careful thought but not advanced training.

If the position for which you are applying is technical or advanced, you will read more advanced, specialized material. If you are already familiar with the basic principles of your field, elementary textbooks would waste your time. Concentrate on advanced textbooks and technical periodicals. Think through the concepts and review difficult problems in your field.

These are all general sources. You can get more ideas on your own initiative, following these leads. For example, training manuals and publications of the government agency which employs workers in your field can be useful, particularly for technical and professional positions. A letter or visit to the government department involved may result in more specific study suggestions, and certainly will provide you with a more definite idea of the exact nature of the position you are seeking.

III. KINDS OF TESTS

Tests are used for purposes other than measuring knowledge and ability to perform specified duties. For some positions, it is equally important to test ability to make adjustments to new situations or to profit from training. In others, basic mental abilities not dependent on information are essential. Questions which test these things may not appear as pertinent to the duties of the position as those which test for knowledge and information. Yet they are often highly important parts of a fair examination. For very general questions, it is almost impossible to help you direct your study efforts. What we can do is to point out some of the more common of these general abilities needed in public service positions and describe some typical questions.

1) General information

Broad, general information has been found useful for predicting job success in some kinds of work. This is tested in a variety of ways, from vocabulary lists to questions about current events. Basic background in some field of work, such as sociology or economics, may be sampled in a group of questions. Often these are principles which have become familiar to most persons through exposure rather than through formal training. It is difficult to advise you how to study for these questions; being alert to the world around you is our best suggestion.

2) Verbal ability

An example of an ability needed in many positions is verbal or language ability. Verbal ability is, in brief, the ability to use and understand words. Vocabulary and grammar tests are typical measures of this ability. Reading comprehension or paragraph interpretation questions are common in many kinds of civil service tests. You are given a paragraph of written material and asked to find its central meaning.

3) Numerical ability

Number skills can be tested by the familiar arithmetic problem, by checking paired lists of numbers to see which are alike and which are different, or by interpreting charts and graphs. In the latter test, a graph may be printed in the test booklet which you are asked to use as the basis for answering questions.

4) Observation

A popular test for law-enforcement positions is the observation test. A picture is shown to you for several minutes, then taken away. Questions about the picture test your ability to observe both details and larger elements.

5) Following directions

In many positions in the public service, the employee must be able to carry out written instructions dependably and accurately. You may be given a chart with several columns, each column listing a variety of information. The questions require you to carry out directions involving the information given in the chart.

6) Skills and aptitudes

Performance tests effectively measure some manual skills and aptitudes. When the skill is one in which you are trained, such as typing or shorthand, you can practice. These tests are often very much like those given in business school or high school courses. For many of the other skills and aptitudes, however, no short-time preparation can be made. Skills and abilities natural to you or that you have developed throughout your lifetime are being tested.

Many of the general questions just described provide all the data needed to answer the questions and ask you to use your reasoning ability to find the answers. Your best preparation for these tests, as well as for tests of facts and ideas, is to be at your physical and mental best. You, no doubt, have your own methods of getting into an exam-taking mood and keeping "in shape." The next section lists some ideas on this subject.

IV. KINDS OF QUESTIONS

Only rarely is the "essay" question, which you answer in narrative form, used in civil service tests. Civil service tests are usually of the short-answer type. Full instructions for answering these questions will be given to you at the examination. But in case this is your first experience with short-answer questions and separate answer sheets, here is what you need to know:

1) Multiple-choice Questions

Most popular of the short-answer questions is the "multiple choice" or "best answer" question. It can be used, for example, to test for factual knowledge, ability to solve problems or judgment in meeting situations found at work.

A multiple-choice question is normally one of three types—
- It can begin with an incomplete statement followed by several possible endings. You are to find the one ending which *best* completes the statement, although some of the others may not be entirely wrong.
- It can also be a complete statement in the form of a question which is answered by choosing one of the statements listed.

- It can be in the form of a problem – again you select the best answer.

Here is an example of a multiple-choice question with a discussion which should give you some clues as to the method for choosing the right answer:

When an employee has a complaint about his assignment, the action which will *best* help him overcome his difficulty is to
    A. discuss his difficulty with his coworkers
    B. take the problem to the head of the organization
    C. take the problem to the person who gave him the assignment
    D. say nothing to anyone about his complaint

In answering this question, you should study each of the choices to find which is best. Consider choice "A" – Certainly an employee may discuss his complaint with fellow employees, but no change or improvement can result, and the complaint remains unresolved. Choice "B" is a poor choice since the head of the organization probably does not know what assignment you have been given, and taking your problem to him is known as "going over the head" of the supervisor. The supervisor, or person who made the assignment, is the person who can clarify it or correct any injustice. Choice "C" is, therefore, correct. To say nothing, as in choice "D," is unwise. Supervisors have and interest in knowing the problems employees are facing, and the employee is seeking a solution to his problem.

2) True/False Questions

The "true/false" or "right/wrong" form of question is sometimes used. Here a complete statement is given. Your job is to decide whether the statement is right or wrong.

SAMPLE: A roaming cell-phone call to a nearby city costs less than a non-roaming call to a distant city.

This statement is wrong, or false, since roaming calls are more expensive.
This is not a complete list of all possible question forms, although most of the others are variations of these common types. You will always get complete directions for answering questions. Be sure you understand *how* to mark your answers – ask questions until you do.

V. RECORDING YOUR ANSWERS

Computer terminals are used more and more today for many different kinds of exams.
For an examination with very few applicants, you may be told to record your answers in the test booklet itself. Separate answer sheets are much more common. If this separate answer sheet is to be scored by machine – and this is often the case – it is highly important that you mark your answers correctly in order to get credit.
An electronic scoring machine is often used in civil service offices because of the speed with which papers can be scored. Machine-scored answer sheets must be marked with a pencil, which will be given to you. This pencil has a high graphite content which responds to the electronic scoring machine. As a matter of fact, stray dots may register as answers, so do not let your pencil rest on the answer sheet while you are pondering the correct answer. Also, if your pencil lead breaks or is otherwise defective, ask for another.

Since the answer sheet will be dropped in a slot in the scoring machine, be careful not to bend the corners or get the paper crumpled.

The answer sheet normally has five vertical columns of numbers, with 30 numbers to a column. These numbers correspond to the question numbers in your test booklet. After each number, going across the page are four or five pairs of dotted lines. These short dotted lines have small letters or numbers above them. The first two pairs may also have a "T" or "F" above the letters. This indicates that the first two pairs only are to be used if the questions are of the true-false type. If the questions are multiple choice, disregard the "T" and "F" and pay attention only to the small letters or numbers.

Answer your questions in the manner of the sample that follows:

32. The largest city in the United States is
    A. Washington, D.C.
    B. New York City
    C. Chicago
    D. Detroit
    E. San Francisco

1) Choose the answer you think is best. (New York City is the largest, so "B" is correct.)
2) Find the row of dotted lines numbered the same as the question you are answering. (Find row number 32)
3) Find the pair of dotted lines corresponding to the answer. (Find the pair of lines under the mark "B.")
4) Make a solid black mark between the dotted lines.

VI. BEFORE THE TEST

Common sense will help you find procedures to follow to get ready for an examination. Too many of us, however, overlook these sensible measures. Indeed, nervousness and fatigue have been found to be the most serious reasons why applicants fail to do their best on civil service tests. Here is a list of reminders:

- Begin your preparation early – Don't wait until the last minute to go scurrying around for books and materials or to find out what the position is all about.
- Prepare continuously – An hour a night for a week is better than an all-night cram session. This has been definitely established. What is more, a night a week for a month will return better dividends than crowding your study into a shorter period of time.
- Locate the place of the exam – You have been sent a notice telling you when and where to report for the examination. If the location is in a different town or otherwise unfamiliar to you, it would be well to inquire the best route and learn something about the building.
- Relax the night before the test – Allow your mind to rest. Do not study at all that night. Plan some mild recreation or diversion; then go to bed early and get a good night's sleep.
- Get up early enough to make a leisurely trip to the place for the test – This way unforeseen events, traffic snarls, unfamiliar buildings, etc. will not upset you.
- Dress comfortably – A written test is not a fashion show. You will be known by number and not by name, so wear something comfortable.

- Leave excess paraphernalia at home – Shopping bags and odd bundles will get in your way. You need bring only the items mentioned in the official notice you received; usually everything you need is provided. Do not bring reference books to the exam. They will only confuse those last minutes and be taken away from you when in the test room.
- Arrive somewhat ahead of time – If because of transportation schedules you must get there very early, bring a newspaper or magazine to take your mind off yourself while waiting.
- Locate the examination room – When you have found the proper room, you will be directed to the seat or part of the room where you will sit. Sometimes you are given a sheet of instructions to read while you are waiting. Do not fill out any forms until you are told to do so; just read them and be prepared.
- Relax and prepare to listen to the instructions
- If you have any physical problem that may keep you from doing your best, be sure to tell the test administrator. If you are sick or in poor health, you really cannot do your best on the exam. You can come back and take the test some other time.

VII. AT THE TEST

The day of the test is here and you have the test booklet in your hand. The temptation to get going is very strong. Caution! There is more to success than knowing the right answers. You must know how to identify your papers and understand variations in the type of short-answer question used in this particular examination. Follow these suggestions for maximum results from your efforts:

1) Cooperate with the monitor

The test administrator has a duty to create a situation in which you can be as much at ease as possible. He will give instructions, tell you when to begin, check to see that you are marking your answer sheet correctly, and so on. He is not there to guard you, although he will see that your competitors do not take unfair advantage. He wants to help you do your best.

2) Listen to all instructions

Don't jump the gun! Wait until you understand all directions. In most civil service tests you get more time than you need to answer the questions. So don't be in a hurry. Read each word of instructions until you clearly understand the meaning. Study the examples, listen to all announcements and follow directions. Ask questions if you do not understand what to do.

3) Identify your papers

Civil service exams are usually identified by number only. You will be assigned a number; you must not put your name on your test papers. Be sure to copy your number correctly. Since more than one exam may be given, copy your exact examination title.

4) Plan your time

Unless you are told that a test is a "speed" or "rate of work" test, speed itself is usually not important. Time enough to answer all the questions will be provided, but this does not mean that you have all day. An overall time limit has been set. Divide the total time (in minutes) by the number of questions to determine the approximate time you have for each question.

5) Do not linger over difficult questions

If you come across a difficult question, mark it with a paper clip (useful to have along) and come back to it when you have been through the booklet. One caution if you do this – be sure to skip a number on your answer sheet as well. Check often to be sure that you have not lost your place and that you are marking in the row numbered the same as the question you are answering.

6) Read the questions

Be sure you know what the question asks! Many capable people are unsuccessful because they failed to *read* the questions correctly.

7) Answer all questions

Unless you have been instructed that a penalty will be deducted for incorrect answers, it is better to guess than to omit a question.

8) Speed tests

It is often better NOT to guess on speed tests. It has been found that on timed tests people are tempted to spend the last few seconds before time is called in marking answers at random – without even reading them – in the hope of picking up a few extra points. To discourage this practice, the instructions may warn you that your score will be "corrected" for guessing. That is, a penalty will be applied. The incorrect answers will be deducted from the correct ones, or some other penalty formula will be used.

9) Review your answers

If you finish before time is called, go back to the questions you guessed or omitted to give them further thought. Review other answers if you have time.

10) Return your test materials

If you are ready to leave before others have finished or time is called, take ALL your materials to the monitor and leave quietly. Never take any test material with you. The monitor can discover whose papers are not complete, and taking a test booklet may be grounds for disqualification.

VIII. EXAMINATION TECHNIQUES

1) Read the general instructions carefully. These are usually printed on the first page of the exam booklet. As a rule, these instructions refer to the timing of the examination; the fact that you should not start work until the signal and must stop work at a signal, etc. If there are any *special* instructions, such as a choice of questions to be answered, make sure that you note this instruction carefully.

2) When you are ready to start work on the examination, that is as soon as the signal has been given, read the instructions to each question booklet, underline any key words or phrases, such as *least, best, outline, describe* and the like. In this way you will tend to answer as requested rather than discover on reviewing your paper that you *listed without describing*, that you selected the *worst* choice rather than the *best* choice, etc.

3) If the examination is of the objective or multiple-choice type – that is, each question will also give a series of possible answers: A, B, C or D, and you are called upon to select the best answer and write the letter next to that answer on your answer paper – it is advisable to start answering each question in turn. There may be anywhere from 50 to 100 such questions in the three or four hours allotted and you can see how much time would be taken if you read through all the questions before beginning to answer any. Furthermore, if you come across a question or group of questions which you know would be difficult to answer, it would undoubtedly affect your handling of all the other questions.

4) If the examination is of the essay type and contains but a few questions, it is a moot point as to whether you should read all the questions before starting to answer any one. Of course, if you are given a choice – say five out of seven and the like – then it is essential to read all the questions so you can eliminate the two that are most difficult. If, however, you are asked to answer all the questions, there may be danger in trying to answer the easiest one first because you may find that you will spend too much time on it. The best technique is to answer the first question, then proceed to the second, etc.

5) Time your answers. Before the exam begins, write down the time it started, then add the time allowed for the examination and write down the time it must be completed, then divide the time available somewhat as follows:
    - If 3-1/2 hours are allowed, that would be 210 minutes. If you have 80 objective-type questions, that would be an average of 2-1/2 minutes per question. Allow yourself no more than 2 minutes per question, or a total of 160 minutes, which will permit about 50 minutes to review.
    - If for the time allotment of 210 minutes there are 7 essay questions to answer, that would average about 30 minutes a question. Give yourself only 25 minutes per question so that you have about 35 minutes to review.

6) The most important instruction is to *read each question* and make sure you know what is wanted. The second most important instruction is to *time yourself properly* so that you answer every question. The third most important instruction is to *answer every question*. Guess if you have to but include something for each question. Remember that you will receive no credit for a blank and will probably receive some credit if you write something in answer to an essay question. If you guess a letter – say "B" for a multiple-choice question – you may have guessed right. If you leave a blank as an answer to a multiple-choice question, the examiners may respect your feelings but it will not add a point to your score. Some exams may penalize you for wrong answers, so in such cases *only*, you may not want to guess unless you have some basis for your answer.

7) Suggestions
    a. Objective-type questions
        1. Examine the question booklet for proper sequence of pages and questions
        2. Read all instructions carefully
        3. Skip any question which seems too difficult; return to it after all other questions have been answered
        4. Apportion your time properly; do not spend too much time on any single question or group of questions

5. Note and underline key words – *all, most, fewest, least, best, worst, same, opposite,* etc.
6. Pay particular attention to negatives
7. Note unusual option, e.g., unduly long, short, complex, different or similar in content to the body of the question
8. Observe the use of "hedging" words – *probably, may, most likely,* etc.
9. Make sure that your answer is put next to the same number as the question
10. Do not second-guess unless you have good reason to believe the second answer is definitely more correct
11. Cross out original answer if you decide another answer is more accurate; do not erase until you are ready to hand your paper in
12. Answer all questions; guess unless instructed otherwise
13. Leave time for review

b. Essay questions
1. Read each question carefully
2. Determine exactly what is wanted. Underline key words or phrases.
3. Decide on outline or paragraph answer
4. Include many different points and elements unless asked to develop any one or two points or elements
5. Show impartiality by giving pros and cons unless directed to select one side only
6. Make and write down any assumptions you find necessary to answer the questions
7. Watch your English, grammar, punctuation and choice of words
8. Time your answers; don't crowd material

8) Answering the essay question

Most essay questions can be answered by framing the specific response around several key words or ideas. Here are a few such key words or ideas:

M's: manpower, materials, methods, money, management
P's: purpose, program, policy, plan, procedure, practice, problems, pitfalls, personnel, public relations

a. Six basic steps in handling problems:
1. Preliminary plan and background development
2. Collect information, data and facts
3. Analyze and interpret information, data and facts
4. Analyze and develop solutions as well as make recommendations
5. Prepare report and sell recommendations
6. Install recommendations and follow up effectiveness

b. Pitfalls to avoid
1. *Taking things for granted* – A statement of the situation does not necessarily imply that each of the elements is necessarily true; for example, a complaint may be invalid and biased so that all that can be taken for granted is that a complaint has been registered

2. *Considering only one side of a situation* – Wherever possible, indicate several alternatives and then point out the reasons you selected the best one
3. *Failing to indicate follow up* – Whenever your answer indicates action on your part, make certain that you will take proper follow-up action to see how successful your recommendations, procedures or actions turn out to be
4. *Taking too long in answering any single question* – Remember to time your answers properly

IX. AFTER THE TEST

Scoring procedures differ in detail among civil service jurisdictions although the general principles are the same. Whether the papers are hand-scored or graded by machine we have described, they are nearly always graded by number. That is, the person who marks the paper knows only the number – never the name – of the applicant. Not until all the papers have been graded will they be matched with names. If other tests, such as training and experience or oral interview ratings have been given, scores will be combined. Different parts of the examination usually have different weights. For example, the written test might count 60 percent of the final grade, and a rating of training and experience 40 percent. In many jurisdictions, veterans will have a certain number of points added to their grades.

After the final grade has been determined, the names are placed in grade order and an eligible list is established. There are various methods for resolving ties between those who get the same final grade – probably the most common is to place first the name of the person whose application was received first. Job offers are made from the eligible list in the order the names appear on it. You will be notified of your grade and your rank as soon as all these computations have been made. This will be done as rapidly as possible.

People who are found to meet the requirements in the announcement are called "eligibles." Their names are put on a list of eligible candidates. An eligible's chances of getting a job depend on how high he stands on this list and how fast agencies are filling jobs from the list.

When a job is to be filled from a list of eligibles, the agency asks for the names of people on the list of eligibles for that job. When the civil service commission receives this request, it sends to the agency the names of the three people highest on this list. Or, if the job to be filled has specialized requirements, the office sends the agency the names of the top three persons who meet these requirements from the general list.

The appointing officer makes a choice from among the three people whose names were sent to him. If the selected person accepts the appointment, the names of the others are put back on the list to be considered for future openings.

That is the rule in hiring from all kinds of eligible lists, whether they are for typist, carpenter, chemist, or something else. For every vacancy, the appointing officer has his choice of any one of the top three eligibles on the list. This explains why the person whose name is on top of the list sometimes does not get an appointment when some of the persons lower on the list do. If the appointing officer chooses the second or third eligible, the No. 1 eligible does not get a job at once, but stays on the list until he is appointed or the list is terminated.

X. HOW TO PASS THE INTERVIEW TEST

The examination for which you applied requires an oral interview test. You have already taken the written test and you are now being called for the interview test – the final part of the formal examination.

You may think that it is not possible to prepare for an interview test and that there are no procedures to follow during an interview. Our purpose is to point out some things you can do in advance that will help you and some good rules to follow and pitfalls to avoid while you are being interviewed.

What is an interview supposed to test?

The written examination is designed to test the technical knowledge and competence of the candidate; the oral is designed to evaluate intangible qualities, not readily measured otherwise, and to establish a list showing the relative fitness of each candidate – as measured against his competitors – for the position sought. Scoring is not on the basis of "right" and "wrong," but on a sliding scale of values ranging from "not passable" to "outstanding." As a matter of fact, it is possible to achieve a relatively low score without a single "incorrect" answer because of evident weakness in the qualities being measured.

Occasionally, an examination may consist entirely of an oral test – either an individual or a group oral. In such cases, information is sought concerning the technical knowledges and abilities of the candidate, since there has been no written examination for this purpose. More commonly, however, an oral test is used to supplement a written examination.

Who conducts interviews?

The composition of oral boards varies among different jurisdictions. In nearly all, a representative of the personnel department serves as chairman. One of the members of the board may be a representative of the department in which the candidate would work. In some cases, "outside experts" are used, and, frequently, a businessman or some other representative of the general public is asked to serve. Labor and management or other special groups may be represented. The aim is to secure the services of experts in the appropriate field.

However the board is composed, it is a good idea (and not at all improper or unethical) to ascertain in advance of the interview who the members are and what groups they represent. When you are introduced to them, you will have some idea of their backgrounds and interests, and at least you will not stutter and stammer over their names.

What should be done before the interview?

While knowledge about the board members is useful and takes some of the surprise element out of the interview, there is other preparation which is more substantive. It *is* possible to prepare for an oral interview – in several ways:

1) Keep a copy of your application and review it carefully before the interview

This may be the only document before the oral board, and the starting point of the interview. Know what education and experience you have listed there, and the sequence and dates of all of it. Sometimes the board will ask you to review the highlights of your experience for them; you should not have to hem and haw doing it.

2) Study the class specification and the examination announcement

Usually, the oral board has one or both of these to guide them. The qualities, characteristics or knowledges required by the position sought are stated in these documents. They offer valuable clues as to the nature of the oral interview. For example, if the job involves supervisory responsibilities, the announcement will usually indicate that knowledge of modern supervisory methods and the qualifications of the candidate as a supervisor will be tested. If so, you can expect such questions, frequently in the form of a hypothetical situation which you are expected to solve. NEVER go into an oral without knowledge of the duties and responsibilities of the job you seek.

3) Think through each qualification required

Try to visualize the kind of questions you would ask if you were a board member. How well could you answer them? Try especially to appraise your own knowledge and background in each area, *measured against the job sought*, and identify any areas in which you are weak. Be critical and realistic – do not flatter yourself.

4) Do some general reading in areas in which you feel you may be weak

For example, if the job involves supervision and your past experience has NOT, some general reading in supervisory methods and practices, particularly in the field of human relations, might be useful. Do NOT study agency procedures or detailed manuals. The oral board will be testing your understanding and capacity, not your memory.

5) Get a good night's sleep and watch your general health and mental attitude

You will want a clear head at the interview. Take care of a cold or any other minor ailment, and of course, no hangovers.

What should be done on the day of the interview?

Now comes the day of the interview itself. Give yourself plenty of time to get there. Plan to arrive somewhat ahead of the scheduled time, particularly if your appointment is in the fore part of the day. If a previous candidate fails to appear, the board might be ready for you a bit early. By early afternoon an oral board is almost invariably behind schedule if there are many candidates, and you may have to wait. Take along a book or magazine to read, or your application to review, but leave any extraneous material in the waiting room when you go in for your interview. In any event, relax and compose yourself.

The matter of dress is important. The board is forming impressions about you – from your experience, your manners, your attitude, and your appearance. Give your personal appearance careful attention. Dress your best, but not your flashiest. Choose conservative, appropriate clothing, and be sure it is immaculate. This is a business interview, and your appearance should indicate that you regard it as such. Besides, being well groomed and properly dressed will help boost your confidence.

Sooner or later, someone will call your name and escort you into the interview room. *This is it.* From here on you are on your own. It is too late for any more preparation. But remember, you asked for this opportunity to prove your fitness, and you are here because your request was granted.

What happens when you go in?

The usual sequence of events will be as follows: The clerk (who is often the board stenographer) will introduce you to the chairman of the oral board, who will introduce you to the other members of the board. Acknowledge the introductions before you sit down. Do not be surprised if you find a microphone facing you or a stenotypist sitting by. Oral interviews are usually recorded in the event of an appeal or other review.

Usually the chairman of the board will open the interview by reviewing the highlights of your education and work experience from your application – primarily for the benefit of the other members of the board, as well as to get the material into the record. Do not interrupt or comment unless there is an error or significant misinterpretation; if that is the case, do not hesitate. But do not quibble about insignificant matters. Also, he will usually ask you some question about your education, experience or your present job – partly to get you to start talking and to establish the interviewing "rapport." He may start the actual questioning, or turn it over to one of the other members. Frequently, each member undertakes the questioning on a particular area, one in which he is perhaps most competent, so you can expect each member to participate in the examination. Because time is limited, you may also expect some rather abrupt switches in the direction the questioning takes, so do not be upset by it. Normally, a board member will not pursue a single line of questioning unless he discovers a particular strength or weakness.

After each member has participated, the chairman will usually ask whether any member has any further questions, then will ask you if you have anything you wish to add. Unless you are expecting this question, it may floor you. Worse, it may start you off on an extended, extemporaneous speech. The board is not usually seeking more information. The question is principally to offer you a last opportunity to present further qualifications or to indicate that you have nothing to add. So, if you feel that a significant qualification or characteristic has been overlooked, it is proper to point it out in a sentence or so. Do not compliment the board on the thoroughness of their examination – they have been sketchy, and you know it. If you wish, merely say, "No thank you, I have nothing further to add." This is a point where you can "talk yourself out" of a good impression or fail to present an important bit of information. Remember, *you close the interview yourself*.

The chairman will then say, "That is all, Mr. _____, thank you." Do not be startled; the interview is over, and quicker than you think. Thank him, gather your belongings and take your leave. Save your sigh of relief for the other side of the door.

How to put your best foot forward

Throughout this entire process, you may feel that the board individually and collectively is trying to pierce your defenses, seek out your hidden weaknesses and embarrass and confuse you. Actually, this is not true. They are obliged to make an appraisal of your qualifications for the job you are seeking, and they want to see you in your best light. Remember, they must interview all candidates and a non-cooperative candidate may become a failure in spite of their best efforts to bring out his qualifications. Here are 15 suggestions that will help you:

1) Be natural – Keep your attitude confident, not cocky

If you are not confident that you can do the job, do not expect the board to be. Do not apologize for your weaknesses, try to bring out your strong points. The board is interested in a positive, not negative, presentation. Cockiness will antagonize any board member and make him wonder if you are covering up a weakness by a false show of strength.

2) Get comfortable, but don't lounge or sprawl

Sit erectly but not stiffly. A careless posture may lead the board to conclude that you are careless in other things, or at least that you are not impressed by the importance of the occasion. Either conclusion is natural, even if incorrect. Do not fuss with your clothing, a pencil or an ashtray. Your hands may occasionally be useful to emphasize a point; do not let them become a point of distraction.

3) Do not wisecrack or make small talk

This is a serious situation, and your attitude should show that you consider it as such. Further, the time of the board is limited – they do not want to waste it, and neither should you.

4) Do not exaggerate your experience or abilities
In the first place, from information in the application or other interviews and sources, the board may know more about you than you think. Secondly, you probably will not get away with it. An experienced board is rather adept at spotting such a situation, so do not take the chance.

5) If you know a board member, do not make a point of it, yet do not hide it
Certainly you are not fooling him, and probably not the other members of the board. Do not try to take advantage of your acquaintanceship – it will probably do you little good.

6) Do not dominate the interview
Let the board do that. They will give you the clues – do not assume that you have to do all the talking. Realize that the board has a number of questions to ask you, and do not try to take up all the interview time by showing off your extensive knowledge of the answer to the first one.

7) Be attentive
You only have 20 minutes or so, and you should keep your attention at its sharpest throughout. When a member is addressing a problem or question to you, give him your undivided attention. Address your reply principally to him, but do not exclude the other board members.

8) Do not interrupt
A board member may be stating a problem for you to analyze. He will ask you a question when the time comes. Let him state the problem, and wait for the question.

9) Make sure you understand the question
Do not try to answer until you are sure what the question is. If it is not clear, restate it in your own words or ask the board member to clarify it for you. However, do not haggle about minor elements.

10) Reply promptly but not hastily
A common entry on oral board rating sheets is "candidate responded readily," or "candidate hesitated in replies." Respond as promptly and quickly as you can, but do not jump to a hasty, ill-considered answer.

11) Do not be peremptory in your answers
A brief answer is proper – but do not fire your answer back. That is a losing game from your point of view. The board member can probably ask questions much faster than you can answer them.

12) Do not try to create the answer you think the board member wants
He is interested in what kind of mind you have and how it works – not in playing games. Furthermore, he can usually spot this practice and will actually grade you down on it.

13) Do not switch sides in your reply merely to agree with a board member
Frequently, a member will take a contrary position merely to draw you out and to see if you are willing and able to defend your point of view. Do not start a debate, yet do not surrender a good position. If a position is worth taking, it is worth defending.

14) Do not be afraid to admit an error in judgment if you are shown to be wrong

The board knows that you are forced to reply without any opportunity for careful consideration. Your answer may be demonstrably wrong. If so, admit it and get on with the interview.

15) Do not dwell at length on your present job

The opening question may relate to your present assignment. Answer the question but do not go into an extended discussion. You are being examined for a *new* job, not your present one. As a matter of fact, try to phrase ALL your answers in terms of the job for which you are being examined.

Basis of Rating

Probably you will forget most of these "do's" and "don'ts" when you walk into the oral interview room. Even remembering them all will not ensure you a passing grade. Perhaps you did not have the qualifications in the first place. But remembering them will help you to put your best foot forward, without treading on the toes of the board members.

Rumor and popular opinion to the contrary notwithstanding, an oral board wants you to make the best appearance possible. They know you are under pressure – but they also want to see how you respond to it as a guide to what your reaction would be under the pressures of the job you seek. They will be influenced by the degree of poise you display, the personal traits you show and the manner in which you respond.

ABOUT THIS BOOK

This book contains tests divided into Examination Sections. Go through each test, answering every question in the margin. We have also attached a sample answer sheet at the back of the book that can be removed and used. At the end of each test look at the answer key and check your answers. On the ones you got wrong, look at the right answer choice and learn. Do not fill in the answers first. Do not memorize the questions and answers, but understand the answer and principles involved. On your test, the questions will likely be different from the samples. Questions are changed and new ones added. If you understand these past questions you should have success with any changes that arise. Tests may consist of several types of questions. We have additional books on each subject should more study be advisable or necessary for you. Finally, the more you study, the better prepared you will be. This book is intended to be the last thing you study before you walk into the examination room. Prior study of relevant texts is also recommended. NLC publishes some of these in our Fundamental Series. Knowledge and good sense are important factors in passing your exam. Good luck also helps. So now study this Passbook, absorb the material contained within and take that knowledge into the examination. Then do your best to pass that exam.

EXAMINATION SECTION

SAMPLE QUESTIONS
BIOGRAPHICAL INVENTORY

The questions included in the Biographical Inventory ask for information about you and your background. These kinds of questions are often asked during an oral interview. For years, employers have been using interviews to relate personal history, preferences, and attitudes to job success. This Biographical Inventory attempts to do the same and includes questions which have been shown to be related to job success. It has been found that successful employees tend to select some answers more often than other answers, while less successful employees tend to select different answers. The questions in the Biographical Inventory do not have a single correct answer. Every choice is given some credit. More credit is given for answers selected more often by successful employees.

These Biographical Inventory questions are presented for illustrative purposes only. The answers have not been linked to the answers of successful employees; therefore, we cannot designate any "correct" answer(s).

DIRECTIONS: You may only mark ONE response to each question. It is possible that none of the answers applies well to you. However, one of the answers will surely be true (or less inaccurate) for you than others. In such a case, mark that answer. <u>Answer each question honestly.</u> The credit that is assigned to each response on the actual test is based upon how successful employees described themselves when honestly responding to the questions. *PRINT THE LETTER OF THE CORRECT ANSWER IN THE SPACE AT THE RIGHT.*

1. Generally, in your work assignments, would you prefer 1.____
   A. to work on one thing at a time
   B. to work on a couple of things at a time
   C. to work on many things at the same time

2. In the course of a week, which of the following gives you the GREATEST 2.____
   satisfaction?
   A. Being told you have done a good job.
   B. Helping other people to solve their problems.
   C. Coming up with a new or unique way to handle a situation.
   D. Having free time to devote to personal interests.

EXAMINATION SECTION
TEST 1

DIRECTIONS: This inventory contains 50 questions about yourself. You are to read each question and select the answer that best describes you from the choices provided. *PRINT THE LETTER OF YOUR ANSWER IN THE SPACE AT THE RIGHT.*

1. What has given you the most difficulty in any job that you have had?   1.____

    A. A supervisor who watched over my work too closely
    B. A supervisor who gave inconsistent direction
    C. Disagreements or gossip among co-workers
    D. Having to deal with too many insignificant details

2. I _____ put off doing a chore that I could have taken care of right away.   2.____

    A. often   B. sometimes   C. seldom   D. never

3. During high school, the number of clubs or organizations I belonged/ belong to is: 3.____

    A. 0   B. 1 or 2   C. 2 to 3   D. more than 3

4. In the past, when I have given a speech or presentation, I was likely to have prepared ahead of time: 4.____

    A. much less than others did
    B. less than others
    C. more than others
    D. about the same as others

5. When working as a member of a team, I prefer to: 5.____

    A. take on challenging tasks but not take the lead
    B. do less complex tasks
    C. take the lead
    D. keep a low profile

6. Generally, in my work assignments, I would prefer to work: 6.____

    A. on one thing at a time.
    B. on a couple of things at a time.
    C. on many things at the same time.
    D. on something I have never done before.

7. In the course of a week, the thing that gives me the greatest satisfaction is   7.____

    A. coming up with a new or unique way to handle a situation.
    B. helping other people to solve problems.
    C. having free time to devote to personal interests.
    D. being told I have done a good job.

8. My health or fitness has _____ limited my ability to perform certain tasks.   8.___

   A. often   B. sometimes   C. seldom   D. never

9. In the past, when faced with an ethical dilemma, my first step has usually been to   9.___

   A. identify the issues that are in conflict
   B. reflect on the punishment or rewards likely to result from either course of action
   C. try to find someone else who is more appropriate for making such a decision
   D. identify the people and organizations likely to be affected by the decision

10. My leadership style could be best described as   10.___

    A. autocratic   B. democratic/participative
    C. permissive/laissez faire   D. motivational

11. In the past, when I have been part of a team, I most often felt   11.___

    A. as if I were a cut above, and ready to lead
    B. a sense of equality and belonging
    C. uncertain about the next step
    D. isolated and marginalized

12. I usually enjoy thinking about the plusses and minuses of alternative approaches to solving a problem: 12.___

    A. very true for me-describes me perfectly
    B. somewhat true of me
    C. somewhat false for me
    D. absolutely false for me-doesn't describe me at all

13. When I have participated in team activities in the past and found that other group members performed better than I have, I most often   13.___

    A. examined the skills and strategies that made them so successful
    B. made a last-gasp attempt to measure up
    C. tried to reconfigure the team members so that I wouldn't end up looking bad
    D. resented the easier set of circumstances that made such success possible

14. In the past, when I failed to adequately learn a skill, concept or body of knowledge, the failure was most often the result of   14.___

    A. other peoples' interference with my approach to learning or solving the problem
    B. poor instruction
    C. having too little time to adequately study and practice
    D. a study plan that aimed too high, without learning the basics first

15. My energy is usually highest when   15.___

    A. I work as part of a collaborative team
    B. I work completely on my own
    C. I work mostly on my own, with input from others when I ask for it
    D. I work with ongoing evaluations from superiors

16. My own work standards are

    A. usually completely different from those of others
    B. usually in tune with those of others
    C. always frustratingly more demanding than those of others
    D. sometimes different from others, but easily adapted to fit the group

17. In the past, when I have worked with a group on a task for which I had little experience, I have most often

    A. asked questions and contributed as much as I was able
    B. tried to alter the parameters of the task in order to suit my own abilities
    C. asked for direction and hoped for clear guidance
    D. I don't recall being in this situation.

18. How much do you agree with the following statement: "Unless I am assigned to a team that is made up of people just like myself, the team is not likely to succeed."

    A. Strongly agree   B. Agree somewhat
    C. Disagree somewhat   D. Strongly disagree

19. I am _____ giving other people feedback on their work because _____ .

    A. very comfortable; I usually know more about what it takes to succeed than they do
    B. comfortable; it is a normal and useful part of teamwork
    C. uncomfortable; I don't usually have anything to add
    D. very uncomfortable; I'm afraid I will be resented or rejected

20. In my career, I have changed jobs

    A. only through promotion   B. once or twice
    C. on the average, every few years D. never

21. In the past, whenever I've been unable to achieve all that I set out to do in a given time period, I have

    A. tried to figure out where I came up short, and devised new strategies
    B. looked for ways to redefine "success"
    C. felt angry or hopeless
    D. I have never failed to achieve what I've set out to do.

22. Other people have _____ referred to me as an over-achiever.

    A. always   B. often   C. occasionally   D. never

23. When it comes to competitiveness, I am

    A. much more competitive than others
    B. slightly more competitive than others
    C. about as competitive as others
    D. generally less competitive than others

24. In the past, when I have achieved an important goal, I have

    A. not made a big deal of it, as it is only one small step toward an ultimate goal
    B. often gone back and tried to imagine how it could have been achieved mere successfully
    C. enjoyed the feeling of satisfaction for a while, before moving on to another goal
    D. tried to make the feeling of accomplishment last for as long as I could

25. My first impressions of people

    A. are almost always dead-on
    B. usually give an incomplete perception that evolves over time
    C. are often wrong, to my delight
    D. are often wrong, to my disappointment

26. When assigned a task, I believe

    A. success is imperative, and I'll do anything to achieve it
    B. success is important, and I focus on doing my best
    C. my investment in the success of the task correlates to my opinion of the task's importance
    D. my investment in the success of the task correlates to my opinion of the task's achievability

27. When trying to evaluate whether I have succeeded on a certain task, I rely mostly on

    A. my own gut feeling
    B. the opinions of peers
    C. a list of objective criteria
    D. people who fill leadership positions and are in a position to judge

28. If I fail to do something well,

    A. it usually isn't my fault
    B. it's probably time to give someone else a chance
    C. I'll look for feedback, reflect on it, and approach it differently another time
    D. I'll redouble my efforts, and won't give up until I succeed

29. At work or in school, when somebody has stood up to me or disagreed with me, I have tended to

    A. make a mental note that the person is an enemy who can't be trusted
    B. react angrily and heatedly, and then tried to make amends afterward
    C. listen carefully and assume that the person's opinion deserves respect
    D. apologize and try to soothe the person

30. In the past, when an assigned task has been altered during the course of my work, my reaction has usually been to

    A. adapt my strategy to fit the new circumstances
    B. wish that the people who first assigned it could make up their minds
    C. wonder what I've been doing wrong
    D. This has never happened to me

31. When times get tough, I usually

   A. become emotionally fragile or volatile
   B. feel more stressed, but make the effort to meet demands
   C. become depressed and find it more difficult to work
   D. tend to engage in unhealthy behaviors such as overeating or getting less sleep

32. I second-guess my decisions

   A. almost never
   B. when there is evidence to suggest that another way might be better
   C. when I feel poorly about myself or my performance
   D. constantly, always mindful of the different available courses of action

33. When I engage in an activity that requires moderate physical exertion, I usually

   A. push myself to ratchet up the physical demands of the activity
   B. feel challenged and energized
   C. come up with ways to make it less strenuous
   D. feel winded and depleted

34. If it were up to me, my success on a certain task would be defined by

   A. myself alone
   B. a set of fair and objective criteria
   C. my friends
   D. the strictest standards available

35. When I have been assigned to work in a group in the past, I have usually

   A. insisted on a leadership position
   B. been asked to assume a leadership position
   C. participated as an equal, and deferred to others when their opinions merited it
   D. been frozen out of decision-making by the more aggressive group members

36. When my regular work schedule changes, I most often

   A. try to stick with my proven formula for success
   B. feel angry and resentful at the whimsy of outside forces
   C. laugh it off as the result of a bureaucracy that often works against logic
   D. try to go with the flow and produce results

37. If somebody tries to talk me out of a decision, I am most likely to

   A. tell them they are wasting their time
   B. say I agree with them to minimize conflict, and then stick to my original plan
   C. try to figure out where they are coming from
   D. ask what I can do to make them happy

38. When I find a task to be unpleasant, but necessary,

    A. it is usually difficult to motivate myself to work on the task
    B. I try to pass it on to someone who will enjoy it more
    C. I am able to motivate myself to complete the task satisfactorily
    D. I place the task low on my priorities list

39. It seems as if it is _____ case that some people find what I say to be rude or offensive.

    A. always
    B. often
    C. sometimes
    D. never

40. When I have finished a particular task, I usually find that the time it took to complete was

    A. about what I had expected and planned for
    B. more than I had expected and planned for
    C. less than I had expected and planned for
    D. other more or less than I had planned for, with no consistent means of predicting either

41. When I undertake a task with several different parts, I usually

    A. tackle the easiest work first
    B. start organizing the different parts into categories that I can prioritize
    C. start working on them in no particular order it all has to get done anyway
    D. have a difficult time deciding which part to do first

42. When I am assigned a new project, I'm usually

    A. a little apprehensive about adding to my workload
    B. hopeful that it will be more interesting than the drudgery that takes up most of my time
    C. excited to take on something new and different
    D. nervous about whether I'm up to the task

43. On the occasions when I have been in a position to lead others, I have most often tried to lead by

    A. isolating and marginalizing the weak links
    B. offering appropriate rewards and punishments
    C. trying to inspire confidence and innovation
    D. allowing decisions to be made by other group members

44. My own academic career has been one characterized by

    A. achievement beyond even my own expectations
    B. hard work
    C. success without having to try very hard
    D. bitter disappointment in those charged with the task of educating me

45. I believe that when a group composed of talented people fails to achieve an assigned task, it is usually the case that

   A. A the group failed to appoint a leader who could have directed their talents toward a result
   B. the group probably didn't do as good a job at communicating as they could have
   C. some group members were working harder than others
   D. the people who assigned the task had unrealistic expectations

45.____

46. I feel that whatever success I have achieved in life has been attributable largely to

   A. myself alone
   B. hard work and the support of others
   C. the fact that tasks were clearly defined and not too difficult
   D. D. pure luck

46.____

47. In my academic career, I have tended to focus the most energy on course work that

   A. allowed me to express my creativity
   B. I knew would later help to advance my career
   C. challenged me to think in new and different ways
   D. involved memorization and repetition

47.____

48. I usually get a physical workout _____ a week.

   A. 0-1   B. 2-3   C. 3-5   D. 5-7

48.____

49. Of the following, my favorite academic subjects could be most accurately described as

   A. the empirical subjects, such as math and science
   B. expressive and creative subjects such as art
   C. subjects that involved a lot of reading, such as history and English literature
   D. entirely dependent on how the subjects were taught, and in what kind of environment

49.____

50. Of the following, the information sources I tend to trust the most are

   A. network television news programs
   B. Internet blogs
   C. professional and scholarly journals, such as *Scientific American*
   D. other print media such as newspapers and magazines

50.____

**Biodata Inventory
Key to Exercises**

Note: In a biographical inventory, which asks for factual data, there are no right or wrong answers. It may also be true that for a particular question, more than one answer reflects a trait or viewpoint that might qualify one as a special agent: there is no single type of person or personality type that is acceptable. At the same time, there are some qualities or experiences that would probably suggest that a person is less than an ideal candidate. Generally, you are likely to be considered "qualified" if your answers tend to reveal the skills and abilities that the Biodata Inventory is designed to look for:

- *Ability to Organize, Plan, and Prioritize*
- *Ability to Maintain a Positive Image*
- *Ability to Evaluate Information and Make Judgment Decisions*
- *Initiative and Motivation*
- *Ability to Adapt to Changing Situations*
- *Physical Requirements*

The following responses are the ones most indicative of these skills and abilities:

1. No choice here is better than the others; all describe a problem.
2. D
3. D
4. C
5. A or C

6. No answer is inherently better than the others; candidate suitability will probably depend on the task at hand.
7. A or B
8. D
9. A
10. B or D

11. B
12. A or B
13. A
14. D
15. A

16. D
17. A
18. C or D
19. B
20. None is "right," but choice C is the least desirable, labeling you as one who can't stick with a job.

21. A
22. None is "right," but choice D is the least desirable—it's better to have over-achieved at least once or twice.
23. None is "right," but choice D is the least desirable.
24. C
25. B

Biodata Inventory
Key to Exercises (continued)

26. B
27. C
28. C
29. C
30. A

31. B
32. B
33. B
34. B
35. B or C

36. D
37. C
38. C
39. D
40. A

41. B
42. C
43. C
44. B
45. B

46. B
47. C
48. D
49. None is the "right" answer, but A or C are the best choices.
50. C

PERSONALITY/AUTOBIOGRAPHICAL INVENTORY
EXAMINATION SECTION
TEST 1

DIRECTIONS: Each question or incomplete statement is followed by several suggested answers or completions. Select the one that BEST answers the question or completes the statement. *PRINT THE LETTER OF THE CORRECT ANSWER IN THE SPACE AT THE RIGHT.*

1. While a senior in high school, I was absent
   - A. never
   - B. seldom
   - C. frequently
   - D. more than 10 days
   - E. only when I felt bored

2. While in high school, I failed classes
   - A. never
   - B. once
   - C. twice
   - D. more than twice
   - E. at least four times

3. During class discussions in my high school classes, I usually
   - A. listened without participating
   - B. participated as much as possible
   - C. listened until I had something to add to the discussion
   - D. disagreed with others simply for the sake of argument
   - E. laughed at stupid ideas

4. My high school grade point average (on a 4.0 scale) was
   - A. 2.0 or lower
   - B. 2.1 to 2.5
   - C. 2.6 to 3.0
   - D. 3.1 to 3.5
   - E. 3.6 to 4.0

5. As a high school student, I completed my assignments
   - A. as close to the due date as I could manage
   - B. whenever the teacher gave me an extension
   - C. frequently
   - D. on time
   - E. when they were interesting

6. While in high school, I participated in
   - A. athletic and nonathletic extracurricular activities
   - B. athletic extracurricular activities
   - C. nonathletic extracurricular activities
   - D. no extracurricular activities
   - E. mandatory after-school programs

7. In high school, I made the honor roll   7._____
   A. several times
   B. once
   C. more than once
   D. twice
   E. I can't remember if I made the honor role

8. Upon graduation from high school, I received   8._____
   A. academic and nonacademic honors
   B. academic honors
   C. nonacademic honors
   D. no honors
   E. I can't remember if I received honors

9. While attending high school, I worked at a paid job or as a volunteer   9._____
   A. never   B. every so often
   C. 5 to 10 hours a month   D. more than 10 hours a month
   E. more than 15 hours a month

10. During my senior year of high school, I skipped school   10._____
    A. whenever I could   B. once a week
    C. several times a week   D. not at all
    E. when I got bored

11. I was suspended from high school   11._____
    A. not at all
    B. once or twice
    C. once or twice, for fighting
    D. several times
    E. more times than I can remember

12. During high school, my fellow students and teachers considered me   12._____
    A. above average
    B. below average
    C. average
    D. underachieving
    E. underachieving and prone to fighting

13. The ability to _____ is most important to a Police Officer   13._____
    A. draw his/her gun quickly
    B. see over great distances and difficult terrain
    C. verbally and physically intimidate criminals
    D. communicate effectively in circumstances which can be dangerous
    E. hear over great distances

14. I began planning for college   14.____
    A. when my parents told me to
    B. when I entered high school
    C. during my junior year
    D. during my senior hear
    E. when I signed up for my SAT (or other standardized exam)

15. An effective leader is someone who   15.____
    A. inspires confidence in his/her followers
    B. inspires fear in his/her followers
    C. tells subordinates exactly what they should do
    D. creates an environment in which subordinates feel insecure about their
       job security and performance
    E. makes as few decisions as possible

16. I prepared myself for college by   16.____
    A. learning how to get extensions on major assignments
    B. working as many hours as possible at my after-school job
    C. spending as much time with my friends as possible
    D. getting good grades and participating in extracurricular activities
    E. watching television shows about college kids

17. I paid for college by   17.____
    A. supplementing my parents contributions with my own earnings
    B. relying on scholarships, loans, and my own earnings
    C. relying on my parents and student loans
    D. relying on my parents to pay my tuition, room and board
    E. relying on sources not listed here

18. While a college student, I spent my summers and holiday breaks   18.____
    A. in summer or remedial classes   B. traveling
    C. working   D. relaxing
    E. spending time with my friends

19. My final college grade point average (on a 4.0 scale) was   19.____
    A. 3.8 to 4.0   B. 3.5 to 3.8   C. 3.0 to 3.5
    D. 2.5 to 3.0   E. 2.0 to 2.5

20. As a college student, I cut classes   20.____
    A. frequently   B. when I didn't like them
    C. sometimes   D. rarely
    E. when I needed the sleep

21. In college, I received academic honors   21.____
    A. not at all
    B. once
    C. twice
    D. several times
    E. I can't remember if I received academic honors

22. While in college, I declared a major
    A. during my first year   B. during my sophomore year
    C. during my junior year   D. during my senior year
    E. several times

23. While on patrol as a Police Officer, you spot someone attempting to flee the scene of a crime. Your first reaction is to
    A. draw your weapon
    B. observe the person until he or she completes the fleeing
    C. identify yourself as a Police Officer
    D. fire your weapon over the person's head in order to scare him or her
    E. call immediately for backup

24. As a college student, I failed _____ classes.
    A. no   B. two   C. three
    D. four   E. more than four

25. Friends describe me as
    A. introverted   B. hot-tempered   C. unpredictable
    D. quiet   E. easygoing

KEY (CORRECT ANSWERS)

PLEASE NOTE: The answers listed are the best answers. However, you are to answer the exam honestly. Your personal answer may differ from the *best* answers.

1. A
2. A
3. C
4. E
5. D

6. A
7. A
8. A
9. E
10. D

11. A
12. A
13. D
14. B
15. A

16. D
17. B
18. C
19. A
20. D

21. D
22. A
23. C
24. A
25. E

TEST 2

DIRECTIONS: Each question or incomplete statement is followed by several suggested answers or completions. Select the one that BEST answers the question or completes the statement. *PRINT THE LETTER OF THE CORRECT ANSWER IN THE SPACE AT THE RIGHT.*

1. As a Police Officer, you apprehend three men whom you believe are in the country illegally. However, none of the men speaks English, and you don't speak their language.
   Your reaction should be to
   A. draw your weapon so that they understand the seriousness of the situation
   B. take them into custody, where they will have access to a translator
   C. attempt to communicate through hand gestures and shouting
   D. call for a translator to come and meet you at your location
   E. pretend you understand their language and apprehend them

   1._____

2. During my college classes, I preferred to
   A. remain silent during class discussions
   B. do other homework during class discussions
   C. participate frequently in class discussions
   D. argue with others as much as possible
   E. laugh at the stupid opinions of others

   2._____

3. As a Police Officer, you are chasing a small group of people who are running away from the scene of a crime. During your pursuit, one member of the group is left behind. You see that she is injured and in need of medical attention.
   Your reaction is to
   A. fire your weapon at the group members to get them to stop
   B. cease pursuit of the group members and take the woman into custody
   C. continue pursuit of the group members, leaving the woman behind since acting ill is a common trick
   D. radio for backup to stay with the woman while medical help arrives while you continue pursuit of the group members
   E. radio for backup to continue pursuit of the group members while you stay with the woman and wait for medical help to arrive

   3._____

4. As a college student, I was placed on academic probation
   A. not at all   B. once
   C. twice   D. three times
   E. more than three times

   4._____

5. At work, being a team player means to
   A. compromise your ideals and beliefs
   B. compensate for the incompetence of others
   C. count on others to compensate for my inexperience
   D. cooperate with others to get a project finished
   E. rely on others to get the job done

   5._____

6. As a Police Officer, you confront someone you believe has just committed a crime. After identifying yourself, you notice the suspect holding something that looks like a knife.
   Your FIRST reaction should be to
   A. draw your weapon and fire
   B. call immediately for backup
   C. keep your weapon drawn until you get the suspect into a position that is controllable
   D. ask the suspect if he is armed
   E. talk to the suspect without drawing your weapon

6._____

7. My friends from college remember me primarily as a(n)
   A. person who loved to party
   B. ambitious student
   C. athlete
   D. joker
   E. fighter

7._____

8. My college experience is memorable primarily because of
   A. the friends I made
   B. the sorority/fraternity I was able to join
   C. the social activities I participated in
   D. my academic achievements
   E. the money I spent

8._____

9. A friend who is applying for a job asks you to help him pass the mandatory drug test by substituting a sample of your urine for his.
   You should
   A. help him by supplying the sample
   B. help him by supplying the sample and insisting he seek drug counseling
   C. supply the sample, but tell him that this is the only time you'll help in this way
   D. call the police
   E. refuse

9._____

10. As a college student, I handed in my assignments
    A. when they were due
    B. whenever I could get an extension
    C. when they were interesting
    D. when my friends reminded me to
    E. when I was able

10._____

11. At work you are accused of a minor infraction which you didn't commit.
    Your FIRST reaction is to
    A. call a lawyer
    B. speak to your supervisor about the mistake
    C. call the police
    D. yell at the person who did commit the infraction
    E. accept the consequences regardless of your guilt or innocence

11._____

12. While on patrol, you are surprised by a large group of disorderly teenage gang members. You are greatly outnumbered.
    As a Police Officer, your FIRST reaction is to
    A. draw your weapon and identify yourself
    B. get back into your vehicle and wait for help to arrive
    C. call for backup
    D. pretend you are part of a large group of police in the area
    E. identify yourself and get the group members into a controllable position

12.____

13. As a college student, I began to prepare for final exams
    A. the night before taking them
    B. when the professor handed out the review sheets
    C. several weeks before taking them
    D. when my friends began to prepare for their exams
    E. the morning of the exam

13.____

14. As a Police Officer in the field, you confront a small group of people you believe to be wanted criminals.
    Your MOST important consideration during this exchange should be
    A. apprehension of criminals
    B. safety of county citizens in nearby towns
    C. safety of the criminals
    D. number of criminals you must apprehend in order to receive a commendation'
    E. the amount of respect the criminals show to you and your position

14.____

15. At work, I am known as
    A. popular   B. quiet   C. intense
    D. easygoing   E. dedicated

15.____

16. The MOST important quality in a coworker is
    A. friendliness   B. cleanliness
    C. a good sense of humor D. dependability
    E. good listening skills

16.____

17. In the past year, I have stayed home from work
    A. frequently   B. only when I felt depressed
    C. rarely   D. only when I felt overwhelmed
    E. only to run important errands

17.____

18. As a Police Officer, the BEST way to collect information from a suspect during an interview is to
    A. physically intimidate the suspect
    B. verbally intimidate the suspect
    C. threaten the suspect's family and/or friend with criminal prosecution
    D. encourage a conversation with the suspect
    E. sit in silence until the suspect begins speaking

18.____

19. For me, the BEST thing about college was the
    A. chance to strengthen my friendships and develop new ones
    B. chance to test my abilities and develop new ones
    C. number of extracurricular activities and clubs
    D. chance to socialize
    E. chance to try several different majors

19.____

20. As an employee, my WEAKEST skill is
    A. controlling my temper
    B. my organizational ability
    C. my ability to effectively understand directions
    D. my ability to effectively manage others
    E. my ability to communicate my thoughts in writing

20.____

21. As a Police Officer, my GREATEST strength would be
    A. my sense of loyalty   B. my organizational ability
    C. punctuality   D. dedication
    E. my ability to intimidate others

21.____

22. As a Police Officer, you find a group of suspicious youths gathered around a truck which is on fire.
    Your FIRST reaction is to
    A. call the fire department
    B. arrest them all for destruction of property
    C. draw your weapon and begin questioning them
    D. return to your vehicle and wait for the fire department
    E. instruct the group to remain while you return to your vehicle and request backup

22.____

23. If asked by my company to learn a new job-related skill, my reaction would be to
    A. ask for a raise
    B. ask for overtime pay
    C. question the necessity of the skill
    D. cooperate with some reluctance
    E. cooperate with enthusiasm

23.____

24. When I disagree with others, I tend to
    A. listen quietly despite my disagreement
    B. laugh openly at the person I disagree with
    C. ask the person to explain their views before I respond
    D. leave the conversation before my anger gets the best of me
    E. point out exactly why the person is wrong

24.____

25. When I find myself in a situation which is confusing or unclear, my reaction is to
    A. pretend I am not confused
    B. remain calm and, if necessary, ask someone else for clarification
    C. grow frustrated and angry
    D. walk away from the situation
    E. immediately insist that someone explain things to me

25._____

KEY (CORRECT ANSWERS)

PLEASE NOTE: The answers listed are the best answers. However, you are to answer the exam honestly. Your personal answer may differ from the *best* answers.

1.	B		11.	B
2.	C		12.	E
3.	E		13.	C
4.	A		14.	A
5.	D		15.	E
6.	C		16.	D
7.	B		17.	C
8.	D		18.	D
9.	E		19.	B
10.	A		20.	E

21. D
22. A
23. E
24. C
25. B

TEST 3

DIRECTIONS: Each question or incomplete statement is followed by several suggested answers or completions. Select the one that BEST answers the question or completes the statement. *PRINT THE LETTER OF THE CORRECT ANSWER IN THE SPACE AT THE RIGHT.*

1. While on patrol as a Police Officer, you find a dead body lying in the open. Hiding a few feet away, behind some rocks, you find a suspicious person who is holding items which seem to have been taken from the dead body, including a pair of shoes and some jewelry.
   You should
   A. apprehend the suspect and bring him to the station for further questioning
   B. arrest the suspect for murder and robbery
   C. arrest the suspect for murder
   D. subdue the suspect with force and check the area for his accomplices
   E. subdue the suspect with force and call for backup to check the area for his accomplices

   1.____

2. If you were placed in a supervisory position, which of the following abilities would you consider to be MOST important to your job performance?
   A. Stubborness
   B. The ability to hear all sides of a story before making a decision
   C. Kindness
   D. The ability to make and stick to a decision
   E. Patience

   2.____

3. What is your HIGHEST level of education?
   A. Less than a high school diploma
   B. A high school diploma or equivalency
   C. A graduate of community college
   D. A graduate of a four-year accredited college
   E. A degree from graduate school

   3.____

4. When asked to supervise other workers, your approach should be to
   A. ask for management wages since you're doing management work
   B. give the workers direction and supervise every aspect of the process
   C. give the workers direction and then allow them to do the job
   D. and the workers their job specifications
   E. do the work yourself, since you're uncomfortable supervising others

   4.____

5. Which of the following BEST describes you?
   A. Need little or no supervision
   B. Resent too much supervision
   C. Require as much supervision as my peers
   D. Require slightly more supervision than my peers
   E. Require close supervision

   5.____

6. You accept a job which requires an ability to perform several tasks at once. What is the BEST way to handle such a position?
   A. With strong organizational skills and a close attention to detail
   B. By delegating the work to someone with strong organizational skills
   C. Staying focused on one task at a time, no matter what happens
   D. Working on one task at a time until each task is successfully completed
   E. Asking my supervisor to help me

7. As a Police Officer, you take a suspected perpetrator into custody. After returning to the field, you notice that your gun is missing.
   You should
   A. retrace your steps to see if you dropped it somewhere
   B. report the loss immediately
   C. ask your partner to borrow his or her gun
   D. pretend that nothing's happened
   E. rely on your hands for defense and protection

8. Which of the following BEST describes your behavior when you disagree with someone?
   You
   A. state your own point of view as quickly and loudly as you can
   B. listen quietly and keep your opinions to yourself
   C. listen to the other person's perspective and then carefully point out all the flaws in their logic
   D. list all of the ignorant people who agree with the opposing point of view
   E. listen to the other person's perspective and then explain your own perspective

9. As a new Police Officer, you make several mistakes during your first week of work.
   You react by
   A. learning from your mistakes and moving on
   B. resigning
   C. blaming it on your supervisor
   D. refusing to talk about it
   E. blaming yourself

10. My ability to communicate effectively with others is _____ average.
    A. below   B. about   C. above
    D. far above   E. far below

11. In which of the following areas are you MOST highly skilled?
    A. Written communication
    B. Oral communication
    C. Ability to think quickly in difficult situations
    D. Ability to work with a broad diversity of people and personalities
    E. Organizational skills

12. As a Police Officer, you are assigned to work with a partner whom you dislike. You should
    A. immediately report the problem to your supervisor
    B. ask your partner not to speak to you during working hours
    C. tell your colleagues about your differences
    D. tell your partner why you dislike him/her
    E. work with your partner regardless of your personal feelings

13. During high school, what was your MOST common after-school activity?
    A. Remaining after school to participate in various clubs and organizations (such as band, sports, etc.)
    B. Remaining after school to make up for missed classes
    C. Remaining after school as punishment (detention, etc.)
    D. Going straight to an after-school job
    E. Spending the afternoon at home or with friends

14. During high school, in which of the following subjects did you receive the HIGHEST grades?
    A. English, History, Social Studies
    B. Math, Science
    C. Vocational classes
    D. My grades were consistent in all subjects
    E. Classes I liked

15. When faced with an overwhelming number of duties at work, your reaction is to
    A. do all of the work yourself, no matter what the cost
    B. delegate some responsibilities to capable colleagues
    C. immediately ask your supervisor for help
    D. put off as much work as possible until you can get to it
    E. take some time off to relax and clear your mind

16. As a Police Officer, your supervisor informs you that a prisoner whom you arrested has accused you of beating him. You know you are innocent. You react by
    A. quitting your job
    B. hiring a lawyer
    C. challenging your supervisor to prove the charges against you
    D. calmly tell your supervisor what really happened and presenting evidence to support your position
    E. insisting that you be allowed to speak alone to the prisoner

17. Which of the following BEST describes your desk at your current or most recent job?
    A. Messy and disorganized   B. Neat and organized
    C. Messy but organized   D. Neat but disorganized
    E. Messy

18. The _____ BEST describes your reasons for wanting to become a Police Officer.
    A. ability to carry and use a weapon
    B. excitement and challenges of the career
    C. excellent salary and benefits package
    D. chance to tell other people what to do
    E. chance to help people find a better life

19. As a Police Officer in the field, you are approached by a man who is frantic but unable to speak English. After several minutes of trying to communicate, you realize that the man is asking you to come with him in order to help someone who has been hurt.
    You should
    A. ignore him, since it might be a trap
    B. call for backup
    C. immediately offer to help the man
    D. return to your vehicle and wait for the man to leave
    E. radio your position and situation to another officer, then go with the man to offer help

20. When asked to take on extra responsibility at work, in order to help out a coworker who is overwhelmed, your response is to
    A. ask for overtime pay
    B. complain to your supervisor that you are being taken advantage of
    C. help the coworker to the best of your ability
    D. ask the coworker to come back some other time
    E. give the coworker some advice on how to get his/her job done

21. At my last job, I was promoted
    A. not at all   B. once
    C. twice   D. three times
    E. more than three times

22. As a Police Officer, you discover the body of a person whom you suspect to be a gang member. You also suspect that there are several other gang members hiding in the nearby vicinity.
    Your FIRST reaction should be to
    A. begin a search of the nearby area for the other gang members
    B. return to your vehicle and call for backup
    C. return to your vehicle with the body of the person you found
    D. check whether the person you found is dead or alive
    E. draw your weapon and identify yourself

23. You are faced with an overwhelming deadline at work. Your reaction is to
    A. procrastinate until the last minute
    B. procrastinate until someone notices you need some help
    C. notify your supervisor that you can't complete the work on your own
    D. work in silence without asking any questions
    E. arrange your schedule so that you can get the work done before the deadline

24. When you feel yourself under deadline pressures at work, your response is to
    A. make sure you keep to a schedule which allows you to complete the work on time
    B. wait until just before the deadline to complete the work
    C. ask someone else to do the work
    D. grow so obsessive about the work that your coworkers feel compelled to help you
    E. ask your supervisor immediately for help

25. Which of the following BEST describes your appearance at your current or most recent position?
    A. Well-groomed, neat, and clean
    B. Unkempt, but dressed neatly
    C. Messy and dirty clothing
    D. Unshaven and untidy
    E. Clean-shaven, but sloppily dressed

KEY (CORRECT ANSWERS)

PLEASE NOTE: The answers listed are our preferred answers. However, you are to answer the exam honestly. Your personal answer may differ from our answers.

1. A
2. D
3. E
4. C
5. A

6. A
7. B
8. E
9. A
10. C

11. C
12. E
13. A
14. D
15. B

16. D
17. B
18. B
19. E
20. C

21. C
22. D
23. E
24. A
25. A

TEST 4

DIRECTIONS: Each question or incomplete statement is followed by several suggested answers or completions. Select the one that BEST answers the question or completes the statement. *PRINT THE LETTER OF THE CORRECT ANSWER IN THE SPACE AT THE RIGHT.*

1. Which of the following BEST describes the way you react to making a difficult decision?
   A. Consult with the people you're closest to before making the decision
   B. Make the decision entirely on your own
   C. Consult only with those people whom your decision will affect
   D. Consult with everyone you known, in an effort to make a decision that will please everyone
   E. Forget about the decision until you have to make it

1.____

2. If placed in a supervisory role, which of the following characteristics would you rely on most heavily when dealing with the employees you supervise?
   A. Kindness   B. Cheeriness   C. Honesty
   D. Hostility   E. Aloofness

2.____

3. As a Police Officer, you are pursuing a suspect when he turns and pulls something out of his pocket that looks like a gun.
   You should
   A. run away and call for backup
   B. assure the man that you mean him no harm
   C. draw your gun and order the man to stop and drop his weapon
   D. draw your gun and fire a warning shot
   E. draw your gun and fire immediately

3.____

4. In addition to English, in which of the following languages are you also fluent?
   A. Spanish   B. French   C. Italian
   D. German   E. Other

4.____

5. When confronted with gossip at work, your typical reaction is to
   A. participate
   B. listen without participating
   C. notify your supervisor
   D. excuse yourself from the discussion
   E. confront your coworkers about their problem

5.____

6. In the past two years, how many jobs have you held?
   A. None   B. One   C. Two
   D. Three   E. More than three

6.____

7. In your current or most recent job, you favorite part of the job is the part which involves
    A. telling other people what they're doing wrong
    B. supervising others
    C. working without supervision to finish a project
    D. written communication
    E. oral communication

8. Your supervisor asks you about a colleague who is applying for a position which you also want.
   You react by
    A. commenting honestly on the person's work performance
    B. enhancing the person's negative traits
    C. informing your supervisor about your colleague's personal problems
    D. telling your supervisor that would be better in the position
    E. refusing to comment

9. As a Police Officer, you confiscate some contraband which was being imported by an illegal alien who is now in your custody. Your partner asks you not to turn the contraband in to your supervisor.
   Your response is to
    A. inform your supervisor of your partner's request immediately
    B. tell your partner you feel uncomfortable with his request
    C. pretend you didn't hear you partner's request
    D. tell your supervisor and all your colleagues about your partner's request
    E. give the contraband to your partner and let him handle it

10. Which of the following BEST describes your responsibilities in your last job?
    A. Entirely supervisory
    B. Much supervisory responsibility
    C. Equal amounts of supervisory and nonsupervisory responsibility
    D. Some supervisory responsibilities
    E. No supervisory responsibilities

11. How much written communication did your previous or most recent job require of you?
    A. A great deal of written communication
    B. Some written communication
    C. I don't remember
    D. A small amount of written communication
    E. No written communication

12. In the past two years, how many times have you been fired from a job?
    A. None   B. Once
    C. Twice   D. Three times
    E. More than three times

13. How much time have you spent working for volunteer organizations in the past year?
    A. 10 to 20 hours per week
    B. 5 to 10 hours per week
    C. 3 to 5 hours per week
    D. 1 to 3 hours per week
    E. I have spent no time volunteering in the past year

14. Your efforts at volunteer work usually revolve around which of the following types of organizations?
    A. Religious
    B. Community-based organizations working to improve the community
    C. Charity organizations working on behalf of the poor
    D. Charity organizations working on behalf of the infirm or handicapped
    E. Other

15. Which of the following BEST describes your professional history?
    Promoted at _____ coworkers
    A. a much faster rate than
    B. a slightly faster rate than
    C. the same rate as
    D. a slightly slower rate than
    E. a much slower rate than

16. Which of the following qualities do you MOST appreciate in a coworker?
    A. Friendliness   B. Dependability   C. Good looks
    D. Silence   E. Forgiveness

17. When you disagree with a supervisor's instructions or opinion about how to complete a project, your reaction is to
    A. inform your supervisor that you refuse to complete the project according to his or her instructions
    B. inform your colleague of you supervisor's incompetence
    C. accept your supervisor's instructions in silence
    D. voice your concerns and then complete the project according to your own instincts
    E. voice your concerns and then complete the project according to your supervisor's instructions

18. Which of the following BEST describes your reaction to close supervision and specific direction from your supervisor?
    You
    A. listen carefully to the directions, and then figure out a way to do the job more effectively
    B. complete the job according to the given specifications
    C. show some initiative by doing the job your way
    D. ask someone else to do the job for you
    E. listen carefully to the directions, and then figure out a better way to do the job which will save more money

19. How should a Police Officer handle a situation in which he or she is offered a bribe not to issue a traffic ticket?
    A. Pretend the bribe was never offered
    B. Accept the money as evidence and release the person
    C. Draw your weapon and call for backup
    D. Refuse the bribe and then arrest the person
    E. Accept the bribe and then arrest the person

19.____

20. At work you are faced with a difficult decision.
    You react by
    A. seeking advice from your colleagues
    B. following your own path regardless of the consequences
    C. asking your supervisor what you should do
    D. keeping the difficulties to yourself
    E. working for a solution which will please everyone

20.____

21. If asked to work with a person whom you dislike, your response would be
    A. to ask your supervisor to allow you to work with someone else
    B. to ask your coworker to transfer to another department or project
    C. talk to your coworker about the proper way to behave at work
    D. pretend the coworker is your best friend for the sake of your job
    E. to set aside your personal differences in order to complete the job

21.____

22. As a supervisory, which of the following incentives would you use to motivate your employees?
    A. Fear of losing their jobs
    B. Fear of their supervisors
    C. Allowing employees to provide their input on a number of policies
    D. Encouraging employees to file secret reports regarding colleagues' transgressions
    E. All of the above

22.____

23. A fellow Police Officer, with whom you enjoy a close friendship, has a substance-abuse problem which has gone undetected. You suspect the problem may be affecting his job.
    You would
    A. ask the Police Officer if the problem is affecting his job performance
    B. warn the Police Officer that he must seek counseling or you will report him
    C. wait a few weeks to see whether the officer's problem really is affecting his job
    D. discuss it with your supervisor
    E. wait for the supervisor to discover the problem

23.____

24. In the past two months, you have missed work
    A. zero times   B. once
    C. twice   D. three times
    E. more than three times

24.____

5 (#4)

25. As a Police Officer, you are pursuing a group of robbers when you discover two small children who have been abandoned near a railroad crossing.
    You should
    A. tell the children to stay put while you continue your pursuit
    B. lock the children in your vehicle and continue your pursuit
    C. stay with the children and radio for help in the pursuit of the robbers
    D. use the children to set a trap for the robbers
    E. ignore the children and continue your pursuit

25.____

KEY (CORRECT ANSWERS)

PLEASE NOTE: The answers listed are our preferred answers. However, you are to answer the exam honestly. Your personal answer may differ from our answers.

1.	A		11.	B
2.	C		12.	A
3.	C		13.	C
4.	A		14.	B
5.	D		15.	A
6.	B		16.	B
7.	C		17.	E
8.	A		18.	B
9.	A		19.	D
10.	D		20.	A

21. E
22. C
23. D
24. A
25. C

EXAMINATION SECTION
TEST 1

For each of the following items, circle the answer that best reflects the accuracy of the given statement, according to your own values, opinions, and experience.

1. In most situations, I value cooperation over competition.

   A. Very Accurate
   B. Moderately Accurate
   C. Neither Accurate nor Inaccurate
   D. Moderately Inaccurate
   E. Very Inaccurate

2. In work or in school, I've tried to do more than what's expected of me.

   A. Very Accurate
   B. Moderately Accurate
   C. Neither Accurate nor Inaccurate
   D. Moderately Inaccurate
   E. Very Inaccurate

3. Most of my problems are caused by other people.

   A. Very Accurate
   B. Moderately Accurate
   C. Neither Accurate nor Inaccurate
   D. Moderately Inaccurate
   E. Very Inaccurate

4. It's reasonable to say that a person's race is in some way related to the likelihood that he or she will commit a crime.

   A. Very Accurate
   B. Moderately Accurate
   C. Neither Accurate nor Inaccurate
   D. Moderately Inaccurate
   E. Very Inaccurate

5. My respect for a person's authority relies entirely on my respect for them as an individual, and has nothing to do with his or her official position.

   A. Very Accurate
   B. Moderately Accurate
   C. Neither Accurate nor Inaccurate
   D. Moderately Inaccurate
   E. Very Inaccurate

6. When I was in school, I never cheated on a test or assignment.

   A. Very Accurate
   B. Moderately Accurate
   C. Neither Accurate nor Inaccurate
   D. Moderately Inaccurate
   E. Very Inaccurate

7. I feel comfortable around most people, even if they're strangers.

   A. Very Accurate
   B. Moderately Accurate
   C. Neither Accurate nor Inaccurate
   D. Moderately Inaccurate
   E. Very Inaccurate

8. It's acceptable for an employee to borrow property from the workplace if the person who takes it intends to return it when he or she is finished with it.

   A. Very Accurate
   B. Moderately Accurate
   C. Neither Accurate nor Inaccurate
   D. Moderately Inaccurate
   E. Very Inaccurate

9. If it's clear that a person is not likely to receive adequate punishment for a crime or infraction, it's only fair to inflict some form of discipline on that person to make up for any likely lapses injustice.

   A. Very Accurate
   B. Moderately Accurate
   C. Neither Accurate nor Inaccurate
   D. Moderately Inaccurate
   E. Very Inaccurate

10. In previous work experience, I have been reluctant or unable to take on extra work or overtime on short notice.

    A. Very Accurate
    B. Moderately Accurate
    C. Neither Accurate nor Inaccurate
    D. Moderately Inaccurate
    E. Very Inaccurate

11. The casual use of illegal substances, if it's done only recreationally and on weekends, has no effect on a person's performance on the job during the work week.

    A. Very Accurate
    B. Moderately Accurate
    C. Neither Accurate nor Inaccurate
    D. Moderately Inaccurate
    E. Very Inaccurate

12. I am sometimes overwhelmed by events.

    A. Very Accurate
    B. Moderately Accurate
    C. Neither Accurate nor Inaccurate
    D. Moderately Inaccurate
    E. Very Inaccurate

13. If I don't agree with a certain rule, I see nothing wrong with breaking it, as long as it doesn't hurt anyone else.

    A. Very Accurate
    B. Moderately Accurate
    C. Neither Accurate nor Inaccurate
    D. Moderately Inaccurate
    E. Very Inaccurate

14. I get angry easily.

    A. Very Accurate
    B. Moderately Accurate
    C. Neither Accurate nor Inaccurate
    D. Moderately Inaccurate
    E. Very Inaccurate

15. As long as an employee finishes all his work on time at the end of the day, there's nothing wrong with coming back from lunch late.

    A. Very Accurate
    B. Moderately Accurate
    C. Neither Accurate nor Inaccurate
    D. Moderately Inaccurate
    E. Very Inaccurate

16. I enjoy beginning new things.

    A. Very Accurate
    B. Moderately Accurate
    C. Neither Accurate nor Inaccurate
    D. Moderately Inaccurate
    E. Very Inaccurate

17. When I have a number of tasks to be done, I prioritize them and tackle them immediately in order of importance.

    A. Very Accurate
    B. Moderately Accurate
    C. Neither Accurate nor Inaccurate
    D. Moderately Inaccurate
    E. Very Inaccurate

18. I would have no reservations about working for a supervisor who is of a different race or gender than I am.

    A. Very Accurate
    B. Moderately Accurate
    C. Neither Accurate nor Inaccurate
    D. Moderately Inaccurate
    E. Very Inaccurate

19. I'd rather help other people to do better than punish them for doing wrong.

    A. Very Accurate
    B. Moderately Accurate
    C. Neither Accurate nor Inaccurate
    D. Moderately Inaccurate
    E. Very Inaccurate

20. In the past, I've had personality clashes with fellow students or co-workers whom I disliked or with whom I disagreed.

    A. Very Accurate
    B. Moderately Accurate
    C. Neither Accurate nor Inaccurate
    D. Moderately Inaccurate
    E. Very Inaccurate

21. Confrontations are usually unpleasant, but sometimes necessary.

    A. Very Accurate
    B. Moderately Accurate
    C. Neither Accurate nor Inaccurate
    D. Moderately Inaccurate
    E. Very Inaccurate

22. I generally believe that other people have good intentions.

    A. Very Accurate
    B. Moderately Accurate
    C. Neither Accurate nor Inaccurate
    D. Moderately Inaccurate
    E. Very Inaccurate

23. When I have a lot of information to sort through, I have difficulty making up my mind.

    A. Very Accurate
    B. Moderately Accurate
    C. Neither Accurate nor Inaccurate
    D. Moderately Inaccurate
    E. Very Inaccurate

24. In tense situations, I choose my words with care.

    A. Very Accurate
    B. Moderately Accurate
    C. Neither Accurate nor Inaccurate
    D. Moderately Inaccurate
    E. Very Inaccurate

25. A person who works through his or her lunch break should automatically be able to go home early.

   A. Very Accurate
   B. Moderately Accurate
   C. Neither Accurate nor Inaccurate
   D. Moderately Inaccurate
   E. Very Inaccurate

Experiences and Traits

For each of the 25 items, score your response according to the list below. Then add the scores of all 25 items to arrive at a single number.

1. A=4;B=3;C=2;D=1;E=0
2. A=4;B=3;C=2;D=1;E=0
3. A=0;B=1;C=2;D=3;E=4
4. A=0;B=1;C=2;D=3;E=4
5. A=0;B=1;C=2;D=3;E=4

6. A=4;B=3;C=2;D=1;E=0
7. A=4;B=3;C=2;D=1;E=0
8. A=0;B=1;C=2;D=3;E=4
9. A=0;B=1;C=2;D=3;E=4
10. A=0;B=1;C=2;D=3;E=4

11. A=0;B=1;C=2;D=3;E=4
12. A=0;B=1;C=2;D=3;E=4
13. A=0;B=1;C=2;D=3;E=4
14. A=0;B=1;C=2;D=3;E=4
15. A=0;B=1;C=2;D=3;E=4

16. A=4;B=3;C=2;D=1;E=0
17. A=4;B=3;C=2;D=1;E=0
18. A=4;B=3;C=2;D=1;E=0
19. A=4;B=3;C=2;D=1;E=0
20. A=0;B=1;C=2;D=3;E=4

21. A=4;B=3;C=2;D=1;E=0
22. A=4;B=3;C=2;D=1;E=0
23. A=0;B=1;C=2;D=3;E=4
24. A=4;B=3;C=2;D=1;E=0
25. A=0;B=1;C=2;D=3;E=4

The following scores serve as an approximate guide to your compatibility with a career in law enforcement but should not be taken as the final word.

85-100 points	Most compatible
70-84 points	Compatible
50-69 points	Somewhat compatible
0-49 points	Incompatible

TEST 2

For each of the following items, circle the answer that best reflects the accuracy of the given statement, according to your own values, opinions, and experience.

1. I find it difficult to approach people I don't know well.

    A. Very Accurate
    B. Moderately Accurate
    C. Neither Accurate nor Inaccurate
    D. Moderately Inaccurate
    E. Very Inaccurate

2. I'm not really interested in hearing about other people's problems.

    A. Very Accurate
    B. Moderately Accurate
    C. Neither Accurate nor Inaccurate
    D. Moderately Inaccurate
    E. Very Inaccurate

3. Sometimes I don't know why I do the things I do.

    A. Very Accurate
    B. Moderately Accurate
    C. Neither Accurate nor Inaccurate
    D. Moderately Inaccurate
    E. Very Inaccurate

4. I am hesitant to take charge of a group that has no clear leadership.

    A. Very Accurate
    B. Moderately Accurate
    C. Neither Accurate nor Inaccurate
    D. Moderately Inaccurate
    E. Very Inaccurate

5. I enjoy examining myself and the direction my life is taking.

    A. Very Accurate
    B. Moderately Accurate
    C. Neither Accurate nor Inaccurate
    D. Moderately Inaccurate
    E. Very Inaccurate

6. I believe there is no absolute right or wrong.

    A. Very Accurate
    B. Moderately Accurate
    C. Neither Accurate nor Inaccurate
    D. Moderately Inaccurate
    E. Very Inaccurate

7. I always pay my bills on time.

    A. Very Accurate
    B. Moderately Accurate
    C. Neither Accurate nor Inaccurate
    D. Moderately Inaccurate
    E. Very Inaccurate

8. In this world it's difficult to be both honest and successful.

    A. Very Accurate
    B. Moderately Accurate
    C. Neither Accurate nor Inaccurate
    D. Moderately Inaccurate
    E. Very Inaccurate

9. I am intimidated by strong personalities.

    A. Very Accurate
    B. Moderately Accurate
    C. Neither Accurate nor Inaccurate
    D. Moderately Inaccurate
    E. Very Inaccurate

10. In past work experience, I was unable to find value in work that wasn't personally rewarding to me.

    A. Very Accurate
    B. Moderately Accurate
    C. Neither Accurate nor Inaccurate
    D. Moderately Inaccurate
    E. Very Inaccurate

11. I often do things I later regret.

    A. Very Accurate
    B. Moderately Accurate
    C. Neither Accurate nor Inaccurate
    D. Moderately Inaccurate
    E. Very Inaccurate

12. I feel sympathy for those who are worse off than I am.

    A. Very Accurate
    B. Moderately Accurate
    C. Neither Accurate nor Inaccurate
    D. Moderately Inaccurate
    E. Very Inaccurate

13. If a rule gets in the way of my doing my job well, I'll look for ways around it.

    A. Very Accurate
    B. Moderately Accurate
    C. Neither Accurate nor Inaccurate
    D. Moderately Inaccurate
    E. Very Inaccurate

14. I think a person's dress and appearance are important in the work environment.

    A. Very Accurate
    B. Moderately Accurate
    C. Neither Accurate nor Inaccurate
    D. Moderately Inaccurate
    E. Very Inaccurate

15. There have been times when my own personal use of drugs or alcohol has adversely affected my job performance.

    A. Very Accurate
    B. Moderately Accurate
    C. Neither Accurate nor Inaccurate
    D. Moderately Inaccurate
    E. Very Inaccurate

16. In past work or school experience, I have never been in a position to supervise the work of others.

    A. Very Accurate
    B. Moderately Accurate
    C. Neither Accurate nor Inaccurate
    D. Moderately Inaccurate
    E. Very Inaccurate

17. If I need to, I can talk other people into doing what I think is necessary.

    A. Very Accurate
    B. Moderately Accurate
    C. Neither Accurate nor Inaccurate
    D. Moderately Inaccurate
    E. Very Inaccurate

18. I usually prefer order to chaos.

    A. Very Accurate
    B. Moderately Accurate
    C. Neither Accurate nor Inaccurate
    D. Moderately Inaccurate
    E. Very Inaccurate

19. When I'm faced with an ethical dilemma, I listen to my conscience.

    A. Very Accurate
    B. Moderately Accurate
    C. Neither Accurate nor Inaccurate
    D. Moderately Inaccurate
    E. Very Inaccurate

20. When I communicate with other people, I can easily sense their emotional state.

    A. Very Accurate
    B. Moderately Accurate
    C. Neither Accurate nor Inaccurate
    D. Moderately Inaccurate
    E. Very Inaccurate

21. I set high standards for myself and others.

    A. Very Accurate
    B. Moderately Accurate
    C. Neither Accurate nor Inaccurate
    D. Moderately Inaccurate
    E. Very Inaccurate

22. In school or at work, I am never late.

    A. Very Accurate
    B. Moderately Accurate
    C. Neither Accurate nor Inaccurate
    D. Moderately Inaccurate
    E. Very Inaccurate

23. I sometimes make assumptions about people based on their racial or ethnic backgrounds.

    A. Very Accurate
    B. Moderately Accurate
    C. Neither Accurate nor Inaccurate
    D. Moderately Inaccurate
    E. Very Inaccurate

24. I tend to focus on the positive aspects of a complex situation, rather than the negatives.

    A. Very Accurate
    B. Moderately Accurate
    C. Neither Accurate nor Inaccurate
    D. Moderately Inaccurate
    E. Very Inaccurate

25. I can manage several tasks at the same time.

    A. Very Accurate
    B. Moderately Accurate
    C. Neither Accurate nor Inaccurate
    D. Moderately Inaccurate
    E. Very Inaccurate

4 (#2)

Experiences and Traits

For each of the 25 items, score your response according to the list below. Then add the scores of all 25 items to arrive at a single number.

1. A=0;B=1;C=2;D=3;E=4
2. A=0;B=1;C=2;D=3;E=4
3. A=0;B=1;C=2;D=3;E=4
4. A=0;B=1;C=2;D=3;E=4
5. A=4;B=3;C=2;D=1;E=0

6. A=0;B=1;C=2;D=3;E=4
7. A=4;B=3;C=2;D=1;E=0
8. A=0;B=1;C=2;D=3;E=4
9. A=0;B=1;C=2;D=3;E=4
10. A=0;B=1;C=2;D=3;E=4

11. A=0;B=1;C=2;D=3;E=4
12. A=4;B=3;C=2;D=1;E=0
13. A=0;B=1;C=2;D=3;E=4
14. A=4;B=3;C=2;D=1;E=0
15. A=0;B=1;C=2;D=3;E=4

16. A=0;B=1;C=2;D=3;E=4
17. A=4;B=3;C=2;D=1;E=0
18. A=4;B=3;C=2;D=1;E=0
19. A=4;B=3;C=2;D=1;E=0
20. A=4;B=3;C=2;D=1;E=0

21. A=4;B=3;C=2;D=1;E=0
22. A=4;B=3;C=2;D=1;E=0
23. A=0;B=1;C=2;D=3;E=4
24. A=4;B=3;C=2;D=1;E=0
25. A=4;B=3;C=2;D=1;E=0

The following scores serve as an approximate guide to your compatibility with a career in law enforcementbut should not be taken as the final word.

85-100 points	Most compatible
70-84 points	Compatible
50-69 points	Somewhat compatible
0-49 points	Incompatible

EXAMINATION SECTION
TEST 1

DIRECTIONS: This section contains descriptions of problem situations. Each problem situation has four alternative actions that might be taken to deal with the problem. You are to make two judgments for each problem.

First, decide which alternative you would MOST LIKELY choose in response to the problem. It might not be exactly what you would do in that situation, but it should be the alternative that comes closest to what you would actually do. Record your answers on the answer sheet by writing the appropriate letter next to the prompt for MOST LIKELY.

Second, decide which alternative you would be LEAST LIKELY to choose in that situation. Write the letter of that alternative next to the prompt for LEAST LIKELY.

1. You realize that an error has been made in the documentation of evidence for a case. The amount of the cash reported seized at the scene is now significantly less than when it was originally recorded. You would
    A. go back and talk to everyone who was involved in the chain of custody
    B. immediately tell a supervisor about the problem
    C. consider it a clerical error and try to conceal the discrepancy while you try to figure out how it happened but tell a supervisor if you cannot figure out what happened
    D. consider that the mistake was made when the evidence was seized, and alter the log to reflect the existing amount

    Most likely:_____ Least likely:_____

2. You are assigned to lead a search for evidence that may have been deposited somewhere within a large tract of woods. The recovery of this evidence is critical to the prosecution of the suspect in the crime. For this task, you are MOST likely to lead by
    A. blazing a trail for others to follow
    B. helping people choose the best course of action
    C. punishing mistakes
    D. appealing to shared goals and values

    Most likely:_____ Least likely:_____

3. Your partner, who has become your oldest and dearest friend, recently admitted to you that he removed something from the evidence room that might suggest the innocence of a suspect whom he knew without a doubt to be guilty. Your supervisor has discovered that the evidence is missing, and your partner asks you to say that you forgot to log the evidence in. You know that this would easily resolve the situation. You would
    A. not go along with the idea to say the mistake was yours, and tell the supervisor what happened
    B. not go along with the idea, but would say nothing about your partner's admission

C. not go along with the idea, and encourage your partner to own up to what he did
D. go along with your partner; he broke the rules but his intentions were good

Most likely:_____ Least likely:_____

4. You are having a telephone conversation with a supervisor who is leaving a confidential message to another agent in your office about facts pertaining to an important case. You are on your cellphone, in a public area, surrounded by many unfamiliar people. In order to verify that you have correctly taken the message, you
    A. read the message back to the supervisor
    B. ask the supervisor to call you back later
    C. explain that you will call back when you can find a more private location
    D. ask the supervisor to repeat the message

    Most likely:_____ Least likely:_____

5. You're in a conversation with someone who has difficulty finding the proper words to say. You
    A. wait for the person to finish, and then offer a restatement of what you think she was trying to say
    B. gladly interrupt and supply the words for her
    C. wait for her to finish, and then ask a series of clarifying questions
    D. interrupt and ask that she take some time to think about it before speaking

    Most likely:_____ Least likely:_____

6. You are meeting with several other law enforcement officials and community members to determine a course of action for reducing drug trafficking in the area. In order to build a constructive relationship with officials and community members, you
    A. assure the group that you are an expert who has a long record of experience in these matters, and tell them how the problem can be solved
    B. advise them that the solution to the problem can be solved
    C. ask for input from representatives from each group before making suggestions
    D. adopt a completely neutral tone of voice when addressing group members

    Most likely:_____ Least likely:_____

7. When working in a group, someone raises a question that you've already given a lot of thought. You're not sure, however, about how the question should best be answered. You decide to
    A. speak up, briefly explaining the different alternatives that occurred to you
    B. wait for somebody to mention something that has already occurred to you, and then voice your agreement
    C. advise the group that this is a thorny problem that probably can't be solved
    D. keep quiet and listen to the group's discussion, offering feedback when you think it's appropriate

    Most likely:_____ Least likely:_____

8. Completely by accident, you notice a significant error in a colleague's report. The report is about to be released to key decision-makers, and you have absolutely no responsibility for the report. You would MOST likely
    A. spread the word about the error to the colleague's co-workers, in the hope that the information makes its way to the report's author
    B. take a mental note of the error and mention it if anyone asks
    C. keep quiet—it's not your responsibility and you don't want to create friction
    D. find the person who wrote the report and point out the mistake

    Most likely:_____ Least likely:_____

9. A detective who is often nasty to you and your colleagues has compiled an impressive record of success in her investigations; nearly all have led to arrests, and every one of those arrests has ended in conviction. In going over one of the detective's reports, you notice that she has neglected to properly document the chain of custody for a piece of evidence. You aren't that familiar with the case, and don't know how important it is to the case. You have a feeling that the detective will be angry if you point out her mistake. You
    A. do nothing and let her deal with the consequences
    B. pull her aside and tell her about the mistake
    C. tell her you noticed a mistake in her report, and ask her if she is interested in knowing what it is
    D. inform her supervisor and her partner about the mistake

    Most likely:_____ Least likely:_____

10. A crime was recently committed. You believe that, among the following, the MOST useful interview subject would probably be a(n)
    A. informant   B. victim   C. suspect   D. witness

    Most likely:_____ Least likely:_____

11. In order to complete a certain task, you need to ask a favor of a colleague whom you don't know very well. The BEST way to do this would be to
    A. ask the colleague briefly for assistance, stating your reasons for asking
    B. ask the colleague and offer to do something for him in return
    C. tell the colleague there will be many intangible rewards associated with his cooperation
    D. explain that one of the ways the colleague can gain favor with his superiors is to cooperate with you

    Most likely:_____ Least likely:_____

12. A team composed of you and your colleagues encounters a problem similar to one you have encountered when working within another team in the past. Together, you and your team come up with a solution that has the potential for success, even though it is significantly different from the one that worked for you in the past. Your reaction to this new solution is to

A. feel good about the team's originality and go along for the ride on this new plan
B. be concerned about the possibility of failure with the new solution, but accept that there may be more than one way to solve the problem
C. tell them there is a proven way to succeed in solving this problem, and insist that they adopt your solution
D. tell colleagues you're uneasy with the unknowns and variables involved in this new solution, and then urge them to go with your proven success

Most likely:_____ Least likely:_____

13. You have become so proficient at the documentation/paperwork part of your job that you actually now have some time to spare during work hours. With this extra time, you decide to
    A. take initiative and propose a new project to the supervisor
    B. see your supervisor and tell him or her you are ready for more work
    C. take care of some personal errands that you have been unable to do because of work
    D. take some of the pressure off existing work and take more time to complete existing tasks

Most likely:_____ Least likely:_____

14. Your investigative team is having a disagreement about strategy that has become a heated debate, with members divided nearly equally between two strategic choices. You think both choices have some merit, and don't feel strongly one way or the other about which is selected. You
    A. take the side of the group that contains more of your friends and associates
    B. calmly wait for them to work out their differences
    C. try to figure out which side is more likely to win the argument before taking sides
    D. calmly point out the benefits of both plans and suggest a compromise

Most likely:_____ Least likely:_____

15. You turn the corner at the office one day and spot an agent altering the evidence log, which has been left unattended. Later, you look and see that the entry was for an amount of an illicit substance, and the new entry appears to match the amount that exists in the evidence room. You are not sure how much of the substance was initially collected. You would
    A. ask the agent to return the missing evidence and tell him/her that if you see it happen again you will tell your supervisor
    B. tell the agent you saw him making the change, and ask him why it was necessary
    C. let the matter drop; you don't know that anything untoward occurred, and bringing it up will only result in bad feelings
    D. tell other colleagues and try to confront the agent as a group to try to deal with the problem on your own

Most likely:_____ Least likely:_____

16. In developing a plan for investigating a crime spree that has taken place on both sides of the state line, a team encounters problems in how to coordinate the input of federal and state resources. The FIRST step in solving this problem would be to
    A. gather information
    B. define the problem as completely as possible
    C. envision contingencies
    D. develop a plan for solving the problem

    Most likely:_____ Least likely:_____

17. Because your work unit has recently become severely understaffed, you are asked to perform a task that you believe is far beneath the skills and capabilities associated with your position. You respond to this request by
    A. performing the task slowly or inadequately before resuming your more important work, in order to insure that you won't be asked again
    B. doing what is asked, but asking a supervisor to make sure these tasks are evenly distributed among co-workers until the unit can be fully staffed
    C. refusing it on the grounds of professional integrity
    D. complying cheerfully and accepting the task as part of a new expanded job description

    Most likely:_____ Least likely:_____

18. Your supervisor has decided to transfer you to an unfamiliar department as part of an agency restructuring of your organization. The department is in the same building and there will be no changes in compensation or benefits. Your reaction is to be
    A. thrilled at the opportunity to push yourself and learn new skills
    B. not to mind the transfer, because it is likely to teach you something new
    C. entirely neutral, since you won't have to relocate or take a pay cut
    D. disappointed that you will have to change your regular routine

    Most likely:_____ Least likely:_____

19. Your investigative team has developed a plan for investigating a series of violent crimes that have occurred in the tri-state area. In developing the plan, your team must balance the need to conduct the investigation "by the book" meticulously gathering and documenting a body of evidence and testimony, with the need to catch the criminal before another person becomes a victim. The plan, in attempting to balance these concerns, includes a few procedures that involve certain risks. The team should attempt to minimize the consequences of risk-taking by
    A. keeping the focus on capturing the suspect as soon as possible, and dealing with the consequences as they come
    B. reworking the plan to avoid risk whenever possible
    C. setting aside emotional concerns about victims and assembling an airtight case
    D. planning ahead and preparing for each outcome

    Most likely:_____ Least likely:_____

20. An informant has come forward to offer information about a crime. You believe it is important to understand the informant's motivation for coming forward, so you ask him about this
    A. when he least expects it
    B. after he has given an account, but before you have asked any questions
    C. at the conclusion of the interview
    D. at the beginning of the interview

    Most likely:_____ Least likely:_____

21. You are faced with a problem that, try as you might, you're unable to solve. You
    A. ask your most trusted associate
    B. ask for input from several people who you know will have different viewpoints
    C. drop it, hope that it won't become a significant concern, and move on to another task
    D. shift your focus to another problem for a while before giving this problem a fresh look

    Most likely:_____ Least likely:_____

22. You are interviewing several witnesses to a particularly violent crime that was committed recently. One of the witnesses, an older woman, is so upset that she can barely speak coherently. Her testimony does not seem to make much sense, especially when compared to that of others. In continuing to interview her, you make a mental note to document her emotional state when you write up the interview, because strong emotional responses are likely to affect a person's
    A. prior knowledge   B. intelligence
    C. perceptions of current reality D. reflexes

    Most likely:_____ Least likely:_____

23. An informant in an ongoing investigation tells you that he resents having to work with you because you have adopted a superior attitude with him and made work unpleasant. The informant is working on the investigation as a condition of a prior court plea. Your BEST response would be to
    A. tell the informant that you are not interested in his opinion of you; he is required to cooperate on the case
    B. try to find out why the offender cannot work with you and tell him that his work is important to the case
    C. consider the informant as rebellious, and inform the court that the terms of his sentencing have been violated
    D. apologize to the offender and tell him you have been under a lot of strain

    Most likely:_____ Least likely:_____

24. Within a few days, you will meet with supervisors for a scheduled work evaluation. For the review, you will
    A. take the evaluation as it comes and improvise your responses
    B. prepare a list of your accomplishments, skills, and ideas for how to contribute more to the organization

C. assume that your performance will be criticized, and prepare for the attack
D. undertake a little reflection on your failures and successes, but nothing elaborate

Most likely:_____ Least likely:_____

25. You and your partner are in the middle of a very heated argument about the conduct of an investigation. You normally like your partner and get along very well with her, but you are so furious that you are about to say something very nasty that you know will hurt her feelings. Your MOST likely reaction would be to
    A. walk away immediately without saying a word
    B. say what is on your mind and sort it out later
    C. say that you are too angry to talk right now and give yourself time to calm down
    D. leave the room while mumbling the comment in a low voice

    Most likely:_____ Least likely:_____

26. In casual conversation, a person asks you for information about your work as an FBI agent. You should
    A. explain that you are not supposed to talk about your responsibilities to outsiders
    B. refer the person to the public relations department
    C. speak vaguely and give out as few facts as possible
    D. be frank and tell the person as much factual information as you can about your general responsibilities

    Most likely:_____ Least likely:_____

27. In the field, you are in an isolated and rural area and find yourself in a situation with circumstances you have never encountered before. You would be MOST likely to use your own judgment
    A. when existing policy and rules appear to be unfair in their application
    B. when immediate action is necessary and the rules do not cover the situation
    C. only if a superior is present
    D. whenever a situation is not covered by established rules

    Most likely:_____ Least likely:_____

28. One of your colleagues has gone on vacation and his mother, an elderly woman who lives in another state, has filed a complaint with your office; she thinks she may have been defrauded via an e-mail scam. The case has been assigned to Agent Broom, who works in your office. Your colleague phones you from his vacation and asks if you can find out more about her case. Your reaction is to
    A. simply refuse to answer your colleague's questions
    B. find the case file and tell the colleague what he wants to know
    C. speak to your supervisor, explain the situation and ask for the information that your colleague wants
    D. ask the mother if she gives permission for you to find out more from Agent Broom

    Most likely:_____ Least likely:_____

29. When working with team members, you offer what you think is a well-reasoned solution to a problem. Your team members reject it out of hand, saying that it could never work. In a later meeting with mid-level administrators, your supervisor makes the same suggestion. You
    A. say nothing to the supervisor, but later make sure your team members understand that they should be more deferential to your judgment
    B. make sure the supervisor knows you suggested the same solution, but were ignored
    C. feel vindicated by the supervisor's concurrence, but don't feel the need to say anything
    D. demand an apology from your team members for being so closed-minded

    Most likely:_____ Least likely:_____

30. After your partner conducts an interview with an informant, the informant emerges from the interrogation room with some swelling around his right eye. You are pretty sure the swelling was not present when the informant entered the room. You
    A. do nothing; you can't be certain your partner did anything wrong
    B. immediately report the partner's abuse to a supervisor
    C. ask other agents in the office if anything like this has ever happened before
    D. confront your partner and ask what happened

    Most likely:_____ Least likely:_____

31. You and another agent in your unit do not get along, to put it mildly. The problem is, you and she have been assigned to direct an investigation together, and in order to have a good outcome, the two of you need to get along. You
    A. realize the destructive potential for run-ins with her, and quietly get yourself assigned to another case
    B. make an effort to be civil, but if she isn't returning the favor, try to keep a low profile and get the work done
    C. take this as a personal challenge and make it your mission to win her over
    D. try to get your supervisors to understand the seriousness of the friction between you, and ask that they reassign her to another case

    Most likely:_____ Least likely:_____

32. At the end of a busy day at work, you accidentally send an e-mail containing an attachment with some confidential case file information to the wrong person. Which of the following would be the BEST thing to do?
    A. Forget what happened and send the e-mail to the correct person
    B. Leave the office for the day and deal with it tomorrow
    C. Explain to your supervisor what has happened and let her handle the issue
    D. Immediately send another e-mail to the 'wrong' person explaining your mistake

    Most likely:_____ Least likely:_____

33. A crime has just been committed at a bank, and you arrive at the scene first, before any local law enforcement personnel. Before the police arrive, a handful of bank officials arrive and ask to enter the crime scene. You would
    A. request their cooperation in remaining outside the scene until the area can be properly secured
    B. keep them out by any means necessary
    C. tell them to take it up with the police when they arrive
    D. defer to their wishes

    Most likely:_____ Least likely:_____

34. You are interviewing the victim of a crime that was committed only about an hour ago. During the course of the interview you try to
    A. maintain a calm and steady demeanor
    B. make sure at least one other agent is present before beginning
    C. get the facts by any means necessary
    D. keep the victim away from others who are familiar to him/her

    Most likely:_____ Least likely:_____

35. You inherit a large sum of money, and your financial advisor suggests two types of investments. In the first, you invest a moderate, set amount each year, and receive a modest guaranteed payoff at the end of the investment period. The second choice includes a much larger investment (most of your inheritance), but also has a larger potential payoff, with the possibility of losing all your money in an economic downturn. Which type of investment would you choose?
    A. A combination of the two
    B. The first type of investment
    C. The second type of investment
    D. Neither. You wouldn't risk your savings on investments.

    Most likely:_____ Least likely:_____

36. You and your partner are working on a complex project that demands a great deal of effort from both of you. Your partner is frequently absent as a result of burnout and stress from his personal problems. You do not know much about the circumstances, nor have you known him for long. Your partner contributes very little to the project, and, as a result, you are putting in an excessive amount of overtime in order to keep the project moving ahead. You feel that your health may begin to suffer if you continue to work this many hours. You handle this situation by
    A. raising the issue with your supervisor and request additional help to ensure that the project is completed on schedule
    B. offering to help your partner deal with his personal problems
    C. continuing to put in overtime to keep the project moving ahead
    D. meeting with your partner to request that he does his share of the work

    Most likely:_____ Least likely:_____

37. For the first time, you are assigned the lead on a case. You oversee a team of about five people. Your supervisor has assigned you a fairly clear-cut case, and in the end, despite a few logistical and technical problems, you and your team wrap things up fairly quickly. After a speedy conviction, you meet with a group of three supervisors, who congratulate you on your success. They then launch a critique of your leadership of the case that, while pointing out your strengths as a leader, can only be interpreted as somewhat unfavorable, given the team's logistical and technical problems. Most likely, your reaction is to feel that
    A. it probably would not be a good idea for you to assume leadership of a more difficult case in the future
    B. you should keep this critique in mind the next time you take charge of a team
    C. the bottom line is that the case resulted in a conviction, and this is the only measure that really matters
    D. the members of your team really let you down with their mistakes

    Most likely:_____ Least likely:_____

38. You and another agent are conducting an investigation together. You have noticed that the other agent is taking some shortcuts as he collects evidence and obtains statements from the victims and witnesses. These shortcuts are reducing the quality of the investigation. You would MOST likely
    A. point out to the trooper the impact his shortcuts will have on the traffic investigation
    B. notify your supervisor of the shortcuts being taken by the other agent
    C. go back and redo those aspects of the investigation on which the agent has taken shortcuts
    D. ignore the agent's work performance, since it is not your responsibility to monitor his performance

    Most likely:_____ Least likely:_____

39. During a meeting, you and a group of supervisors are discussing your performance on a recently completed project. Using a list of objective criteria, the supervisors explain where you performed most successfully. They then shift their focus to areas in which your performance fell short of the standards. Your reaction is to
    A. launch a vigorous defense of your performance and explain why you think the standards are not appropriate in your case
    B. listen carefully, ask for clarification when necessary, and then discuss with them why these shortcomings occurred
    C. tell them you are very sorry and promise to do better in the future
    D. explain that you did your best and are skeptical that any of them could have done better, given the circumstances

    Most likely:_____ Least likely:_____

40. While you are conducting an investigation at a crime scene, a citizen walks past you and makes a demeaning and derogatory comment about your law enforcement responsibilities. You would MOST likely

11 (#1)

   A. ask the person to come back and explain why he made such a comment
   B. ask the person to show you some identification, so that you can take his name down in case of further trouble
   C. ignore the comment and continue with your work
   D. confront the individual and demand an apology for the comment

   Most likely:_____ Least likely:_____

41. You are working on a case under the direct supervision of a regional supervisor. In your opinion, she has her mind set on a plan that is mediocre, uninspired, and likely to meet only a minimal set of objectives. She is happy with having finally made a decision, wants to finalize, and makes a point of telling you not to try to talk her out of her plan. You think the plan is a waste of resources and perhaps even a mistake, even though most of your colleagues have already told you to let it go. How would you deal with the situation?
    A. Quietly work to get transferred to another project
    B. Tell the supervisor that she is making a mistake, and try to convince her to change her mind
    C. Resist the temptation to try changing her mind
    D. Ask if she is certain she doesn't want to think it over one last time

    Most likely:_____ Least likely:_____

42. When interviewing a potential witness, you notice that she has a tendency to wander off the subject and talk about herself and her family for expended intervals. When you ask her where she was at about noon the day before yesterday, she launches into a long description of her normal daily routine. You respond by
    A. telling her sternly that your time is limited and you would like her to stick to answering your questions
    B. waiting for a pauses in her speech during which you can politely steer the conversation back toward her whereabouts yesterday at noon
    C. cutting her off and repeating the question, as if she hadn't been speaking at all
    D. letting her "talk herself out" and then repeating the question, this time in a more closed-ended format

    Most likely:_____ Least likely:_____

43. You are the leader of an investigative team, and wonder about the role of praise in the team's success. As the leader, your philosophy about praise is that it
    A. can improve performance if it is given when it is most appropriate
    B. should almost always be withheld in order to make team members understand there is always room for improvement
    C. should be given sparely, and reserved for truly exceptional achievements
    D. should be given to team members even, and perhaps especially, when they perform poorly, in order to boost their self-esteem

    Most likely:_____ Least likely:_____

44. You are assigned to an investigation with Agent Stark, who is known to be somewhat inattentive to detail. His mistakes or omissions have resulted in at least one case dismissal that you know of. Throughout the course of the investigation, you
    A. make it a point to be involved in every aspect of the investigation, accompanying Agent Stark on every interview, and insisting on collaboration in written work
    B. leave Agent Stark mostly alone, and then go back and make corrections to his work and documentation when they are necessary
    C. work to block Agent Stark's access to important witnesses, evidence, and case files, thereby minimizing the harm he is likely to do
    D. document every one of Agent Stark's missteps and report them to your superiors as they occur, in order to avoid jeopardizing the case

    Most likely:_____ Least likely:_____

45. An interview has strayed far beyond what you had intended. To redirect the subject's response, you say
    A. "I'm interested in what you were saying a few minutes ago. Can you tell me more about it?"
    B. "Why are we talking about this?"
    C. "Let me ask the rest of the questions I need answered, then we can talk."
    D. "This is interesting, but it isn't related to the business of this interview."

    Most likely:_____ Least likely:_____

46. You have been asked to recruit a new detective to come work for your regional office. She is an up-and-coming star with a lot of potential, and you and your supervisor both feel she would be a good fit for your office. Unfortunately, despite your best efforts, she ends up seeking and receiving an assignment elsewhere. You later find out through your supervisor that you came off as seeming a little too aggressive and desperate. Your supervisor offers you some suggestions for how to handle this situation if it ever comes up again. Your reaction is to think that
    A. putting you in charge of the detective's recruitment was a terrible idea to begin with
    B. the detective's choice was her own loss; you made it clear that your office had the most to offer
    C. you wish there was some way you could make it up to your supervisor
    D. maybe you did come on too strong and should re-examine your methods

    Most likely:_____ Least likely:_____

47. You have become aware that a colleague, who is nearing retirement and now working only part-time for the bureau, has been using office phone and tax facilities to run his own private investigation business. You think that he may have been warned about this once before and that he promised to stop. You have just found a fax for his business placed in your mailbox by mistake. You would MOST likely
    A. Put the fax in your colleague's mailbox without saying anything to anyone
    B. Politely inform your colleague that you will tell your supervisor the next time you catch him using agency resources for his own private business.

C. Put the fax in your supervisor's mailbox without saying anything to anyone
D. Give the fax to your co-worker and remind her that office equipment is not supposed to be used for personal use.

48. You are working on a case with a detective in another regional office who has, once again, rescheduled your meeting appointment at the last minute. Apparently, he left a last-minute message for you this time, but you didn't get it because you were already on your way. This is not the first time you have canceled prior engagements to accommodate his schedule. Each time you have been inconvenienced and very irritated, but this is a very important case and he is a good detective when he is at work. How do you react to this person?
    A. Tell the detective it is disrespectful and inconvenient when he makes last-minute changes to your schedule
    B Don't let on that you are irritated, but ask the detective to give you longer notice the next time he has to cancel.
    C. Maintain a cold professionalism when rescheduling the appointment
    D. Don't let on that you are irritated, but make a point to subject the detective to a few last-minute cancellations of his own, so he'll know how it feels

    Most likely:_____ Least likely:_____

49. A pharmacist has complained to the police department that several drug addicts in his neighborhood have been attempting to obtain drugs illegally, often by passing fake prescriptions. Based only on this information during a stakeout of the prescription counter, you would be MOST likely to find suspicious
    A. a young African-American male in a hooded sweatshirt on a hot day
    B. a woman in her thirties who glances around furtively and brings a large amount of nonprescription items to the counter for purchase
    C. a middle-aged man who appears homeless and is poorly groomed
    D. none of the above should be regarded as suspicious on the basis of their appearance alone

    Most likely:_____ Least likely:_____

50. At a work meeting, your supervisor mentions an interesting new assignment that has not been assigned yet. It sounds like something you could handle, though it would be demanding. You
    A. grow increasingly nervous about the possibility that you would be assigned the job
    B. immediately volunteer to handle the project yourself
    C. tell the supervisor that you would be willing to take it on, but ask if it might be possible to delegate some of your current workload
    D. tell the supervisor that you would be willing to take it on, but only if you receive a raise in pay

    Most likely:_____ Least likely:_____

SITUATIONAL JUDGMENT
KEY TO EXERCISES

NOTE: While a few situations in the examination have one choice that is clearly better or worse than the others, some have two or even three choices that would be equally as good or bad as the rest. The key that follows should be taken as a rough guideline and not a definitive formula for success on the test. The answers below reflect the fact that the situational judgment test is designed to measure your:
- Ability to Organize, Plan, and Prioritize
- Ability to Relate Effectively with Others
- Ability to Maintain a Positive Image
- Ability to Evaluate Information and Make Judgment Decisions
- Ability to Adapt to Changing Situations Integrity

1. Most Likely: B; Least Likely: D
2. Most Likely: D, Least Likely: C
3. Most Likely: A or C; Least Likely: D
4. Most Likely: D; Least Likely: A
5. Most Likely: A or C; Least Likely: D

6. Most Likely: C; Least Likely; A or B
7. Most Likely: A; Least Likely: C
8. Most Likely: D; Least Likely: C
9. Most Likely: B; Least Likely: A
10. Most Likely: D; Least Likely: C

11. Most Likely: A; Least Likely: D
12. Most Likely: B; Least Likely: C
13. Most Likely: B; Least Likely: C or D
14. Most Likely: D; Least Likely: A, B, or C
15. Most Likely: B; Least Likely: A

16. Most Likely: B; Least Likely: A, C, or D
17. Most Likely: B; Least Likely: C
18. Most Likely: B; Least Likely: D
19. Most Likely: D; Least Likely: A, B, or C
20. Most Likely: C; Least Likely: A, B, or D

21. Most Likely: B; Least Likely: C
22. Most Likely: C; Least Likely: A, B, or D
23. Most Likely: B; Least Likely: C
24. Most Likely: B; Least Likely: C
25. Most Likely: C; Least Likely: B

15 (#1)

26. Most Likely: D; Least Likely: A
27. Most Likely: B; Least Likely: D
28. Most Likely: C; Least Likely: A
29. Most Likely: C; Least Likely: D
30. Most Likely: D; Least Likely: A

31. Most Likely: C; Least Likely: A or D
32. Most Likely: C; Least Likely: A
33. Most Likely: A; Least Likely: B, C, or D
34. Most Likely: A; Least Likely: C or D
35. Most Likely: A; Least Likely: D

36. Most Likely: A; Least Likely: C
37. Most Likely: B; Least Likely: A, C, or D
38. Most Likely: A; Least Likely: D
39. Most Likely: B; Least Likely: C or D
40. Most Likely: C; Least Likely: A, B, or D

41. Most Likely: D; Least Likely: A
42. Most Likely: B; Least Likely: A
43. Most Likely: A; Least Likely: B or D
44. Most Likely: A; Least Likely: C
45. Most Likely: A; Least Likely: B

46. Most Likely: D; Least Likely: A or B
47. Most Likely: D; Least Likely: A
48. Most Likely: B; Least Likely: D
49. Most Likely: D; Least Likely: A, B, or C
50. Most Likely: C; Least Likely: A or D

EXAMINATION SECTION
TEST 1

DIRECTIONS: Each question or incomplete statement is followed by several suggested answers or completions. Select the one that BEST answers the question or completes the statement. *PRINT THE LETTER OF THE CORRECT ANSWER IN THE SPACE AT THE RIGHT.*

Questions 1-3.

DIRECTIONS: Answer Questions 1 to 3 based on the following situation.

You are a school counselor in an academic and commercial high school. A senior boy by the name of Peter informs you that for years he has wished to prepare for the practice of medicine. His parents urged him to make this choice when an uncle, who was a doctor, promised to pay part of his college expenses, provided he enrolled in the medical course.

You have listened with interest to Peter's problem as he related it. You have talked to all of his teachers, studied his school records, checked his grades, and given him a battery of tests. All of his grades were below average. Tests revealed that he had slightly less than an average mental ability. Personality and adjustment tests revealed nothing wrong except a slight tendency to be dissatisfied with his family relationship. His clerical aptitude test score was low. Three mechanical aptitude tests, however, revealed high promise. Further questioning revealed that for years Peter had tinkered in his own shop with tools.

It appears that unwise family pressures had caused Peter to choose a life work beyond his ability to achieve.

1. Your FIRST step in handling this problem should be to

    A. tell the parents that they must agree to a search for another life goal
    B. inform the boy's parents that their son does not have the ability to succeed in a profession
    C. confer with the boy's parents and get them to, have the boy keep trying to gain entrance to a medical school
    D. see the boy's parents and suggest that they forget about his choice of a vocation for the present

2. You later arranged a meeting with Peter and during your interview with him, he stated that he wanted to learn more about various types of work before he chose. Under these conditions, you should

    A. advise him to take a variety of subjects as tryouts so that he will be able to make a wiser choice
    B. suggest that he learn something about the requirements of other jobs
    C. take him to the library and show him books to read on various types of work and try to given him insight into his abilities and interests
    D. tell him you feel that he is old enough to decide now

3. After thinking about it, Peter finally decided to prepare for work as a garage mechanic. You should then

   A. advise him to change to a trade school and take auto mechanics or machine shop and do that kind of work during the summer
   B. advise him to drop chemistry and biology but not give up completely the idea of becoming a doctor
   C. advise him to remain in school and take several more science subjects
   D. try to interest him in getting a job in a garage and attending night school

4. You are a judge in a juvenile court in a large city. A young girl fifteen years of age is brought before you. She is charged with the theft of a dress, perfume, and handbag from a large department store. The total value of the articles is $437. This is the first time the girl has been caught. She is from a middle class family. Her mother works in a factory in the daytime, and her father is employed in a local bank as an assistant cashier. Their combined income is about $40,000 a year. She is an only child. Her school record is good, and one test showed that she had better than average mental ability.
After having had a talk with the girl, it is your duty to make a decision. You FIRST would

   A. give her a severe scolding and release her, but make her pay the bill
   B. counsel with the girl and her parents and then give her another chance
   C. talk with the mother to find out whether the girl had ever been neglected
   D. inform the girl that you are thinking of sending her to a girls' training school

5. Wally is a bright five-year-old boy in a kindergarten group. Every day he wastes the time of the group by being slow in putting away materials at the end of the activity period. You, his teacher, know that at home his toys are picked up and put away by his mother or father when he tires of them. He is an only child.
You should

   A. tell his parents to force him to pick up things at home so that he will put away his materials when he is at school
   B. tell him to hurry because the group is waiting for him
   C. help him to put away his materials so the group will not be forced to wait
   D. send the group to the gymnasium to play a game which Wally likes, and have Wally lose out on the fun while he puts away his materials

6. Jimmy, a first-grade pupil, is active on the playground. In the schoolroom, however, he refuses to take part and frequently cries when told to do so.
In trying to remedy this situation, you, as his teacher, should

   A. advise him to take part at once because you think that he is afraid
   B. ask his parents to keep him at home for a year in the belief that he is not yet mature enough to begin school
   C. keep harmony in the class by permitting him to take part when he chooses to do so
   D. encourage him to take part gradually

7. Ralph, who is in the sixth grade, likes to make things with tools and seems to enjoy helping you keep the library books in order and the room decorated nicely. He finds arithmetic very difficult and often avoids it. He plays truant quite often.
In handling this truancy problem, you should

A. discuss why his offense is serious and try to get him to see the error of his ways
B. attempt to discover the causes of his difficulty and tell him you will excuse him from arithmetic if he does not skip school
C. compliment him on his mechanical ability and at the proper time assign him mechanical work in which arithmetic would be useful
D. tell him that staying out of school is an offense not to be tolerated

8. Harry sprinkled a foul-smelling drug around the classroom. The odor was so bad that it made some of the pupils ill and thus almost broke up school for the day. When the teacher discovered who did it, she forced Harry to apologize to the school and to stand before the class each morning for a week taking a smell of the drug from a vial which she kept in her possession.
In your judgment, this form of punishment

   A. will cure him
   B. is not quite severe enough for the offense
   C. was carried on too long even though it produced the desired results
   D. is apt to fail

9. For more than a month, various articles had been disappearing from the lockers in the school hallway. Finally, the instructor caught Jerry going through the coats in the lockers. He admitted the thefts. The instructor knew that Jerry's parents were very poor. He had no spending money, and his meals did not meet his needs.
His instructor should

   A. give him a weekly amount which he can pay back sometime and also give him an apple, a sandwich, or candy when possible
   B. help him find work so that he can take care of his own needs
   C. show him that a thief always gets caught and then promise him a still worse penalty if he does it again
   D. make an example of him by telling the students that he stole the articles

10. Jack, in the eighth grade, is always doing something to attract the attention of his classmates. He makes *bright* remarks during class, insists on talking more than his share of the time, acts up as he walks around the room to obtain a laugh, and even dresses, walks, and combs his hair in an unusual manner to attract attention.
His teachers think that

    A. he should be separated from the group or otherwise punished until he learns not to disturb
    B. the best way to handle him is to join with his classmates in smiling at his remarks and tricks because this cannot do a great deal of harm
    C. the teacher should give him the attention he desires whenever he earns it by doing something worthwhile
    D. the teacher should refuse to notice his behavior so it will return to normal again

11. The teacher has noticed lately that Mildred, age eight, answers out of turn, speaks when others are speaking, and wants to be the center of attention in every activity. She pouts or cries if another child is selected to do something for the teacher which she wishes to do. She has no sister but has a new baby brother.
The MOST probable explanation of her behavior is that

A. her behavior changed because she now has new duties at home
B. she is no longer the center of attention at home and is seeking more attention at school
C. she is being disobedient because she has been spoiled from babyhood
D. Mildred is probably suffering from some illness

12. You are an employment officer. It is your duty to talk with and refer individuals who are trying to secure work. There have been many inquiries regarding a particularly fine automotive mechanic's job in a well-known shop in the city. It offers a good chance to anyone who obtains it. It is up to you to fill this opening from a large group of men applying for this work.
You should select the man who

   A. showed that he knew his trade and showed you the best set of written references and recommendations from his former employers
   B. appeared to be most highly recommended by such previous employers as you were able to contact and answered the trade questions most satisfactorily
   C. told you he had the best training and had the longest experience in the automotive field
   D. appeared the most intelligent and answered the oral trade questions correctly

13. As head nurse in a leading hospital, you are faced with a serious problem. Two of your very efficient nurses are unable to cooperate and to avoid trouble. You have attempted to improve the situation by talking to both of them but their attitudes and relations have not improved.
It would be BEST to

   A. dismiss the less efficient nurse and secure a more satisfactory employee to take her position
   B. overlook their attitude toward each other as much as possible
   C. assign each to unpleasant duties and thereby attempt to teach both that they should try to cooperate better with each other
   D. place them on duty in different wards of the hospital so that they will not need to work together

14. You are a nurse in a city hospital assigned to a patient who demands too much of your time, thus causing you to neglect other duties.
The situation would BEST be handled agreeably by

   A. referring her case to the hospital authorities
   B. doing things requested by her to avoid offending her
   C. explaining pleasantly but firmly why you are unable to grant all of her requests
   D. paying no attention to her occasionally so she will not ask so often

15. You are a social case worker from a public welfare agency. You are charged with advising and assisting poor families which supposedly are in need of financial or medical aid. You are asked to investigate a family of six small children whose father is a ne'er-do-well and who is in a drunken condition most of the time. The mother has been frail and sickly for years.
Under these conditions, you should

   A. give them a monthly allowance despite the father's drinking
   B. refuse them all help so that the father might feel forced to work

C. take the children from the family and advise the mother to secure a divorce
D. give them a monthly allowance and have the father sent to a sanitarium or other institution for medical help

16. Virginia is an attractive girl in the ninth grade with ability somewhat above the average. She is nervous and worries a great deal about her schoolwork and about life in general. Her mother is very anxious for her to excel in school. She criticizes Virginia if her marks are not high and urges her to work harder.
If you were Virginia's teacher, the method you would use in helping Virginia is to

    A. show the other pupils what fine work Virginia is doing, using her case as a model to inspire the others
    B. talk to the mother, explaining that it may be dangerous to urge Virginia to earn high marks
    C. encourage Virginia and her mother to continue as at present since it is likely to lead to high scholarship
    D. tell Virginia that she should not study hard

16.____

17. The attitudes of three teachers in discussing the behavior of their pupils is shown in the four paragraphs that follow.
Which do you regard as BEST from the standpoint of development of the child?

    A. When a child does what is wrong, he should be withdrawn from the group so that he may think over his poor behavior.
    B. Teachers should watch children, stopping them promptly the instant they get into mischief. Privileges should be temporarily withdrawn because of offenses.
    C. When a child misbehaves, he should be punished.
    D. When a child misbehaves, the adult should explain what the right mode of behavior is and why it is right.

17.____

18. Teacher X will never admit that she is wrong. Every question in the classroom is taken as a challenge to her authority. Every comment on her work is regarded as unfair criticism. She makes sarcastic comments to her fellow workers but never apologizes. She can usually prove to her own satisfaction that she is right. She interrupts friends or students so often that no one is able to finish a discussion in her presence.
If you were the principal, you would

    A. put up with the behavior since in a few more years she will be obliged to retire
    B. tell her that she may lose her position if she does not change
    C. have a serious talk with her and force her to see her behavior is educationally unsound
    D. arrange for a psychiatrist to help her to understand her behavior and alter it

18.____

19. Dale shows shyness on the playground. He seems afraid to enter into the games and is so awkward when he plays that the boys do not like to choose him on their side. You are the director.
How can you assist him in overcoming this fear? You should

    A. give him some easy task connected with the games, such as keeping score
    B. allow him to watch or to do something with another pupil
    C. advise him to learn to play
    D. insist that he get into the games and play

19.____

20. A ten-year-old boy in the fourth grade suddenly begins to stutter. He is ashamed, and the   20.____
children in his class are amused.
The teacher should

    A. advise the parents to keep him out of school for a while because of his nervousness
    B. compel him to recite in front of the class so that he will cure his stuttering
    C. tell him he can stop if he wants to and then attempt to overlook the condition if it occurs again
    D. refer him to a clinic for help

KEY (CORRECT ANSWERS)

1.	D	11.	B
2.	C	12.	B
3.	A	13.	D
4.	B	14.	C
5.	D	15.	D
6.	D	16.	B
7.	C	17.	D
8.	D	18.	D
9.	B	19.	A
10.	C	20.	D

TEST 2

DIRECTIONS: Each question or incomplete statement is followed by several suggested answers or completions. Select the one that BEST answers the question or completes the statement. *PRINT THE LETTER OF THE CORRECT ANSWER IN THE SPACE AT THE RIGHT.*

Questions 1-8.

DIRECTIONS: If you were judging social workers, which of the following personality traits would you consider the MOST important for a successful person in this type of work? Select ONE in each group, and mark its letter in the space at the right.

1. A. Aggressive and persuasive
   B. Determined and hard working
   C. Prudent and careful
   D. Helpful and kindly

   1.____

2. A. Ambitious and spirited
   B. Tactful and diplomatic
   C. Persuasive and overbearing
   D. Cautious and prudent

   2.____

3. A. *Slippery* and critical
   B. Pleasant appearing and apologetic
   C. Selfish and self-reliant
   D. Well-balanced and interested in people

   3.____

4. A. Persevering and determined
   B. Considerate and understanding
   C. Outstanding and superior
   D. Friendly and spirited

   4.____

5. A. Sympathetic and condescending
   B. Determined and superior
   C. Practical and experienced
   D. Self-confident and changeable

   5.____

6. A. Sociable and sincere
   B. Self-reliant and theoretical
   C. Overbearing and forward
   D. Agreeable and congenial

   6.____

7. A. Self-confident and assured
   B. Energetic and tactless
   C. Intelligent and ambitious
   D. Industrious and tolerant

   7.____

8. A. Enthusiastic and eager
   B. Cheerful and apologetic
   C. Cordial and tolerant
   D. Analytical and intelligent

   8.____

9. Geraldine, a junior in high school, is boasting constantly about something that she has done, or about the members of her family. Her companions think that she is conceited. A close study of her case shows the following possibilities.
The MOST likely cause of her boastful conduct is that

   A. her father is a prominent man in town, highly respected by his fellow citizens
   B. she has ability above the average and generally earns good marks
   C. she lacks self-confidence and occasionally hints to her teacher that she is not quite as capable as her classmates
   D. she has been spoiled by having had too much attention

10. Skippy, a high school senior, is a poor athlete. No matter how hard he tries, he seems unable to do well in sports. This worries him. He has expressed the opinion that he does not amount to much. He has had a physical examination and his poor athletic ability is not due to physical causes. Skippy can *probably* be helped if

    A. his teachers urge him to put forth every effort to become good in athletics
    B. teachers let him alone to fight the battle that everyone must fight sooner or later when he learns that someone else is better than he
    C. his teachers study his case and help him to discover other things that he can do well
    D. the coach places him in a special class known as the awkward squad and teaches him to improve his athletic ability

11. In order to help a child to avoid developing the feeling that others are ALWAYS better than he is, you should

    A. assist him in becoming as successful as possible in the things he attempts
    B. try to get him to see that he is as competent as anyone else
    C. tell him never to admit that he is beaten
    D. help him to be as successful as possible in the things he attempts and help him to do some one thing especially well

12. With pupils of extremely low mental ability, it is MOST justifiable to

    A. give them the same work as the others get but realize that it will take them longer to do it
    B. give them the same type of work as the others get but less of it
    C. assign more extra curricular work and less from the regular curriculum; for example, use more handwork
    D. place all of them in manual arts courses

13. You are a personnel manager in a large industrial plant engaged in the manufacture of vital instruments. It is your job to maintain good employee-employer relationships, increase the amount of work done, and keep the men happy and satisfied in their work. In other words, you are active in keeping up high standards of work by keeping everyone happy.
One of your experienced employees, Mr. Ryan, is engaged in the final inspection of shuttle o-rings. He apparently has fallen down in his work rating without any known reason. He holds an important job and must maintain a high degree of skill. The plant physician, after a thorough physical examination, says there is nothing wrong with him physically.
Under these conditions, you should

A. suggest that he might lose his job if he does not increase the quality and amount of work he does
B. talk with him and attempt to determine what is causing his trouble or what is worrying him
C. drop a word of praise occasionally so he might be helped to do better
D. suggest that it might help if he changed to a different type of work

14. Suppose that you found that Mr. Ryan was upset at work because of difficulties with his wife and his envy of a man who was promoted over him.
You should

   A. try to explain to him why this man was promoted over him
   B. to satisfy him, tell him that your plant promotes those first who were employed first, and casually suggest that his wife drop in to see you
   C. give him some marital advice and suggest that he may be better off if he separated from his wife for a while
   D. tell him you are interested only in his output and that he will have to work out his personal affairs by himself

14.____

15. You are a Red Cross director with an army unit in the field. A soldier, Jones, approaches you and tells you there is serious illness in his family, and he would like to go home. You agree, but upon looking into the matter the next day, you find that no one is actually sick in the soldier's family.
Under these conditions, you should

   A. take no further action at present but later get the man a furlough because you can see that he is under serious strain and may become very ill
   B. treat it as a humorous incident but be on the lookout so that it does not occur again
   C. notify the commanding officer and get his opinion
   D. deny the request and try to find out the real cause for the man's behavior

15.____

16. If Jones then saw you again, you should

   A. tell him to pour out his troubles to you
   B. scold him for his actions and explain the seriousness of such dishonesty
   C. explain that taking vacations whenever he feels like it is impossible; offer assistance and try to find something to interest him
   D. explain to him in a nice manner that you have shortened his furlough a few days

16.____

17. Jones then told you that he was sick and tired of the army and wanted to get away from it for a while.
You should

   A. warn him of what would happen if he deserted and obtain a furlough for him
   B. notify his commanding officer that the man should be watched
   C. suggest an appointment be made for him with the psychiatrist
   D. refuse to interest yourself in his problem because it is not your concern

17.____

18. If Jones also told you that his first sergeant was picking on him, you should

   A. look into the matter to determine the truth by talking to a few people who know him
   B. call the soldier's commanding officer and tell him about the situation

18.____

C. tell him to forget the incident since it really was not very serious
D. try to arrange to get the soldier transferred to another company

19. You are a dean in a secondary school. An intelligent child, Bob, sixteen years of age who is about to fail, has been referred to you. Prior to this time, the boy has been a good student and a very likable boy. Suddenly, he began to neglect his work.
Under these conditions, you should

   A. go to the principal and suggest that the boy be deprived of a few privileges around school until his behavior improves
   B. have a casual talk with the boy
   C. learn about the boy's home life and outside activities
   D. have a talk with the boy and tell him he must apply himself

20. If you should have a talk with Bob, your FIRST step will be to try to

   A. make him feel that by improving his behavior it will please you
   B. gain his confidence so he will feel free to tell his problem
   C. impress him with the importance of your position
   D. show him that he is developing some bad habits

21. You discover that one reason for Bob's poor attitude is the fact that he feels he is being left out of things.
Knowing this, you should

   A. ask his friends to aid him in his studies
   B. force him to engage in sports
   C. tell him not to worry as things are bound to turn out all right
   D. seek the help of his friends

22. If, in two months, you heard nothing more concerning Bob, you should

   A. have one of his teachers send him to you
   B. look into his current activities and then drop in and talk to him about how well he is progressing in his classes and social relations
   C. inquire about him and then drop in casually and observe him
   D. look at his school record to determine whether he had improved

23. Near the close of the school year, you notice a great improvement in Bob's behavior, and his grades have improved.
You then should

   A. call the boy in and tell him you were disappointed in the amount of improvement shown because you knew he could do better
   B. say nothing to him but inform his parents that he has improved
   C. go to him and comment on his splendid improvement
   D. give him a two-day holiday as a reward for the splendid improvement shown

24. Which of these teacher's opinions is CORRECT?

   A. Mr. W. - "I think some children are naturally quite mischievous and must be dealt with sternly."
   B. Mr. X. - "I have a pupil who causes a great deal of trouble. After I scold him, he quiets down and behaves himself."

C. Mr. Y. - "*Since every bit of misconduct has a cause, we should not be angry with a child who misbehaves any more than we should get angry at one who is ill.*"
D. Mr. Z. - "*Most misconduct can be traced right back to the home. It is the parents' fault.*"

25. You are a social case worker from a public welfare agency. One of your cases is Mr. Backus, an aged man whose failing health makes nursing care necessary.
Mr. Backus is dependent upon relief. An agency reports that he suffers from *senility and paralysis.* His only son is confined in the Veterans Hospital. There are no other relatives. Mr. Backus is receiving $320 per month, but he feels he should be receiving at least $600 per month on which to live since the high cost of living makes it very hard to get along on less. He has no savings. His landlady says that she does not wish to have him remain there because she cannot care for an invalid.
After a complete investigation of this case, you then should

   A. arrange to increase Mr. Backus' pension to $600 a month and then try to get the landlady to keep him
   B. place him in a home for old people at public expense
   C. increase his pension to $600 a month and make arrangements with the owner of a nursing home to care for Mr. Backus
   D. try to have the son support him

KEY (CORRECT ANSWERS)

1.	D		11.	D
2.	B		12.	C
3.	D		13.	B
4.	B		14.	A
5.	C		15.	D
6.	A		16.	C
7.	D		17.	C
8.	C		18.	A
9.	C		19.	C
10.	C		20.	B

21. D
22. B
23. C
24. C
25. C

READING COMPREHENSION
UNDERSTANDING AND INTERPRETING WRITTEN MATERIAL
EXAMINATION SECTION
TEST 1

DIRECTIONS: Each question or incomplete statement is followed by several suggested answers or completions. Select the one that BEST answers the question or completes the statement. *PRINT THE LETTER OF THE CORRECT ANSWER IN THE SPACE AT THE RIGHT.*

Questions 1-2.

DIRECTIONS: Questions 1 and 2 are to be answered SOLELY on the basis of the information given in the following paragraph.

It is argued by some that the locale of the trial should be given little or no consideration. Facts are facts, they say, and if presented properly to a jury panel they will be productive of the same results regardless of where the trial is held. However, experience shows great differences in the methods of handling claims by juries. In some counties, large demands in personal injury suits are viewed with suspicion by the jury. In others, the jurors are liberal in dealing with someone else's funds.

1. According to the above paragraph, it would be ADVISABLE for an examiner on a personal injury case to

    A. get information as to the kind of verdicts that are usually awarded by juries in the county of trial
    B. give little or no consideration to the locale of the trial
    C. look for incomplete and improper presentation of facts to the jury if the verdict was not justified by the facts
    D. offer a high but realistic initial settlement figure so that no temptation is left to the claimant to gamble on the jury's verdict

2. According to the above statement, the argument that the location of a trial in a personal injury suit CANNOT counteract the weight of the evidence is

    A. basically sound
    B. disproven by the differences in awards for similar claims
    C. substantiated in those cases where the facts are properly and carefully presented to the injury
    D. supported by experience which shows great differences in the methods of handling claims by juries

Questions 3-6.

DIRECTIONS: Questions 3 through 6 are to be answered SOLELY on the basis of the following excerpt from a recorded annual report of the police department. This material should be read first and then referred to in answering these questions.

LEGAL BUREAU

One of the more important functions of this bureau is to analyze and furnish the department with pertinent information concerning Federal and State statutes and local laws which affect the department, law enforcement or crime prevention. In addition, all measure introduced in the State Legislature and the City Council which may affect this department are carefully reviewed by members of the Legal Bureau and, where necessary, opinions and recommendations thereon are prepared.

Another important function of this office is the prosecution of cases in the Criminal Courts. This is accomplished by assignment of attorneys who are members of the Legal Bureau to appear in those cases which are deemed to raise issues of importance to the department or questions of law which require technical presentation to facilitate proper determination; and also in those cases where request is made for such appearances by a judge or magistrate, some other official of the city, or a member of the force.

Proposed legislation was prepared and sponsored for introduction in the State Legislature and, at this writing, one of these proposals has already been enacted into law and five others are presently on the Governor's desk awaiting executive action. The new law prohibits the sale or possession of a hypodermic syringe or needle by an unauthorized person. The bureau's proposals awaiting executive action pertain to an amendment to the Criminal Procedure Law prohibiting desk officers from taking bail in gambling cases or in cases mentioned in the Criminal Procedure Law, including confidence men and swindlers as jostlers in the Penal Law; prohibiting the sale of switchblade knives of any size to children under 16 and bills extending the licensing period of gunsmiths.

The Legal Bureau has regularly cooperated with the Corporation Counsel and the District Attorneys in respect to matters affecting this department, and has continued to advise and represent the Police Athletic League, the Police Sports Association, the Police Relief Fund, and the Police Pension Fund.

3. Members of the Legal Bureau frequently appear in Criminal Court for the purpose of

    A. defending members of the Police Force
    B. raising issues of important to the Police Department
    C. prosecuting all offenders arrested by members of the Force
    D. facilitating proper determination of questions of law requiring technical presentation

4. The Legal Bureau sponsored a bill that would

    A. extend the licenses of gunsmiths
    B. prohibit the sale of switchblade knives to children of any size
    C. place confidence men and swindlers in the same category as jostlers in the Penal Law
    D. prohibit desk officers from admitting gamblers, confidence men, and swindlers to bail

5. One of the functions of the Legal Bureau is to 5._____

   A. review and make recommendations on proposed Federal laws affecting law enforcement
   B. prepare opinions on all measures introduced in the State Legislature and the City Council
   C. furnish the Police Department with pertinent information concerning all new Federal and State laws
   D. analyze all laws affecting the work of the Police Department

6. The one of the following that is NOT a function of the Legal Bureau is 6._____

   A. law enforcement and crime prevention
   B. prosecution of all cases in Women's Court
   C. advise and represent the Police Sports Association
   D. lecturing at the Police Academy

7. It is usual in public service for recruits to serve a probationary period before they receive tenured positions. The objective of this is to observe them in actual service, to teach them the duties of their position, and to provide a means for eliminating those who prove they are not suited for this kind of work. During this period, firings may be made at the discretion of the chief. 7._____
   Which one of the following is BEST supported by the above selection?

   A. Demonstrated fitness for the job is the basis for retention of probationary employees.
   B. Trial appointments protect the appointee from unfair dismissal practices.
   C. Public service employees need experience and instruction before permanent appointment.
   D. Exams must be given to determine the ability of probationary employees.

8. As the fundamental changes sought to be brought about in the inmates of a correctional institution can be accomplished only under good leadership, it follows that the quality of the staff whose duty it is to influence and guide the inmates in the right direction is more important than the physical facilities of the institution. 8._____
   Of the following, the MOST accurate conclusion based on the preceding statement is that

   A. the development of leadership is the fundamental change brought about in inmates by good quality staff
   B. the physical facilities of an institution are not very important in bringing about fundamental changes in the inmates
   C. with proper training the entire staff of a correctional institution can be developed into good leaders
   D. without good leadership the basic changes desired in the inmates of a correctional institution cannot be brought about

Questions 9-11.

DIRECTIONS: Questions 9 through 11 are to be answered SOLELY on the basis of the following paragraph.

The law enforcement agency is one of the most important agencies in the field of juvenile delinquency prevention. This is so not because of the social work connected with this problem, however, for this is not a police matter, but because the officers are usually the first to come in contact with the delinquent. The manner of arrest and detention makes a deep impression upon him and affects his life-long attitude toward society and the law. The juvenile court is perhaps the most important agency in this work. Contrary to the general opinion, however, it is not primarily concerned with putting children into correctional schools. The main purpose of the juvenile court is to save the child and to develop his emotional make-up in order that he can grow up to be a decent and well-balanced citizen. The system of probation is the means whereby the court seeks to accomplish these goals.

9. According to this paragraph, police work is an important part of a program to prevent juvenile delinquency because

    A. social work is no longer considered important in juvenile delinquency prevention
    B. police officers are the first to have contact with the delinquent
    C. police officers jail the offender in order to be able to change his attitude toward society and the law
    D. it is the first step in placing the delinquent in jail

10. According to this paragraph, the CHIEF purpose of the juvenile court is to

    A. punish the child for his offense
    B. select a suitable correctional school for the delinquent
    C. use available means to help the delinquent become a better person
    D. provide psychiatric care for the delinquent

11. According to this paragraph, the juvenile court directs the development of delinquents under its care CHIEFLY by

    A. placing the child under probation
    B. sending the child to a correctional school
    C. keeping the delinquent in prison
    D. returning the child to his home

Questions 12-14.

DIRECTIONS: Questions 12 through 14 are to be answered on the basis of the following paragraph.

An assassination is an act that consists of a plotted, attempted or actual murder of a prominent political figure by an individual who performs this act in other than a governmental role. This definition draws a distinction between political execution and assassination. An execution may be regarded as a political killing, but it is initiated by the organs of the state, while an assassination can always be characterized as an illegal act. A prominent figure must be the target of the killing, since the killing of lesser members of the political community is included within a wider category of internal political turmoil, namely, terrorism. Assassination is also to be distinguished from homicide. The target of the aggressive act must be a political figure rather than a private person. The killing of a prime minister by a member of an insurrectionist or underground group clearly qualifies as an assassination. So does an act by a deranged individual who tries to kill not just any individual, but the individual in his political role - as President, for example.

12. Assume that a nationally prominent political figure is charged with treason by the state, tried in a court of law, found guilty, and hanged by the state. According to the above passage, it would be MOST appropriate to regard his death as a(n)

    A. assassination
    B. execution
    C. aggressive act
    D. homicide

13. According to the above passage, which of the following statements is CORRECT?

    A. The assassination of a political figure is an illegal act.
    B. A private person may be the target of an assassination attempt.
    C. The killing of an obscure member of a political community is considered an assassination event.
    D. An execution may not be regarded as a political killing.

14. Of the following, the MOST appropriate title for this passage would be

    A. ASSASSINATION - LEGAL ASPECTS
    B. POLITICAL CAUSES OF ASSASSINATION
    C. ASSASSINATION - A DEFINITION
    D. CATEGORIES OF ASSASSINATION

Questions 15-17.

DIRECTIONS: Questions 15 through 17 are to be answered SOLELY on the basis of the following paragraph.

All applicants for an original license to operate a catering establishment shall be fingerprinted. This shall include the officers, employees, and stockholders of the company and the members of a partnership. In case of a change, by addition or substitution, occurring during the existence of a license, the person added or substituted shall be fingerprinted. However, in the case of a hotel containing more than 200 rooms, only the officer or manager filing the application is required to be fingerprinted. The police commissioner may also, at his discretion, exempt the employees and stockholders of any company. The fingerprints shall be taken on one copy of Form C.E. 20 and on two copies of C.E. 21. One copy of Form C.E. 21 shall accompany the application. Fingerprints are not required with a renewal application.

15. According to the above paragraph, an employee added to the payroll of a licensed catering establishment which is not in a hotel must be fingerprinted

    A. always
    B. unless he has been previously fingerprinted for another license
    C. unless exempted by the police commissioner
    D. only if he is the manager or an officer of the company

16. According to the above paragraph, it would be MOST accurate to state that

    A. Form C.E. 20 must accompany a renewal application
    B. Form C.E. 21 must accompany all applications
    C. Form C.E. 21 must accompany an original application
    D. both Forms C.E. 20 and C.E. 21 must accompany all applications

17. A hotel of 270 rooms has applied for a license to operate a catering establishment on the premises.
According to the instructions for fingerprinting given in the above paragraph, the _____ shall be fingerprinted.

   A. officers, employees, and stockholders
   B. officers and the manager
   C. employees
   D. officer filing the application

17.____

Questions 18-24.

DIRECTIONS: Read the following two paragraphs. Then answer the questions by selecting the answer
   A - if the paragraphs indicate it is TRUE
   B - if the paragraphs indicate it is PROBABLY true
   C - if the paragraphs indicate it is PROBABLY false
   D - if the paragraphs indicate it is FALSE

The fallacy underlying what some might call the eighteenth and nineteenth century misconceptions of the nature of scientific investigations seems to lie in a mistaken analogy. Those who said they were investigating the structure of the universe imagined themselves as the equivalent of the early explorers and map makers. The explorers of the fifteenth and sixteenth centuries had opened up new worlds with the aid of imperfect maps; in their accounts of distant lands, there had been some false and many ambiguous statements. But by the time everyone came to believe the world was round, the maps of distant continents were beginning to assume a fairly consistent pattern. By the seventeenth century, methods of measuring space and time had laid the foundations for an accurate geography.

On this basic issue there is far from complete agreement among philosophers *of* science today. You can, each of you, choose your side and find highly distinguished advocates for the point of view you have selected. However, in view of the revolution in physics, anyone who now asserts that science is an exploration of the universe must be prepared to shoulder a heavy burden of proof. To my mind, the analogy between the map maker and the scientist is false. A scientific theory is not even the first approximation to a map; it is not a need; it is a policy -- an economical and fruitful guide to action, by scientific investigators.

18. The author thinks that 18th and 19th century science followed the same technique as the 15th century geographers. 18.____

19. The author disagrees with the philosophers who are labelled realists. 19.____

20. The author believes there is a permanent structure to the universe. 20.____

21. A scientific theory is an economical guide to exploring what cannot be known absolutely. 21.____

22. Philosophers of science accept the relativity implications of recent research in physics. 22.____

23. It is a matter of time and effort before modern scientists will be as successful as the geographers. 23.____

24. The author believes in an indeterminate universe. 24.____

25. Borough X reports that its police force makes fewer arrests per thousand persons than any of the other boroughs.
    From this statement, it is MOST probable that

    A. sufficient information has not been given to warrant any conclusion
    B. the police force of Borough X is less efficient
    C. fewer crimes are being committed in Borough X
    D. fewer crimes are being reported in Borough X

KEY (CORRECT ANSWERS)

1.	A	11.	A
2.	B	12.	B
3.	D	13.	A
4.	C	14.	C
5.	D	15.	C
6.	A	16.	C
7.	A	17.	D
8.	D	18.	D
9.	B	19.	B
10.	C	20.	D

21. A
22. D
23. D
24. B
25. A

TEST 2

DIRECTIONS: Each question or incomplete statement is followed by several suggested answers or completions. Select the one that BEST answers the question or completes the statement. *PRINT THE LETTER OF THE CORRECT ANSWER IN THE SPACE AT THE RIGHT.*

Questions 1-2.

DIRECTIONS: Questions 1 and 2 are to be answered on the basis of the information given in the following passage.

Assume that a certain agency is having a problem at one of its work locations because a sizable portion of the staff at that location is regularly tardy in reporting to work. The management of the agency is primarily concerned about eliminating the problem and is not yet too concerned about taking any disciplinary action. An investigator is assigned to investigate to determine, if possible, what might be causing this problem.

After several interviews, the investigator sees that low morale created by poor supervision at this location is at least part of the problem. In addition, there is a problem of tardiness and lack of interest.

1. Given the goals of the investigation and assuming that the investigator was using a non-directive approach in this interview, of the following, the investigator's MOST effective response should be:

    A. You know, you are building a bad record of tardiness
    B. Can you tell me more about this situation?
    C. What kind of person is your superior?
    D. Do you think you are acting fairly towards the agency by being late so often?

1.____

2. Given the goals of the investigation and assuming the investigator was using a directed approach in this interview, of the following, the investigator's response should be:

    A. That doesn't seem like much of an excuse to me
    B. What do you mean by saying that you've lost interest?
    C. What problems are there with the supervision you are getting?
    D. How do you think your tardiness looks in your personnel record?

2.____

Questions 3-5.

DIRECTIONS: Questions 3 through 5 are to be answered SOLELY on the basis of the following passage.

As investigators, we are more concerned with the utilitarian than the philosophical aspects of ethics and ethical standards, procedures, and conduct. As a working consideration, we might view ethics as the science of doing the right thing at the right time in the right manner in conformity with the normal, everyday standards imposed by society; and in conformity with the judgment society would be expected to make concerning the rightness or wrongness of what we have done.

An ethical code might be considered a basic set of rules and regulations to which we must conform in the performance of investigative duties. Ethical standards, procedures, and conduct might be considered the logical workings of our ethical code in its everyday application to our work. Ethics also necessarily involves morals and morality. We must eventually answer the self-imposed question of whether or not we have acted in the right way in conducting our investigative activities in their individual and total aspects.

3. Of the following, the MOST suitable title for the above passage is

    A. THE IMPORTANCE OF RULES FOR INVESTIGATORS
    B. THE BASIC PHILOSOPHY OF A LAWFUL SOCIETY
    C. SCIENTIFIC ASPECTS OF INVESTIGATIONS
    D. ETHICAL GUIDELINES FOR THE CONDUCT OF INVESTIGATIONS

4. According to the above passage, ethical considerations for investigators involve

    A. special standards that are different from those which apply to the rest of society
    B. practices and procedures which cannot be evaluated by others
    C. individual judgments by investigators of the appropriateness of their own actions
    D. regulations which are based primarily upon a philosophical approach

5. Of the following, the author's PRINCIPAL purpose in writing the above passage seems to have been to

    A. emphasize the importance of self-criticism in investigative activities
    B. explain the relationship that exists between ethics and investigative conduct
    C. reduce the amount of unethical conduct in the area of investigations
    D. seek recognition by his fellow investigators for his academic treatment of the subject matter

Questions 6-8.

DIRECTIONS: Questions 6 through 8 are to be answered SOLELY on the basis of the following passage.

The investigator must remember that acts of omission can be as effective as acts of commission in affecting the determination of disputed issues. Acts of omission, such as failure to obtain available information or failure to verify dubious information, manifest themselves in miscarriages of justice and erroneous adjudications. An incomplete investigation is an erroneous investigation because a conclusion predicated upon inadequate facts is based on quicksand.

When an investigator throws up his hands and admits defeat, the reason for this action does not necessarily lie in his possible laziness and ineptitude. It is more likely that the investigator has made his conclusions after exhausting only those avenues of investigation of which he is aware. He has exercised good faith in his belief that nothing else can be done.

This tendency must be overcome by all investigators if they are to operate at top efficiency. If no suggestion for new or additional action can be found in any authority, an investigator should use his own initiative to cope with a given situation. No investigator should ever hesitate to set precedents. It is far better in the final analysis to attempt difficult solutions, even if the chances of error are obviously present, than it is to take refuge in the spineless adage: If you don't do anything, you don't do it wrong.

6. Of the following, the MOST suitable title for the above passage is

   A. THE NEED FOR RESOURCEFULNESS IN INVESTIGATIONS
   B. PROCEDURES FOR COMPLETING AN INVESTIGATION
   C. THE DEVELOPMENT OF STANDARDS FOR INVESTIGATORS
   D. THE CAUSES OF INCOMPLETE INVESTIGATIONS

7. Of the following, the author of this passage considers that the LEAST important consideration in developing new investigative methods is

   A. efficiency
   B. caution
   C. imagination
   D. thoroughness

8. According to this passage, which of the following statements is INCORRECT?

   A. Lack of creativity may lead to erroneous investigations.
   B. Acts of omission are sometimes as harmful as acts of commission.
   C. Some investigators who give up on a case are lazy or inept.
   D. An investigator who gives up on a case is usually not acting in good faith.

Questions 9-12.

DIRECTIONS: Questions 9 through 12 are to be answered on the basis of the following paragraph.

A report of investigation should not be weighed down by a mass of information which is hardly material or only remotely relevant, or which fails to prove a point, clarify an issue, or aid the inquiry even by indirection. Some investigative agencies, however, value the report for its own sake, considering it primarily as a justification of the investigative activity contained therein. Every step is listed to show that no logical measure has been overlooked and to demonstrate that the reporting agent is beyond criticism. This system serves to provide reviewing authorities with a ready means of checking subordinates and provides order, method, and routine to investigative activity. In addition, it may offer supervisors and investigators a sense of security; the investigator would know within fairly exact limits what is expected of him and the supervisor may be comforted by the knowledge that his organization may not be reasonably criticized in a particular case on the grounds of obvious omissions or inertia. To the state's attorney and others, however, who must take administrative action on the basis of the report, the irrelevant and immaterial information thwarts the purpose of the investigation by dimming the issues and obscuring the facts that are truly contributory to the proof.

9. From the point of view of the supervising investigator, a drawback of having the investigator prepare the type of report which the state's attorney would like is that it

   A. gives a biased and one-sided view of what should have been an impartial investigation
   B. has only limited usefulness as an indication that all proper investigative methods were used by the investigator
   C. overlooks logical measures, removing the responsibility for taking those measures which the investigator should otherwise have been expected to take
   D. sets fairly exact limits to what the supervisor can expect of the investigator

10. District attorneys do not like reports of investigations in which every step is listed because

   A. their administrative action is then based on irrelevant and immaterial information
   B. it places the investigator beyond criticism, making the responsibility of the district attorney that much greater
   C. of the difficulty of finding among the mass of information the portion which is meaningful and useful
   D. the inclusion of indirect or hardly material information is not in accord with the order in which the steps were taken

10.____

11. As expressed in the above paragraph, the type of report which MOST investigators prefer to prepare is

   A. a step-by-step account of their activities, including both fruitful and unfruitful steps, since to do so provides order and method and gives them a sense of security
   B. not made clear, even though current practice in some agencies is to include every step taken in the investigation
   C. one from which useless and confusing information has been excluded because it is not helpful and is poor practice
   D. one not weighed down by a mass of irrelevant information but one which shows within fairly exact limits what was expected of them

11.____

12. With regard to the type of information which an investigator should include in his report, the above paragraph expresses the opinion that

   A. it is best to include in the report only that information which supports the conclusions of the investigator
   B. reports should include all relevant and clarifying information and exclude information on inquiries which had no productive result
   C. reports should include sufficient information to demonstrate that the investigator has been properly attending to his duties and all the information which contributes toward proof of what occurred in the case
   D. the most logical thing to do is to list every step in the investigation and its result

12.____

Questions 13-17.

DIRECTIONS: Questions 13 through 17 are to be answered SOLELY on the basis of the following paragraph.

Those statutes of limitations which are of interest to a claim examiner are the ones affecting third party actions brought against an insured covered by a liability policy of insurance. Such statutes of limitations are legislative enactments limiting the time within which such actions at law may be brought. Research shows that such periods differ from state to state and vary within the states with the type of action brought. The laws of the jurisdiction in which the action is brought govern and determine the period within which the action may be instituted, regardless of the place of the cause of action or the residence of the parties at the time of cause of action. The period of time set by a statute of limitations for a tort action starts from the moment the alleged tort is committed. The period usually extends continuously until its expiration, upon which legal action may no longer be brought. However, there is a suspension of the running of the period when a defendant has concealed himself in order to avoid service of legal process. The suspension continues until the defendant discontinues his concealment and then the period starts running again. A defendant may, by his agreement or conduct, be legally barred from asserting the statute of limitations as a defense to an action. The insurance carrier for the defendant may, by the misrepresentation of the claims man, cause such a bar against use of the statute of limitations by the defendant. If the claim examiner of the insurance carrier has by his conduct or assertion lulled the plaintiff into a false sense of security by false representations, the defendant may be barred from setting up the statute of limitations as a defense.

13. Of the following, the MOST suitable title for the above paragraph is

    A. FRAUDULENT USE OF THE STATUTE OF LIMITATIONS
    B. PARTIES AT INTEREST IN A LAWSUIT
    C. THE CLAIM EXAMINER AND THE LAW
    D. THE STATUTE OF LIMITATIONS IN CLAIMS WORK

14. The period of time during which a third party action may be brought against an insured covered by a liability policy depends on

    A. the laws of the jurisdiction in which the action is brought
    B. where the cause of action which is the subject of the suit took place
    C. where the claimant lived at the time of the cause of action
    D. where the insured lived at the time of the cause of action

15. Time limits in third party actions which are set by the statutes of limitations described above are

    A. determined by claimant's place of residence at start of action
    B. different in a state for different actions
    C. the same from state to state for the same type of action
    D. the same within a state regardless of type of action

16. According to the above paragraph, grounds which may be legally used to prevent a defendant from using the statute of limitations as a defense in the action described are

    A. defendant's agreement or concealment; a charge of liability for death and injury
    B. defendant's agreement or conduct; misrepresentation by the claims man
    C. fraudulent concealment by claim examiner; a charge of liability for death or injury; defendant's agreement
    D. misrepresentation by claim examiner of carrier; defendant's agreement; plaintiff's concealment

17. Suppose an alleged tort was commited on January 1, 2008 and that the period in which action may be taken is set at three years by the statute of limitations. Suppose further that the defendant, in order to avoid service of legal process, had concealed himself from July 1, 2010 through December 31, 2010.
    In this case, the defendant may not use the statute of limitations as a defense unless action is brought by the plaintiff after _____, 2011.

    A. January 1   B. February 28
    C. June 30   D. August 1

Questions 18-20.

DIRECTIONS: Questions 18 through 20 are to be answered SOLELY on the basis of information contained in the following passage.

No matter how well the interrogator adjusts himself to the witness and how precisely he induces the witness to describe his observations, mistakes still can be made. The mistakes made by an experienced interrogator may be comparatively few, but as far as the witness is concerned, his path is full of pitfalls. Modern *witness psychology* has shown that even the most honest and trustworthy witnesses are apt to make grave mistakes in good faith. It is, therefore, necessary that the interrogator get an idea of the weak links in the testimony in order to check up on them in the event that something appears to be strange or not quite satisfactory.

Unfortunately, modern witness psychology does not yet offer any means of directly testing the credibility of testimony. It lacks precision and method, in spite of worthwhile attempts on the part of learned men. At the same time, witness psychology, through the gathering of many experiences concerning the weaknesses of human testimony, has been of invaluable service. It shows clearly that only evidence of a technical nature has absolute value as proof.

Testimony may be separated into the following stages: (1) perception, (2) observation, (3) mind fixation of the observed occurrences, in which fantasy, association of ideas, and personal judgment participate, and (4) expression in oral or written form, where the testimony is transferred from one witness to another or to the interrogator.

Each of these stages offers innumerable possibilities for the distortion of testimony.

18. The above passage indicates that having witnesses talk to each other before testifying is a practice which is GENERALLY

    A. *desirable,* since the witnesses will be able to correct each other's errors in observation before testimony
    B. *undesirable,* since the witnesses will collaborate on one story to tell the investigator
    C. *undesirable,* since one witness may distort his testimony because of what another witness may erroneously say
    D. *desirable,* since witnesses will become aware of discrepancies in their own testimony and can point out the discrepancies to the investigator

19. According to the above passage, the one of the following which would be the MOST reliable for use as evidence would be the testimony of a

    A. handwriting expert about a signature on a forged check
    B. trained police officer about the identity of a criminal
    C. laboratory technician about an accident he has observed
    D. psychologist who has interviewed any witnesses who relate conflicting stories

20. Concerning the validity of evidence, it is CLEAR from the above passage that

    A. only evidence of a technical nature is at all valuable
    B. the testimony of witnesses is so flawed that it is usually valueless

C. an investigator, by knowing modern witness psychology, will usually be able to perceive mistaken testimony
D. an investigator ought to expect mistakes in even the most reliable witness testimony

Questions 21-22.

DIRECTIONS: Questions 21 and 22 are to be answered SOLELY on the basis of the information contained in the passage below. This passage represents a report prepared by a subordinate superior concerning a school demonstration.

On April 1, a group of students, each holding an anti-apartheid sign, was involved in a demonstration on the grounds of Columbia University. The students began by locking the main entrance doors to the Administration Building and preventing faculty and students from entering or leaving the building.

The C.O. of the police detail at the scene requested additional assistance of four female detectives, an Emergency Service van, and a police photographer equipped with a Polaroid instamatic camera.

When the additional assistance arrived, the Commanding Officer directed the students to disperse. His justification for the order was that the demonstrators were violating the rights of other students and certain faculty members by denying them access to the Administration Building. The students ignored the order to disperse and the Commanding Officer of the police detail ordered them to be removed.

Another group of students who had been standing in front of the library were sympathetic toward the demonstrators and charged the police. Several police officers were injured during the ensuing hostilities.

Eventually, order was restored. That evening, the television coverage presented a neutral and fairly accurate account of the incident.

21. Which of the following statements MOST clearly and accurately reflects the contents of the report?   21._____

 A. A large group of students, all of whom were holding anti-apartheid signs, was involved in a demonstration on the grounds of Columbia University.
 B. A large group of students, some of whom were holding anti-apartheid signs, was involved in a demonstration on the grounds of Columbia University.
 C. Each of a group of Columbia students carrying anti-apartheid signs was involved in a demonstration on the grounds of Columbia University.
 D. Each of the students involved in the demonstration on the grounds of Columbia University was holding an anti-apartheid sign.

22. Which of the following statements MOST clearly and accurately reflects the contents of the report?   22._____

A. The Commanding Officer of the police detail justified his order that the demonstrators disperse when the additional assistance arrived.
B. When the additional assistance arrived, the Commanding Officer of the police detail justified his order that the demonstrators disperse.
C. The Commanding Officer of the police detail directed the students to disperse when the additional assistance arrived.
D. The Commanding Officer of the police detail requested additional assistance because the student demonstrators were violating the rights of other students and certain faculty members.

23. Which of the following statements MOST clearly and accurately reflects the contents of the report?   23.____

    A. Another group of students charged the police because they were sympathetic toward the police.
    B. The evening television coverage of the demonstration was fair and accurate.
    C. The group of students who had been standing in front of the library was sympathetic toward the demonstrators.
    D. Several police officers were injured during the hostilities which took place in front of the library.

Questions 24-25.

DIRECTIONS: Questions 24 and 25 are to be answered SOLELY on the basis of the information given in the following paragraph.

Credibility of a witness is usually governed by his character and is evidenced by his reputation for truthfulness. Personal or financial reasons or a criminal record may cause a witness to give false information to avoid being implicated. Age, sex, physical and mental abnormalities, loyalty, revenge, social and economic status, indulgence in alcohol, and the influence of other persons are some of the many factors which may affect the accuracy, willingness, or ability with which witnesses observe, interpret, and describe occurrences.

24. According to the above paragraph, a witness may, for personal reasons, give wrong information about an occurrence because he   24.____

    A. wants to protect his reputation for truthfulness
    B. wants to embarrass the investigator
    C. doesn't want to become involved
    D. doesn't really remember what happened

25. According to the above paragraph, factors which influence the witness of an occurrence may affect   25.____

    A. not only what he tells about it but what he was able and wanted to see of it
    B. only what he describes and interprets later but not what he actually sees at the time of the event
    C. what he sees but not what he describes
    D. what he is willing to see but not what he is able to see

KEY (CORRECT ANSWERS)

1. B
2. C
3. D
4. C
5. B

6. A
7. B
8. D
9. B
10. C

11. B
12. B
13. D
14. A
15. B

16. B
17. C
18. C
19. A
20. D

21. D
22. C
23. C
24. C
25. A

READING COMPREHENSION
UNDERSTANDING AND INTERPRETING WRITTEN MATERIAL
EXAMINATION SECTION
TEST 1

DIRECTIONS: Each question or incomplete statement is followed by several suggested answers or completions. Select the one that *BEST* answers the question or completes the statement. *PRINT THE LETTER OF THE CORRECT ANSWER IN THE SPACE AT THE RIGHT.*

Questions 1-5.

DIRECTIONS: The following passage is to be used as the *SOLE* basis for answering Questions 1 to 5. Read the selection carefully and base your answers *ONLY* on the information contained therein.

PASSAGE

Politicians, preachers, and moralists frequently inveigh against the breakdown of family and community morality. According to one variant of this position, it is because of a "moral breakdown" that we find so much "crime in the streets." This line of reasoning has a persuasive message for many white Americans – it carries surface plausibility and underlying racial prejudice. Family "breakdown," "immoral" delinquent gangs and African-Americans are all disproportionately found in the urban slums. There is, however, an important flaw in the implied argument of this modern morality tale. It is apparent that lower-class families have difficulty in maintaining control over their children. According to the modern morality tale, if parents were more responsible and less perverse, and exercised control over their children, there would be less delinquency. The parents, and later their children, are the villains. But the lack of control stems not from parental perversity but from parental poverty, that is, from the deprivations of lower-class status. Of course, personalities do vary, even in their degree of "perversity"; and there are undoubtedly elements of "perversity" among some parents who do not maintain control over their children. But the magnitude of the problem stems from major social forces that have a pervasive influence over the lives of so many people.

By increasing the amount and awareness of legitimate opportunities, and reducing the attractiveness of delinquent gangs and illegitimate behavior, it may be possible to reduce delinquency. But overcoming these deprivations may also have an indirect effect upon delinquency by influencing family structure. The key problem in the lower class family is the weak occupational economic position of the man. Since, in the United States, the man is expected to be the breadwinner above all else, he performs inadequately at his major role within the family. As a result the lower class man is not esteemed, even within his own family. Under these circumstances, he may also leave his family. It can therefore be expected that improvements made in occupational and economic opportunities for lower class men will strengthen their position within the family and thereby strengthen the stability of the family as a whole. It will also heighten the attractiveness of the father and the family in the eyes of the children and make additional resources available within the family. Such changes will make it possible for the family to maintain stronger controls over its children.

Some argue that the provision of opportunities is not enough–that lower class people differ in their subculture, or values, or goals, or motivations so that they would not take advantage of these opportunities. Although value modifications generally take place within the lower class to make life's values more in accord with life's circumstances, it appears that middle class values and goals are still retained. Lower class people frequently find it necessary to stretch their values and aspirations downward to accord with realistic opportunities, but they do not abandon middle class values. They may lessen their commitment to values so that some of the sting will be taken out of life's deprivations, but they do not abandon all values. In short, providing additional opportunities seems to be the key area for change.

QUESTIONS

1. According to the passage, which of the following statements concerning street crime and moral breakdown is CORRECT?

   A. The irresponsibility of parents in slum-areas is the root cause of moral breakdown and street crime.
   B. Moral breakdown is basically a result of street crime.
   C. Moral breakdown and street crime are aspects of larger and widespread social problems.
   D. Street crime is basically a result of moral breakdown.
   E. Moral breakdown and street crime are a response to the prejudice of many white Americans.

2. According to the passage, the problem of juvenile delinquency is basically a result of

   A. the overrepresentation of minority groups in lower class neighborhoods
   B. the poor social and economic conditions that are an inherent part of lower class life
   C. the unwillingness of parents to accept their responsibilities and exercise discipline
   D. the breakdown in family morality that is most pervasive among the lower class
   E. personality variations among lower class parents which prevent them from maintaining control over their children

3. According to the passage, the *central* problem of the lower class family is the

   A. absence of goal motivated behavior
   B. failure to develop a distinct subculture within poor communities
   C. dissatisfaction with middle class values
   D. inability of the father to adequately support his family
   E. attractiveness of delinquency and illegitimate behavior

4. According to the passage, providing greater occupational opportunities for lower class men will result in all of the following EXCEPT

   A. allowing families to maintain greater control over their children
   B. improving the standing of lower class fathers within their families
   C. reducing the amount of juvenile delinquency so that lower class neighborhoods are as safe as others in the city
   D. increasing the stability of lower class families
   E. enhancing the image of the family itself for lower class children

5. According to the passage, lower class people often make adjustments in their values. As a result, their values *generally*

    A. reflect the opportunities that are actually available to the lower class
    B. coincide exactly with middle class values
    C. depend upon a family structure that lacks a strong father figure
    D. include goals and aspirations that exceed their economic situation
    E. deny responsibility for the delinquent behavior of their children

Questions 6-10.

DIRECTIONS: Questions 6 to 10 are to be answered SOLELY on the basis of the following passage.

PASSAGE

Of all the groups claiming interference by restrictions on the dissemination of news, the one with the most pressing claim is the law enforcement agency. Due to the combination of a morbid interest in crimes of violence and fear that a vicious criminal may be at large, there is a demand by the public for a showing by the police of capability in solving a crime. Perhaps unwilling to acknowledge the existence of, and accept responsibility for, a degenerate element in its midst, the public tends to cast the blame for a successful crime on police failure to prevent it. Thus there is constant pressure on the police to demonstrate that the case is nearing solution and that the perpetrator will soon be in custody. To avoid the accusation of suppressing information to cover up malfeasance, there is a legitimate tendency on the part of the police to cooperate with the press and thus escape being cast in an unfavorable light. The ideal solution – from the point of view of the police – would be to allow them free rein in releasing information to reassure the public. However, this would not be consonant with the right of the accused to a fair trial with the presumption of innocence.

A distinguished committee of lawyers and jurists has developed a comprehensive code for police and law enforcement agencies. The committee's recommendations include the following:

A. Concerning the Defendant

    1. The release of information concerning the defendant shall be limited to his name, age, occupation, marital status, and personal data not related to the crime or the character of the defendant. His criminal record, prior medical and psychiatric history, or military disciplinary record, if any, shall not be released. No other information that is clearly prejudicial to the defendant shall be released.

    2. No statement of any nature made by the defendant, or the substance thereof, shall be released. No reference shall be made to any test taken by the defendant or that he has refused to take.

    3. The announcement of the arrest of the defendant may include, in addition to the information authorized above, the time, place, and manner of apprehension as well as the text or summary of the charge, information, or indictment. No comments shall be made relating to his guilt or innocence.

    4. News media shall not be permitted to interview the defendant with or without his attorney's consent, while he is in police custody.

    5. News media shall not be permitted to photograph or televise the defendant while he is in police custody except in a public place. This prohibition extends to such instances as where he is being interrogated, where he is being processed ("booked") following arrest, where he is in a lockup or detention facility, or where he is at a hospital bedside for identification purposes.

    6. Where the defendant is still at large, and it appears that he is a fugitive from justice, additional information that may reasonably and directly aid in effecting his apprehension, including his photograph, may be released.

B. Concerning the Crime, the Investigation, and the Arrest
   1. A general description of the crime shall be made available to the news media. Gruesome or sordid aspects which tend unduly to inflame public emotions shall not be released. Witnesses shall not be identified by name or otherwise, nor shall any comment be made concerning their credibility, their testimony, or their identification of the defendant.
   2. No comment on the apparent motivation or character of the perpetrator shall be made.
   3. No information concerning scientific evidence such as laboratory or ballistics tests or fingerprints shall be released.
C. General
   1. A member of the police agency shall be designated as the Information Officer responsible for the dissemination of all information to the news media. It will be the responsibility of the Information Officer to supervise the enforcement of these regulations and to solicit and encourage full cooperation of news media. No member of a police agency may furnish any information to news media without prior approval by the Information Officer. No interviews shall be permitted with investigating or arresting officers.
   2. Wherever feasible, the Information Officer will encourage news media to enter into pool arrangements so as to reduce confusion and interference with the orderly processes of law enforcement. It shall be a prime responsibility of the Information Officer to insure a calm and orderly atmosphere during the dissemination of information to the news media.

QUESTIONS

6. According to the passage, the tendency of the police to cooperate with the press by releasing information is based on the

   A. public's desire for evidence that the police are able to bring criminals to justice
   B. deterrent effect on other criminals which results from reports of police efficiency
   C. requirement of the courts for full disclosure of pertinent information
   D. assistance which unrestricted publicity provides in apprehending perpetrators who are still at large
   E. belief that charges of corruption cannot be avoided in any other way

7. Of the following, the *BASIC* purpose of the recommendations contained in the passage is to

   A. satisfy the public's curiosity concerning crime
   B. expedite the dissemination of information to the news media
   C. protect the defendant's right to a fair trial
   D. enhance the reputation of the police
   E. reduce interference by the news media in essential police functions

8. According to the recommendations contained in the passage, it would *NOT* be proper for a law enforcement agency to

   A. release information pertaining to how the defendant was caught
   B. discuss the testimony given by eyewitnesses
   C. distribute a written copy or synopsis of the indictment
   D. provide a general description of the crime in question
   E. disclose the occupation and marital status of the defendant

9. According to the recommendations contained in the passage, law enforcement agencies, under certain circumstances, would be able to

    A. permit a defendant to make a statement to the news media
    B. release information concerning the defendant's medical history which is not pertinent to the case
    C. describe to the news media evidence against the defendant in terms of probable guilt or innocence
    D. allow a defendant to be televised while in their custody in a non-public place
    E. provide a photograph of the defendant to the news media

10. According to the passage, the Information Officer in a police department is responsible for all of the following EXCEPT

    A. coordinating interviews of arresting officers by members of the news media
    B. enforcing regulations concerning dissemination of information to the news media
    C. fostering the use of pool arrangements by the news media
    D. approving in advance all requests by the news media for information
    E. preventing hectic and unruly situations when information is provided to the news media.

KEY (CORRECT ANSWERS)

1. C
2. B
3. D
4. C
5. A

6. A
7. C
8. B
9. E
10. A

TEST 2

DIRECTIONS: Each question or incomplete statement is followed by several suggested answers or completions. Select the one that *BEST* answers the question or completes the statement. *PRINT THE LETTER OF THE CORRECT ANSWER IN THE SPACE AT THE RIGHT.*

Questions 1-5.

DIRECTIONS: Questions 1 to 5 are to be answered *SOLELY* on the basis of the following passage.

PASSAGE

There is a hazy boundary between grateful citizens paying their respects to a proud profession, and "good" citizens involved in corruption, wishing to buy future favors. Once begun, however, the acceptance of small bribes and favors or similar practices can become "norms" or informal standards of cliques of policemen. A recruit can be socialized into accepting these illegal practices by mild, informal negative sanctions such as the withholding of group acceptance. If these unlawful practices are embraced, the recruit's membership group – the police force – and his reference group – the clique involved in illegal behavior – are no longer one and the same. In such circumstances the norms of the reference group (the illegal-oriented clique) would clearly take precedence over either the formal requisites of the membership group (police department regulations) or the formalized norms (legal statutes) of the larger society. When such conflicts are apparent a person can

1. conform to one, take the consequences of non-conformity to the other;
2. seek a compromise position by which he attempts to conform in part, though not wholly, to one or more sets of role expectations, in the hope that sanctions applied will be minimal.

If these reference group norms involving illegal activity become routinized with use they become an identifiable informal "code." Such codes are not unique to the police profession. A fully documented case study of training at a military academy, in which an informal pattern of behavior was assimilated along with the formal standards, clearly outlined the function of the informal norms, their dominance when in conflict with formal regulations, and the secretive nature of their existence to facilitate their effectiveness and subsequent preservation. This same secrecy could be demanded of a police "code" to insure its preservation. Although within the clique the code must be well defined, the ignorance of the lay public to even its existence would be a requisite to its continuous and effective use. Through participation in activity regimented by the "code," an increased group identity and cohesion among "code" practitioners would emerge.

Group identity requires winning of acceptance as a member of the inner group and, thereby, gaining access to the secrets of the occupation which are acquired through informal contacts with colleagues. Lack of this acceptance not only bars the neophyte from the inner secrets of the profession, but may isolate him socially and professionally from his colleagues and even his superiors. There is the added fear that, in some circumstances in which he would need their support, they would avoid becoming involved, forcing him to face personal danger or public ridicule alone.

QUESTIONS

1. According to the passage, the reference group of a recruit who accepts corrupt practices is

   A. the police force of which the recruit is a member
   B. a loosely-structured group from which the recruit learns both formal and informal norms
   C. the coterie of officers who are involved in illegal activities
   D. society as a whole, of which the police are a component
   E. a professional organization which instructs the recruit in his responsibilities

   1._____

2. According to the passage, allegiance by policemen to informally codified standards of behavior is *most likely* to result in

   A. increased attempts by most citizens to bribe police officers
   B. a decrease of mutual support among policemen
   C. greater awareness on the part of the public of such behavior
   D. decreased secrecy about police department practices
   E. stronger group identification among such policemen

   2._____

3. According to the passage, the police recuit who is NOT accepted by the group which is involved in illegal behavior will

   A. be prevented from learning many confidential aspects of police work
   B. face less risk of public ridicule or personal danger
   C. be held in high esteem by his superiors
   D. gain social and professional stature among his colleagues
   E. be more likely to expose the activities of the group to the public

   3._____

4. According to the passage, informal codes of illegal behavior function effectively only when they

   A. are tacitly accepted by the entire society
   B. permit formal standards to predominate whenever there is a conflict
   C. exist without being known to outsiders
   D. minimize the use of informal negative sanctions
   E. complement pre-existing norms within the police profession

   4._____

5. According to the passage, a recruit who must deal with conflicting norms of different groups may

   A. not be able to distinguish between ordinary citizens and those involved in graft
   B. try to accommodate himself to the different roles he is expected to play
   C. be unaware of the informal codes of behavior within the police department
   D. accept one set of standards and thereby avoid any unpleasant consequences
   E. find that he is able to solve the problem by bringing the competing norms into conformity

   5._____

Questions 6-10.

DIRECTIONS: Questions 6 to 10 are to be answered *SOLELY* on the basis of the following passage.

PASSAGE
THE CONCEPT OF AN OFFENSIVELY DEPLOYED PATROL FORCE

Police forces, in general, are defensively deployed, both in their organization and operation. That is, they are principally designed to act efficiently during or after the commission of a crime. This concept becomes quite clear when the distribution of available manpower of a police force is examined.

The defensive enforcement attitude is prevalent in the philosophy of the individual policeman. Most law enforcement officers seem to view the making of an arrest as one of their major goals. The reason for this attitude is obvious. Police administrators do not have available a measuring technique for evaluating an officer's crime prevention efforts, while an arrest is a measure of his defensive effectiveness.

One of the most serious drawbacks for any police force that is committed to a defensive action during a period of rising crime, is that it becomes, of necessity, a retrograde operation; that is, as more crime is committed, more manpower is utilized for investigation, with a corresponding decrease in crime prevention activities, thus encouraging more crime, more manpower for investigation, etc., etc. The logical extension of this situation is a police force that is completely overloaded with investigations, while crime runs rampant.

It is now appropriate to inquire into the effectiveness of defensive police strategy in the present crime situation. Determining the effectiveness of a police system and its strategy requires the use of absolute measurements. In particular, the effectiveness should be measured in terms of how well it attains its goals. By these measures, the defensive strategy used by the police does not appear to be effective.

If the goal of police action is to eliminate or substantially reduce crime, it is not succeeding. The number of crimes as well as the crime rate is increasing.

It seems completely self-evident that if it were possible to station a policeman at or about every house and building in the city, the amount of crime would be significantly reduced. It would be reduced not because a criminal would be caught after he committed a crime, but because he would not commit the crime, because of the fear of being caught. Thus the crime rate would be reduced by preventing the crime from happening, not by punishing the criminal (if caught) after the crime has been committed.

The solution is, of course, not a practical one but, nevertheless, it should serve as an ideal for an offensively deployed police force. In practice, the force should create the appearance of being everywhere at once.

In contrast to the defensive force, whose operation is retrograde, such an offensive force would be progressive in nature; that is, by preventing a crime from occurring, the manpower required for investigation would be reduced. Hence, it could be diverted toward the prevention of more crime, which would further reduce the investigations and manpower needed, etc. The logical extension of this situation is a force that is completely deployed to prevent crime.

The offensive force depicted above is, of course, a patrol force, but not in the sense of the conventional police patrol, which is very inflexible with regard to the time and place it can be deployed, which is heavily committed to answering complaints, and which is managed by "seat of the pants" techniques.

The specifications for an offensively deployed patrol force are as follows:
1. A patrol unit must pass by every point in the city, on the average of once every ten minutes.

2. The patrol unit must not be sent on a complaint, unless the complaint can be disposed of in less than ten minutes, or there is a crime or equivalent emergency situation in progress. If a unit does become involved, its territory must be covered by adjacent patrol units.
3. The patrol force must be deployed with due regard to the expected type and location of crime, based on an analysis of previous criminal activity for the particular season of the year, day of the week, hour of the day, etc.

QUESTIONS

6. Assume that a certain city has changed the nature of its motor patrol force from a defensive force to offensive deployment.
Which one of the following results will *MOST* logically follow if the patrol force is functioning in line with the principles discussed in the passage? The

   A. arrest rate for burglary will decrease
   B. number of complaints received will increase
   C. number of aggravated assaults will increase
   D. number of miles that the patrol vehicles travel will increase
   E. number of complaints answered by the patrol force will increase

7. According to the passage, which one of the following *MOST* accurately states the underlying purpose of offensively deployed patrol? To

   A. leave the patrol unit free to perform offensive patrol
   B. increase the number of criminals that are caught and punished
   C. catch so many criminals that the criminals are afraid to commit offenses
   D. make offenders so fearful of being caught that they refrain from committing offenses
   E. have a patrol unit pass every point in the city on the average of once every ten minutes

8. A certain police department has accepted the concept of offensive deployment. In implementing this concept, it has adopted a policy defining the basic responsibility for making initial investigations or crimes.
Which one of the following is *MOST* likely the policy this department has adopted, if it followed the terms of the passage?

   A. Basic responsibility for initial investigation of crimes is assigned to the patrol force.
   B. Basic responsibility for initial criminal investigation is assigned somewhere other than to the patrol units.
   C. As crime increases above normal levels, the basic responsibility for initial investigation of crime retrogrades to the patrol force.
   D. As crime increases above normal levels, the basic responsibility for initial investigation of crime retrogrades to the Detective Division.
   E. When crime is normal, basic responsibility for initial investigation of crime is divided between the Detective Division and the patrol force, depending on the availability of manpower in each.

9. Assume the following facts: The police department of a certain city has implemented the concept of an offensively deployed police force based on the recommendations contained in the passage.
Which one of the following results would MOST logically indicate that the patrol force is functioning ineffectively? The

   A. crime rate has decreased
   B. number of crime investigations by the patrol units has increased
   C. percentage of crimes cleared by arrest has increased
   D. number of prosecutions for crimes cleared by arrest has increased
   E. average amount of time spent by the average officer answering complaints has decreased

10. According to the passage, which one of the following is the MOST probable reason why many individual policemen have accepted the philosophy of defensive enforcement? Because

    A. of the retrograde philosophy
    B. no technique exists for evaluating an officer's offensive efforts
    C. most policemen believe in the effectiveness of the crime-investigation cycle
    D. the goal of police action is to eliminate or substantially reduce crime
    E. the effectiveness of defensive police strategy has never been evaluated

KEY (CORRECT ANSWERS)

1. C
2. E
3. A
4. C
5. B
6. D
7. D
8. B
9. B
10. B

EVALUATING CONCLUSIONS IN LIGHT OF KNOWN FACTS
EXAMINATION SECTION
TEST 1

DIRECTIONS: Each question or incomplete statement is followed by several suggested answers or completions. Select the one that BEST answers the question or completes the statement. *PRINT THE LETTER OF THE CORRECT ANSWER IN THE SPACE AT THE RIGHT.*

Questions 1-9.

DIRECTIONS: In Questions 1 through 9, you will read a set of facts and a conclusion drawn from them. The conclusion may be valid or invalid, based on the facts—it's your task to determine the validity of the conclusion.

For each question, select the letter before the statement that BEST expresses the relationship between the given facts and the conclusion that has been drawn from them. Your choices are:
  A. The facts prove the conclusion;
  B. The facts disprove the conclusion; or
  C. The facts neither prove nor disprove the conclusion.

1. FACTS: If the supervisor retires, James, the assistant supervisor, will not be transferred to another department. James will be promoted to supervisor if he is not transferred. The supervisor retired.

   CONCLUSION: James will be promoted to supervisor.
     A. The facts prove the conclusion.
     B. The facts disprove the conclusion.
     C. The facts neither prove nor disprove the conclusion.

2. FACTS: In the town of Luray, every player on the softball team works at Luray National Bank. In addition, every player on the Luray softball team wear glasses.

   CONCLUSIONS: At least some of the people who work at Luray National Bank wear glasses.
     A. The facts prove the conclusion.
     B. The facts disprove the conclusion.
     C. The facts neither prove nor disprove the conclusion.

3. FACTS: The only time Henry and June go out to dinner is on an evening when they have childbirth classes. Their childbirth classes meet on Tuesdays and Thursdays.

CONCLUSION: Henry and June never go out to dinner on Friday or Saturday.
  A. The facts prove the conclusion.
  B. The facts disprove the conclusion.
  C. The facts neither prove nor disprove the conclusion.

4. FACTS: Every player on the field hockey team has at least one bruise. Everyone on the field hockey team also has scarred knees.

   CONCLUSION: Most people with both bruises and scarred knees are field hockey players.
   A. The facts prove the conclusion.
   B. The facts disprove the conclusion.
   C. The facts neither prove nor disprove the conclusion.

4._____

5. FACTS: In the chess tournament, Lance will win his match against Jane if Jane wins her match against Mathias. If Lance wins his match against Jane, Christine will not win her match against Jane.

   CONCLUSION: Christine will not win her match against Jane if Jane wins her match against Mathias.
   A. The facts prove the conclusion.
   B. The facts disprove the conclusion.
   C. The facts neither prove nor disprove the conclusion.

5._____

6. FACTS: No green lights on the machine are indicators for the belt drive status. Not all of the lights on the machine's upper panel are green. Some lights on the machine's lower panel are green.

   CONCLUSION: The green lights on the machine's lower panel may be indicators for the belt drive status.
   A. The facts prove the conclusion.
   B. The facts disprove the conclusion.
   C. The facts neither prove nor disprove the conclusion.

6._____

7. FACTS: At a small, one-room country school, there are eight students: Amy, Ben, Carla, Dan, Elliot, Francine, Greg, and Hannah. Each student is in either the 6th, 7th, or 8th grade. Either two or three students are in each grade. Amy, Dan, and Francine are all in different grades. Ben and Elliot are both in the 7th grade. Hannah and Carl are in the same grade.

   CONCLUSION: Exactly three students are in the 7th grade.
   A. The facts prove the conclusion.
   B. The facts disprove the conclusion.
   C. The facts neither prove nor disprove the conclusion.

7._____

8. FACTS: Two married couples are having lunch together. Two of the four people are German and two are Russian, but in each couple the nationality of the spouse is not necessarily the same as the other's. One person in the group is a teacher, the other a lawyer, one an engineer, and the other a writer. The teacher is a Russian man. The writer is Russian, and her husband is an engineer. One of the people, Mr. Stern, is German.

   CONCLUSION: Mr. Stern's wife is a writer.
   A. The facts prove the conclusion.
   B. The facts disprove the conclusion.
   C. The facts neither prove nor disprove the conclusion.

   8.____

9. FACTS: The flume ride at the county fair is open only to children who are at least 36 inches tall. Lisa is 30 inches tall. John is shorter than Henry, but more than 10 inches taller than Lisa.

   CONCLUSION: Lisa is the only one who can't ride the flume ride.
   A. The facts prove the conclusion.
   B. The facts disprove the conclusion.
   C. The facts neither prove nor disprove the conclusion.

   9.____

Questions 10-17.

DIRECTIONS: Questions 10 through 17 are based on the following reading passage. It is not your knowledge of the particular topic that is being tested, but your ability to reason based on what you have read. The passage is likely to detail several proposed courses of action and factors affecting these proposals. The reading passage is followed by a conclusion or outcome based on the facts in the passage, or a description of a decision taken regarding the situation. The conclusion is followed by a number of statements that have a possible connection to the conclusion. For each statement, you are to determine whether:
   A. The statement proves the conclusion.
   B. The statement supports the conclusion but does not prove it.
   C. The statement disproves the conclusion.
   D. The statement weakens the conclusion but does not disprove it.
   E. The statement has no relevance to the conclusion.

Remember that the conclusion after the passage is to be accepted as the outcome of what actually happened, and that you are being asked to evaluate the impact each statement would have had on the conclusion.

PASSAGE:

The Grand Army of Foreign Wars, a national veteran's organization, is struggling to maintain its National Home, where the widowed spouses and orphans of deceased members are housed together in a small village-like community. The Home is open to spouses and children who are bereaved for any reason, regardless of whether the member's death was related to military service, but a new global conflict has led to a dramatic surge in the number of members' deaths: many veterans who re-enlisted for the conflict have been killed in action.

The Grand Army of Foreign Wars is considering several options for handling the increased number of applications for housing at the National Home, which has been traditionally supported by membership due. At its national convention, it will choose only one of the following:

The first idea is a one-time $50 tax on all members, above and beyond the dues they pay already. Since the organization has more than a million member, this tax should be sufficient for the construction and maintenance of new housing for applicants on the existing grounds of the National Home. The idea is opposed, however, by some older members who live on fixed incomes. These members object in principle to the taxation of Grand Army members. The Grand Army has never imposed a tax on its members.

The second idea is to launch a national fundraising drive the public relations campaign that will attract donations for the National Home. Several national celebrities are members of the organization, and other celebrities could be attracted to the cause. Many Grand Army members are wary of this approach, however: in the past, the net receipts of some fundraising efforts have been relatively insignificant, given the costs of staging them.

A third approach, suggested by many of the younger members, is to have new applicants share some of the costs of construction and maintenance. The spouses and children would pay an up-front "enrollment" fee, based on a sliding scale proportionate to their income and assets, and then a monthly fee adjusted similarly to contribute to maintenance costs. Many older members are strongly opposed to this idea, as it is in direct contradiction to the principles on which the organization was founded more than a century ago.

The fourth option is simply to maintain the status quo, focus the organization's efforts on supporting the families who already live at the National Home, and wait to accept new applicants based on attrition.

CONCLUSION: At its annual national convention, the Grand Army of Foreign Wars votes to impose a one-time tax of $10 on each member for the purpose of expanding and supporting the National Home to welcome a larger number of applicants. The tax is considered to be the solution most likely to produce the funds needed to accommodate the growing number of applicants.

10. Actuarial studies have shown that because the Grand Army's membership consists mostly of older veterans from earlier wars, the organization's membership will suffer a precipitous decline in numbers in about five years.
    A. The statement proves the conclusion.
    B. The statement supports the conclusion but does not prove it.
    C. The statement disproves the conclusion.
    D. The statement weakens the conclusion but does not disprove it.
    E. The statement has no relevance to the conclusion.

11. After passage of the funding measure, a splinter group of older members appeals for the "sliding scale" provision to be applied to the tax, so that some members may be allowed to contribute less based on their income.
    A. The statement proves the conclusion.
    B. The statement supports the conclusion but does not prove it.
    C. The statement disproves the conclusion.
    D. The statement weakens the conclusion but does not disprove it.
    E. The statement has no relevance to the conclusion.

5 (#1)

12. The original charter of the Grand Army of Foreign Wars specifically states that the organization will not levy taxes or duties on its members beyond its modest annual dues. It takes a super-majority of attending delegates at the national convention to make alterations to the charter.
    A. The statement proves the conclusion.
    B. The statement supports the conclusion but does not prove it.
    C. The statement disproves the conclusion.
    D. The statement weakens the conclusion but does not disprove it.
    E. The statement has no relevance to the conclusion.

12.____

13. Six months before Grand Army of Foreign Wars' national convention, the Internal Revenue Service rules that because it is an organization that engages in political lobbying, the Grand Army must no longer enjoy its own federal tax-exempt status.
    A. The statement proves the conclusion.
    B. The statement supports the conclusion but does not prove it.
    C. The statement disproves the conclusion.
    D. The statement weakens the conclusion but does not disprove it.
    E. The statement has no relevance to the conclusion.

13.____

14. Two months before the national convention, Dirk Rockwell, arguably the country's most famous film actor, announces in a nationally televised interview that he has been saddened to learn of the plight of the National Home, and that he is going to make it his own personal crusade to see that it is able to house and support a greater number of widowed spouses and orphans in the future.
    A. The statement proves the conclusion.
    B. The statement supports the conclusion but does not prove it.
    C. The statement disproves the conclusion.
    D. The statement weakens the conclusion but does not disprove it.
    E. The statement has no relevance to the conclusion.

14.____

15. The Grand Army's final estimate is that the cost of expanding the National Home to accommodate the increased number of applicants will be about $61 million.
    A. The statement proves the conclusion.
    B. The statement supports the conclusion but does not prove it.
    C. The statement disproves the conclusion.
    D. The statement weakens the conclusion but does not disprove it.
    E. The statement has no relevance to the conclusion.

15.____

16. Just before the national convention, the Federal Department of Veterans Affairs announces steep cuts in the benefits package that is currently offered to the widowed spouses and orphans of veterans.
    A. The statement proves the conclusion.
    B. The statement supports the conclusion but does not prove it.
    C. The statement disproves the conclusion.
    D. The statement weakens the conclusion but does not disprove it.
    E. The statement has no relevance to the conclusion.

16.____

17. After the national convention, the Grand Army of Foreign Wars begins charging a modest "start-up" fee to all families who apply for residence at the national home.
    A. The statement proves the conclusion.
    B. The statement supports the conclusion but does not prove it.
    C. The statement disproves the conclusion.
    D. The statement weakens the conclusion but does not disprove it.
    E. The statement has no relevance to the conclusion.

17._____

Questions 18-25.

DIRECTIONS: Questions 18 through 25 each provide four factual statements and a conclusion based on these statements. After reading the entire question, you will decide whether:
    A. The conclusion is proved by statements I-IV;
    B. The conclusion is disproved by statements I-IV.
    C. The facts are not sufficient to prove or disprove the conclusion.

18. FACTUAL STATEMENTS:
    I. In the Field Day high jump competition, Martha jumped higher than Frank.
    II. Carl jumped higher than Ignacio.
    III. Ignacio jumped higher than Frank.
    IV. Dan jumped higher than Carl.

    CONCLUSION: Frank finished last in the high jump competition.
    A. The conclusion is proved by statements I-IV;
    B. The conclusion is disproved by statements I-IV.
    C. The facts are not sufficient to prove or disprove the conclusion.

18._____

19. FACTUAL STATEMENTS:
    I. The door to the hammer mill chamber is locked if light 6 is red.
    II. The door to the hammer mill chamber is locked only when the mill is operating.
    III. If the mill is not operating, light 6 is blue.
    IV. Light 6 is blue.

    CONCLUSION: The door to the hammer mill chamber is locked.
    A. The conclusion is proved by statements I-IV;
    B. The conclusion is disproved by statements I-IV.
    C. The facts are not sufficient to prove or disprove the conclusion.

19._____

20. FACTUAL STATEMENTS:
    I. Ziegfried, the lion tamer at the circus, has demanded ten additional minutes of performance time during each show.
    II. If Ziegfried is allowed his ten additional minutes per show, he will attempt to teach Kimba the tiger to shoot a basketball.
    III. If Kimba learns how to shoot a basketball, then Ziegfried was not given his ten additional minutes.
    IV. Ziegfried was given his ten additional minutes.

20._____

7 (#1)

CONCLUSION: Despite Ziegfried's efforts, Kimba did not learn how to shoot a basketball.
   A. The conclusion is proved by statements I-IV;
   B. The conclusion is disproved by statements I-IV.
   C. The facts are not sufficient to prove or disprove the conclusion.

21. FACTUAL STATEMENTS:
    I. If Stan goes to counseling, Sara won't divorce him.
    II. If Sara divorces Stan, she'll move back to Texas.
    III. If Sara doesn't divorce Stan, Irene will be disappointed.
    IV. Stan goes to counseling.

    CONCLUSION: Irene will be disappointed.
       A. The conclusion is proved by statements I-IV;
       B. The conclusion is disproved by statements I-IV.
       C. The facts are not sufficient to prove or disprove the conclusion.

21.____

22. FACTUAL STATEMENTS:
    I. If Delia is promoted to district manager, Claudia will have to be promoted to team leader.
    II. Delia will be promoted to district manager unless she misses her fourth-quarter sales quota.
    III. If Claudia is promoted to team leader, Thomas will be promoted to assistant team leader.
    IV. Delia meets her fourth-quarter sales quota.

    CONCLUSION: Thomas is promoted to assistant team leader.
       A. The conclusion is proved by statements I-IV;
       B. The conclusion is disproved by statements I-IV.
       C. The facts are not sufficient to prove or disprove the conclusion.

22.____

23. FACTUAL STATEMENTS:
    I. Clone D is identical to Clone B.
    II. Clone B is not identical to Clone A.
    III. Clone D is not identical to Clone C.
    IV. Clone E is not identical to the clones that are identical to Clone B.

    CONCLUSION: Clone E is identical to Clone D.
       A. The conclusion is proved by statements I-IV;
       B. The conclusion is disproved by statements I-IV.
       C. The facts are not sufficient to prove or disprove the conclusion.

23.____

24. FACTUAL STATEMENTS:
    I. In the Stafford Tower, each floor is occupied by a single business.
    II. Big G Staffing is on a floor between CyberGraphics and MainEvent.
    III. Gasco is on the floor directly below CyberGraphics and three floors above Treehorn Audio.
    IV. MainEvent is five floors below EZ Tax and four floors below Treehorn Audio.

24.____

CONCLUSION: EZ Tax is on a floor between Gasco and MainEvent.
  A. The conclusion is proved by statements I-IV;
  B. The conclusion is disproved by statements I-IV.
  C. The facts are not sufficient to prove or disprove the conclusion.

25. FACTUAL STATEMENTS:
  I. Only county roads lead to Nicodemus.
  II. All the roads from Hill City to Graham County are federal highways.
  III. Some of the roads from Plainville lead to Nicodemus.
  IV. Some of the roads running from Hill City lead to Strong City.

  CONCLUSION: Some of the roads from Plainville are county roads.
  A. The conclusion is proved by statements I-IV;
  B. The conclusion is disproved by statements I-IV.
  C. The facts are not sufficient to prove or disprove the conclusion.

25.____

KEY (CORRECT ANSWERS)

1.	A		11.	A
2.	A		12.	D
3.	A		13.	E
4.	C		14.	D
5.	A		15.	B
6.	B		16.	B
7.	A		17.	C
8.	A		18.	A
9.	A		19.	B
10.	E		20.	A

21.	A
22.	A
23.	B
24.	A
25.	A

SOLUTIONS TO PROBLEMS

1. **CORRECT ANSWER: A**
   Given Statement 3, we deduce that James will not be transferred to another department. By Statement 2, we can conclude that James will be promoted.

2. **CORRECT ANSWER: A**
   Since every player on the softball team wears glasses, these individuals compose some of the people who work at the bank. Although not every person who works at the bank plays softball, those bank employees who do play softball wear glasses.

3. **CORRECT ANSWER: A**
   If Henry and June go out to dinner, we conclude that it must be on Tuesday or Thursday, which are the only two days when they have childbirth classes. This implies that if it is not Tuesday or Thursday, then this couple does not go out to dinner.

4. **CORRECT ANSWER: C**
   We can only conclude that if a person plays on the field hockey team, then he or she has both bruises and scarred knees. But there are probably a great number of people who have both bruises and scarred knees but do not play on the field hockey team. The given conclusion can neither be proven or disproven.

5. **CORRECT ANSWER: A**
   From statement 1, if Jane beats Mathias, then Lance will beat Jane. Using statement 2, we can then conclude that Christine will not win her match against Jane.

6. **CORRECT ANSWER: B**
   Statement 1 tells us that no green light can be an indicator of the belt drive status. Thus, the given conclusion must be false.

7. **CORRECT ANSWER: A**
   We already know that Ben and Elliot are in the 7th grade. Even though Hannah and Carl are in the same grade, it cannot be the 7th grade because we would then have at least four students in this 7th grade. This would contradict the third statement, which states that either two or three students are in each grade. Since Amy, Dan, and Francine are in different grade, exactly one of them must be in the 7th grade. Thus, Ben, Elliot, and exactly one of Amy, Dan, and Francine are the three students in the 7th grade.

8. **CORRECT ANSWER: A**
   One man is a teacher, who is Russian. We know that the writer is female and is Russian. Since her husband is an engineer, he cannot be the Russian teacher. Thus, her husband is of German descent, namely Mr. Stern. This means that Mr. Stern's wife is the writer. Note that one couple consists of a male Russian teacher and a female German lawyer. The other couple consists of a male German engineer and a female Russian writer.

9. CORRECT ANSWER: A
Since John is more than 10 inches taller than Lisa, his height is at least 46 inches. Also, John is shorter than Henry, so Henry's height must be greater than 46 inches. Thus, Lisa is the only one whose height is less than 36 inches. Therefore, she is the only one who is not allowed on the flume ride.

18. CORRECT ANSWER: A
Dan jumped higher than Carl, who jumped higher than Ignacio, who jumped higher than Frank. Since Martha jumped higher than Frank, every person jumped higher than Frank. Thus, Frank finished last.

19. CORRECT ANSWER: B
If the light is red, then the door is locked. If the door is locked, then the mill is operating. Reversing the logical sequence of these statements, if the mill is not operating, then the door is not locked, which means that the light is blue. Thus, the given conclusion is disproved.

20. CORRECT ANSWER: A
Using the contrapositive of statement III, Ziegfried was given his ten additional minutes, then Kimba did not learn how to shoot a basketball. Since statement IV is factual, the conclusion is proved.

21. CORRECT ANSWER: A
From Statements IV and I, we conclude that Sara doesn't divorce Stan. Then statement III reveals that Irene will be disappointed. Thus, the conclusion is proved.

22. CORRECT ANSWER: A
Statement II can be rewritten as "Delia is promoted to district manager or she misses her sales quota." Furthermore, this statement is equivalent to "If Delia makes her sales quota, then she is promoted to district manager." From statement I, we conclude that Claudia is promoted to team leader. Finally, by statement III, Thomas is promoted to assistant team leader.

23. CORRECT ANSWER: B
By statement IV, Clone E is not identical to any clones identical to Clone B. Statement I tells us that Clones B and D are identical. Therefore, Clone E cannot be identical to Clone D. The conclusion is disproved.

24. CORRECT ANSWER: A
Based on all four statements, CyberGraphics is somewhere below MainEvent. Gasco is one floor below CyberGraphics. EZ Tax is two floors below Gasco. Treehorn Audio is one floor below EZ Tax. MainEvent is four floors below Treehorn Audio. Thus, EZ Tax is two floors below Gasco and five floors above MainEvent. The conclusion is proved.

25. CORRECT ANSWER: A
From statement III, we know that some of the roads from Plainville lead to Nicodemus. But statement I tells us that only county roads lead to Nicodemus. Therefore, some of the roads from Plainville must be county roads. The conclusion is proved.

TEST 2

DIRECTIONS: Each question or incomplete statement is followed by several suggested answers or completions. Select the one that BEST answers the question or completes the statement. *PRINT THE LETTER OF THE CORRECT ANSWER IN THE SPACE AT THE RIGHT.*

Questions 1-9.

DIRECTIONS: In Questions 1 through 9, you will read a set of facts and a conclusion drawn from them. The conclusion may be valid or invalid, based on the facts—it's your task to determine the validity of the conclusion.

For each question, select the letter before the statement that BEST expresses the relationship between the given facts and the conclusion that has been drawn from them. Your choices are:
   A. The facts prove the conclusion;
   B. The facts disprove the conclusion; or
   C. The facts neither prove nor disprove the conclusion.

1. FACTS: Some employees in the testing department are statisticians. Most of the statisticians who work in the testing department are projection specialists. Tom Wilks works in the testing department.

   CONCLUSION: Tom Wilks is a statistician.
      A. The facts prove the conclusion.
      B. The facts disprove the conclusion.
      C. The facts neither prove nor disprove the conclusion.

2. FACTS: Ten coins are split among Hank, Lawrence, and Gail. If Lawrence gives his coins to Hank, then Hank will have more coins than Gail. If Gail gives her coins to Lawrence, then Lawrence will have more coins than Hank.

   CONCLUSION: Hank has six coins.
      A. The facts prove the conclusion.
      B. The facts disprove the conclusion.
      C. The facts neither prove nor disprove the conclusion.

3. FACTS: Nobody loves everybody. Janet loves Ken. Ken loves everybody who loves Janet.

   CONCLUSION: Everybody loves Janet.
      A. The facts prove the conclusion.
      B. The facts disprove the conclusion.
      C. The facts neither prove nor disprove the conclusion.

4. FACTS: Most of the Torres family lives in East Los Angeles. Many people in East Los Angeles celebrate Cinco de Mayo. Joe is a member of the Torres family.

   CONCLUSION: Joe lives in East Los Angeles.
   A. The facts prove the conclusion.
   B. The facts disprove the conclusion.
   C. The facts neither prove nor disprove the conclusion.

5. FACTS: Five professionals each occupy one story of a five-story office building. Dr. Kane's office is above Dr. Assad's. Dr. Johnson's office is between Dr. Kane's and Dr. Conlon's. Dr. Steen's office is between Dr. Conlon's and Dr. Assad's. Dr. Johnson is on the fourth story.

   CONCLUSION: Dr. Kane occupies the top story.
   A. The facts prove the conclusion.
   B. The facts disprove the conclusion.
   C. The facts neither prove nor disprove the conclusion.

6. FACTS: To be eligible for membership in the Yukon Society, a person must be able to either tunnel through a snowbank while wearing only a T-shirt and short, or hold his breath for two minutes under water that is 50°F. Ray can only hold his breath for a minute and a half.

   CONCLUSION: Ray can still become a member of the Yukon Society by tunneling through a snowbank while wearing a T-shirt and shorts.
   A. The facts prove the conclusion.
   B. The facts disprove the conclusion.
   C. The facts neither prove nor disprove the conclusion.

7. FACTS: A mark is worth five plunks. You can exchange four sharps for a tinplot. It takes eight marks to buy a sharp.

   CONCLUSION: A sharp is the most valuable.
   A. The facts prove the conclusion.
   B. The facts disprove the conclusion.
   C. The facts neither prove nor disprove the conclusion.

8. FACTS: There are gibbons, as well as lemurs, who like to play in the trees at the monkey house. All those who like to play in the trees at the monkey house are fed lettuce and bananas.

   CONCLUSION: Lemurs and gibbons are types of monkeys.
   A. The facts prove the conclusion.
   B. The facts disprove the conclusion.
   C. The facts neither prove nor disprove the conclusion.

9. FACTS: None of the Blackfoot tribes is a Salishan Indian tribe. Salishan Indians came from the northern Pacific Coast. All Salishan Indians live each of the Continental Divide.

   CONCLUSION: No Blackfoot tribes live east of the Continental Divide.
   A. The facts prove the conclusion.
   B. The facts disprove the conclusion.
   C. The facts neither prove nor disprove the conclusion.

9.____

Questions 10-17.

DIRECTIONS: Questions 10 through 17 are based on the following reading passage. It is not your knowledge of the particular topic that is being tested, but your ability to reason based on what you have read. The passage is likely to detail several proposed courses of action and factors affecting these proposals. The reading passage is followed by a conclusion or outcome based on the facts in the passage, or a description of a decision taken regarding the situation. The conclusion is followed by a number of statements that have a possible connection to the conclusion. For each statement, you are to determine whether:
   A. The statement proves the conclusion.
   B. The statement supports the conclusion but does not prove it.
   C. The statement disproves the conclusion.
   D. The statement weakens the conclusion but does not disprove it.
   E. The statement has no relevance to the conclusion.

Remember that the conclusion after the passage is to be accepted as the outcome of what actually happened, and that you are being asked to evaluate the impact each statement would have had on the conclusion.

PASSAGE:

On August 12, Beverly Willey reported that she was in the elevator late on the previous evening after leaving her office on the 16th floor of a large office building. In her report, she states that a man got on the elevator at the 11th floor, pulled her off the elevator, assaulted her, and stole her purse. Ms. Willey reported that she had seen the man in the elevators and hallways of the building before. She believes that the man works in the building. Her description of him is as follows: he is tall, unshaven, with wavy brown hair and a scar on his left cheek. He walks with a pronounced limp, often dragging his left foot behind his right.

CONCLUSION: After Beverly Willey makes her report, the police arrest a 43-year-old man, Barton Black, and charge him with her assault.

4 (#2)

10. Barton Black is a former Marine who served in Vietnam, where he sustained shrapnel wounds to the left side of his face and suffered nerve damage in his left leg.
    A. The statement proves the conclusion.
    B. The statement supports the conclusion but does not prove it.
    C. The statement disproves the conclusion.
    D. The statement weakens the conclusion but does not disprove it.
    E. The statement has no relevance to the conclusion.

10._____

11. When they arrived at his residence to question him, detectives were greeted at the door by Barton Black, who was tall and clean-shaven.
    A. The statement proves the conclusion.
    B. The statement supports the conclusion but does not prove it.
    C. The statement disproves the conclusion.
    D. The statement weakens the conclusion but does not disprove it.
    E. The statement has no relevance to the conclusion.

11._____

12. Barton Black was booked into the county jail several days after Beverly Willey's assault.
    A. The statement proves the conclusion.
    B. The statement supports the conclusion but does not prove it.
    C. The statement disproves the conclusion.
    D. The statement weakens the conclusion but does not disprove it.
    E. The statement has no relevance to the conclusion.

12._____

13. Upon further investigation, detectives discover that Beverly Willey does not work at the office building.
    A. The statement proves the conclusion.
    B. The statement supports the conclusion but does not prove it.
    C. The statement disproves the conclusion.
    D. The statement weakens the conclusion but does not disprove it.
    E. The statement has no relevance to the conclusion.

13._____

14. Upon further investigation, detectives discover that Barton Black does not work at the office building.
    A. The statement proves the conclusion.
    B. The statement supports the conclusion but does not prove it.
    C. The statement disproves the conclusion.
    D. The statement weakens the conclusion but does not disprove it.
    E. The statement has no relevance to the conclusion.

14._____

15. In the spring of the following year, Barton Black is convicted of assaulting Beverly Willey on August 11.
    A. The statement proves the conclusion.
    B. The statement supports the conclusion but does not prove it.
    C. The statement disproves the conclusion.
    D. The statement weakens the conclusion but does not disprove it.
    E. The statement has no relevance to the conclusion.

15._____

16. During their investigation of the assault, detectives determine that Beverly Willey 16._____
was assaulted on the 12th floor of the office building.
   A. The statement proves the conclusion.
   B. The statement supports the conclusion but does not prove it.
   C. The statement disproves the conclusion.
   D. The statement weakens the conclusion but does not disprove it.
   E. The statement has no relevance to the conclusion.

17. The day after Beverly Willey's assault, Barton Black fled the area and was never 17._____
seen again.
   A. The statement proves the conclusion.
   B. The statement supports the conclusion but does not prove it.
   C. The statement disproves the conclusion.
   D. The statement weakens the conclusion but does not disprove it.
   E. The statement has no relevance to the conclusion.

Questions 18-25.

DIRECTIONS: Questions 18 through 25 each provide four factual statements and a conclusion based on these statements. After reading the entire question, you will decide whether:
   A. The conclusion is proved by statements I-IV;
   B. The conclusion is disproved by statements I-IV.
   C. The facts are not sufficient to prove or disprove the conclusion.

18. FACTUAL STATEMENTS: 18._____
   I. Among five spice jars on the shelf, the sage is to the right of the parsley.
   II. The pepper is to the left of the basil.
   III. The nutmeg is between the sage and the pepper.
   IV. The pepper is the second spice from the left.

   CONCLUSION: The safe is the farthest to the right.
   A. The conclusion is proved by statements I-IV;
   B. The conclusion is disproved by statements I-IV.
   C. The facts are not sufficient to prove or disprove the conclusion.

19. FACTUAL STATEMENTS: 19._____
   I. Gear X rotates in a clockwise direction if Switch C is in the OFF position.
   II. Gear X will rotate in a counter-clockwise direction is Switch C is ON.
   III. If Gear X is rotating in a clockwise direction, then Gear Y will not be rotating at all.
   IV. Switch C is ON.

   CONCLUSION: Gear X is rotating in a counter-clockwise direction.
   A. The conclusion is proved by statements I-IV;
   B. The conclusion is disproved by statements I-IV.
   C. The facts are not sufficient to prove or disprove the conclusion.

20. FACTUAL STATEMENTS:
    I. Lane will leave for the Toronto meeting today only if Terence, Rourke, and Jackson all file their marketing reports by the end of the work day.
    II. Rourke will file her report on time only if Ganz submits last quarter's data.
    III. If Terence attends the security meeting, he will attend it with Jackson, and they will not file their marketing reports by the end of the work day.

    CONCLUSION: Lane will leave for the Toronto meeting today.
    A. The conclusion is proved by statements I-IV;
    B. The conclusion is disproved by statements I-IV.
    C. The facts are not sufficient to prove or disprove the conclusion.

20.____

21. FACTUAL STATEMENTS:
    I. Bob is in second place in the Boston Marathon.
    II. Gregory is winning the Boston Marathon.
    III. There are four miles to go in the race, and Bob is gaining on Gregory at the rate of 100 yards every minute.
    IV. There are 1760 yards in a mile and Gregory's usual pace during the Boston Marathon is one mile every six minutes.

    CONCLUSION: Bob wins the Boston Marathon.
    A. The conclusion is proved by statements I-IV;
    B. The conclusion is disproved by statements I-IV.
    C. The facts are not sufficient to prove or disprove the conclusion.

21.____

22. FACTUAL STATEMENTS:
    I. Four brothers are named Earl, John, Gary, and Pete.
    II. Earl and Pete are unmarried.
    III. John is shorter than the youngest of the four.
    IV. The oldest brother is married, and is also the tallest.

    CONCLUSION: Gary is the oldest brother.
    A. The conclusion is proved by statements I-IV;
    B. The conclusion is disproved by statements I-IV.
    C. The facts are not sufficient to prove or disprove the conclusion.

22.____

23. FACTUAL STATEMENTS:
    I. Brigade X is ten miles from the demilitarized zone.
    II. If General Woundwort gives the order, Brigade X will advance to the demilitarized zone, but not quickly enough to reach the zone before the conflict begins.
    III. Brigade Y, five miles behind Brigade X, will not advance unless General Woundwort gives the order.
    IV. Brigade Y advances.

23.____

7 (#2)

CONCLUSION: Brigade X reaches the demilitarized zone before the conflict begins.
  A. The conclusion is proved by statements I-IV;
  B. The conclusion is disproved by statements I-IV.
  C. The facts are not sufficient to prove or disprove the conclusion.

24. FACTUAL STATEMENTS: 24.____
  I. Jerry has decided to take a cab from Fullerton to Elverton.
  II. Chubby Cab charges $5 plus $3 a mile.
  III. Orange Cab charges $7.50 but gives free mileage for the first 5 miles.
  IV. After the first 5 miles, Orange Cab charges $2.50 a mile.

  CONCLUSION: Orange Cab is the cheaper fare from Fullerton to Elverton.
  A. The conclusion is proved by statements I-IV;
  B. The conclusion is disproved by statements I-IV.
  C. The facts are not sufficient to prove or disprove the conclusion.

25. FACTUAL STATEMENTS: 25.____
  I. Dan is never in class when his friend Lucy is absent.
  II. Lucy is never absent unless her mother is sick.
  III. If Lucy is in class, Sergio is in class also.
  IV. Sergio is never in class when Dalton is absent.

  CONCLUSION: If Lucy is absent, Dalton may be in class.
  A. The conclusion is proved by statements I-IV;
  B. The conclusion is disproved by statements I-IV.
  C. The facts are not sufficient to prove or disprove the conclusion.

KEY (CORRECT ANSWERS)

1.	C	11.	E
2.	B	12.	B
3.	B	13.	D
4.	C	14.	E
5.	A	15.	A
6.	A	16.	E
7.	B	17.	C
8.	C	18.	B
9.	C	19.	A
10.	B	20.	C

21.	C
22.	A
23.	B
24.	A
25.	B

SOLUTIONS TO PROBLEMS

1. **CORRECT ANSWER: C**
   Statement 1 only tells us that some employees who work in the Testing Department are statisticians. This means that we need to allow the possibility that at least one person in this department is not a statistician. Thus, if a person works in the Testing Department, we cannot conclude whether or not this individual is a statistician.

2. **CORRECT ANSWER: B**
   If Hank had six coins, then the total of Gail's collection and Lawrence's collection would be four. Thus, if Gail gave all her coins to Lawrence, Lawrence would only have four coins. Thus, it would be impossible for Lawrence to have more coins than Hank.

3. **CORRECT ANSWER: B**
   Statement 1 tells us that nobody loves everybody. If everybody loved Janet, then Statement 3 would imply that Ken loves everybody. This would contradict statement 1. The conclusion is disproved.

4. **CORRECT ANSWER: C**
   Although most of the Torres family lives in East Los Angeles, we can assume that some members of this family do not live in East Los Angeles. Thus, we cannot prove or disprove that Joe, who is a member of the Torres family, lives in East Los Angeles.

5. **CORRECT ANSWER: A**
   Since Dr. Johnson is on the 4th floor, either (a) Dr. Kane is on the 5th floor and Dr. Conlon is on the 3rd floor, or (b) Dr. Kane is on the 3rd floor and Dr. Conlon is on the 5th floor. If option (b) were correct, then since Dr. Assad would be on the 1st floor, it would be impossible for Dr. Steen's office to be between Dr. Conlon and Dr. Assad's office. Therefore, Dr. Kane's office must be on the 5th floor. The order of the doctors' offices, from 5th floor down to the 1st floor is: Dr. Kane, Dr. Johnson, Dr. Conlon, Dr. Steen, Dr. Assad.

6. **CORRECT ANSWER: A**
   Ray does not satisfy the requirement of holding his breath for two minutes under water, since he can only hold is breath for one minute in that setting. But if he tunnels through a snowbank with just a T-shirt and shorts, he will satisfy the eligibility requirement. Note that the eligibility requirement contains the key word "or." So only one of the two clauses separated by "or" need to be fulfilled.

7. **CORRECT ANSWER: B**
   Statement 2 says that four sharps is equivalent to one tinplot. This means that a tinplot is worth more than a sharp. The conclusion is disproved. We note that the order of these items, from most valuable to least valuable are: tinplot, sharp, mark, plunk.

8. **CORRECT ANSWER: C**
   We can only conclude that gibbons and lemurs are fed lettuce and bananas. We can neither prove nor disprove that these animals are types of monkeys.

9. CORRECT ANSWER: C
We know that all Salishan Indians live east of the Continental Divide. But some non-members of this tribe of Indians may also live east of the Continental Divide. Since none of the members of the Blackfoot tribe belong to the Salishan Indian tribe, we cannot draw any conclusion about the location of the Blackfoot tribe with respect to the Continental Divide.

18. CORRECT ANSWER: B
Since the pepper is second from the left and the nutmeg is between the sage and the pepper, the positions 2, 3, and 4 (from the left) are pepper, nutmeg, sage. By statement II, the basil must be in position 5, which implies that the parsley is in position 1. Therefore, the basil, not the sage, is farthest to the right. The conclusion disproved.

19. CORRECT ANSWER: A
Statement II assures us that if switch C is ON, then Gear X is rotating in a counterclockwise direction. The conclusion is proved.

20. CORRECT ANSWER: C
Based on Statement IV, followed by Statement II, we conclude that Ganz and Rourke will file their reports on time. Statement III reveals that if Terence and Jackson attend the security meeting, they will fail to file their reports on time. We have no further information if Terence and Jackson attended the security meeting, so we are not able to either confirm or deny that their reports were filed on time. This implies that we cannot know for certain that Lane will leave for his meeting in Toronto.

21. CORRECT ANSWER: C
Although Bob is in second place behind Gregory, we cannot deduce how far behind Gregory he is running. At Gregory's current pace, he will cover four miles in 24 minutes. If Bob were only 100 yards behind Gregory, he would catch up to Gregory in one minute. But if Bob were very far behind Gregory, for example 5 miles, this is the equivalent of $(5)(1760) = 8800$ yards. Then Bob would need $8800/100 = 88$ minutes to catch up to Gregory. Thus, the given facts are not sufficient to draw a conclusion.

22. CORRECT ANSWER: A
Statement II tells us that neither Earl nor Pete could be the oldest; also, either John or Gary is married. Statement IV reveals that the oldest brother is both married and the tallest. By Statement III, John cannot be the tallest. Since John is not the tallest, he is not the oldest. Thus, the oldest brother must be Gary. The conclusion is proved.

23. CORRECT ANSWER: B
By Statements III and IV, General Woundwort must have given the order to advance. Statement II then tells us that Brigade X will advance to the demilitarized zone, but not soon enough before the conflict begins. Thus, the conclusion is disproved.

11 (#2)

24. CORRECT ANSWER: A
If the distance is 5 miles or less, then the cost for the Orange Cab is only $7.50, whereas the cost for the Chubby Cab is $5 + 3x, where x represents the number of miles traveled. For 1 to 5 miles, the cost of the Chubby Cab is between $8 and $20. This means that for a distance of 5 miles, the Orange Cab costs $7.50, whereas the Chubby Cab costs $20. After 5 miles, the cost per mile of the Chubby Cab exceeds the cost per mile of the Orange Cab. Thus, regardless of the actual distance between Fullerton and Elverton, the cost for the Orange Cab will be cheaper than that of the Chubby Cab.

25. CORRECT ANSWER: B
It looks like "Dalton" should be replaced by "Dan" in the conclusion. Then by statement I, if Lucy is absent, Dan is never in class. Thus, the conclusion is disproved.

LOGICAL REASONING
EVALUATING CONCLUSIONS IN LIGHT OF KNOWN FACTS
EXAMINATION SECTION
TEST 1

COMMENTARY

This section is designed to provide practice questions in evaluating conclusions when you are given specific data to work with.

We suggest you do the questions three at a time, consulting the answer key and then the solution section for any questions you may have missed. It's a good idea to try the questions again a week before the exam.

In the validity of conclusion type of question, you are first given a reading passage which describes a particular situation. The passage may be on any topic, as it is not your knowledge of the topic that is being tested, but your reasoning abilities. The passage is likely to detail several proposed courses of action and factors affecting these proposals. The reading passage is followed by a conclusion based on the facts in the passage, or a description of a decision taken regarding the situation. The conclusion is followed by a number of statements which have a possible connection to the conclusion. For each statement, you are to determine whether:

- A. The statement proves the conclusion.
- B. The statement supports the conclusion but does not prove it.
- C. The statement disproves the conclusion.
- D. The statement weakens the conclusion but does not disprove it.
- E. The statement has no relevance to the conclusion.

Remember that the conclusion after the passage is to be accepted as the outcome of what actually happened, and that you are being asked to evaluate the impact each statement would have had on the conclusion.

Questions 1-8.

DIRECTIONS: Questions 1 through 8 are based on the following paragraph.

In May of 2018, Mr. Bryan inherited a clothing store on Main Street in a small New England town. The store has specialized in selling quality men's and women's clothing since 1920. Business has been stable throughout the years, neither increasing nor decreasing. He has an opportunity to buy two adjacent stores which would enable him to add a wider range and style of clothing. In order to do this, he would have to borrow a substantial amount of money. He also risks losing the goodwill of his present clientele.

CONCLUSION: On November 7, 2018, Mr. Bryan tells the owner of the two adjacent stores that he has decided not to purchase them. He feels that it would be best to simply maintain his present marketing position, as there would not be enough new business to support an expansion.

A. The statement proves the conclusion.
B. The statement supports the conclusion but does not prove it.
C. The statement disproves the conclusion.
D. The statement weakens the conclusion.
E. The statement is irrelevant to the conclusion.

1. A large new branch of the county's community college holds its first classes in September. 1.____

2. The town's largest factory shuts down with no indication that it will reopen. 2.____

3. The United States Census showed that the number of children per household dropped from 2.4 to 2.1 since the last census. 3.____

4. Mr. Bryan's brother tells him of a new clothing boutique specializing in casual women's clothing which is opening soon. 4.____

5. Mr. Bryan's sister buys her baby several items for Christmas at Mr. Bryan's store. 5.____

6. Mrs. McIntyre, the President of the Town Council, brings Mr. Bryan a home-baked pumpkin pie in honor of his store's 100th anniversary. They discuss the changes that have taken place in the town, and she comments on how his store has maintained the same look and feel over the years. 6.____

7. In October, Mr. Bryan's aunt lends him $50,000. 7.____

8. The Town Council has just announced that the town is eligible for funding from a federal project designed to encourage the location of new businesses in the central districts of cities and towns. 8.____

Questions 9-18.

DIRECTIONS: Questions 9 through 18 are based on the following paragraph.

A proposal was put before the legislative body of a country to require air bags in all automobiles manufactured for domestic use in that country after 2019. The air bag, made of nylon or plastic, is designed to inflate automatically within a car at the impact of a collision, thus protecting front-seat occupants from being thrown forward. There has been much support of the measure from consumer groups, the insurance industry, key legislators, and the general public. The country's automobile manufacturers, who contend the new crash equipment would add up to $1,000 to car prices and provide no more protection than existing seat belts, are against the proposed legislation

CONCLUSION: On April 21, 2014, the legislation requiring air bags in all automobiles manufactured for domestic use in that country after 2019.

A. The statement proves the conclusion.
B. The statement supports the conclusion but does not prove it.
C. The statement disproves the conclusion.
D. The statement weakens the conclusion.
E. The statement is irrelevant to the conclusion.

9. A study has shown that 59% of car occupants do not use seat belts. 9.____

10. The country's Department of Transportation has estimated that the crash protection equipment would save up to 5,900 lives each year. 10.____

11. On April 27, 2013, Augusta Raneoni was named head of an advisory committee to gather and analyze data on the costs, benefits, and feasibility of the proposed legislation on air bags in automobiles. 11.____

12. Consumer groups and the insurance industry accuse the legislature of rejecting passage of the regulation for political reasons. 12.____

13. A study by the Committee on Imports and Exports projected that the sales of imported cars would rise dramatically in 2019 because imported cars do not have to include air bags, and can be sold more cheaply. 13.____

14. Research has shown that air bags, if produced on a large scale, would cost about $200 apiece, and would provide more reliable protection than any other type of seat belt. 14.____

15. Auto sales in 2011 increased 3% over the previous year. 15.____

16. A Department of Transportation report in July of 2020 credits a drop in automobile deaths of 4,100 to the use of air bags. 16.____

17. In June of 2014, the lobbyist of the largest insurance company receives a bonus for her work on the passage of the air bag legislation. 17.____

18. In 2020, the stock in crash protection equipment has risen three-fold over the previous year. 18.____

Questions 19-25.

DIRECTIONS: Questions 19 through 25 are based on the following paragraph.

On a national television talk show, Joan Rivera, a famous comedienne, has recently insulted the physical appearances of a famous actress and the dead wife of an ex-President. There has been a flurry of controversy over her comments, and much discussion of the incident has appeared in the press. Most of the comments have been negative. It appears that this tie she might have gone too far. There have been cancellations of two of her five scheduled performances in the two weeks since the show was televised, and Joan's been receiving a lot of negative mail. Because of the controversy, she has an interview with a national news magazine at the end of the week, and her press agent is strongly urging her to apologize publicly. She feels strongly that her comments were no worse than any other she has ever made, and that the whole incident will *blow over* soon. She respects her press agent's judgment, however, as his assessment of public sentiment tends to be very accurate.

CONCLUSION: Joan does not apologize publicly, and during the interview she challenges the actress to a weight-losing contest. For every pound the actress loses, Joan says she will donate $1 to the Cellulite Prevention League.

A. The statement proves the conclusion.
   B. The statement supports the conclusion but does not prove it.
   C. The statement disproves the conclusion.
   D. The statement weakens the conclusion.
   E. The statement is irrelevant to the conclusion.

19. Joan's mother, who she is very fond of, is very upset with Joan's comments.   19.____

20. Six months after the interview, Joan's income has doubled.   20.____

21. Joan's agent is pleased with the way Joan handles the interview.   21.____

22. Joan's sister has been appointed Treasurer of the Cellulite Prevention League In her report, she states that Joan's $12 contribution is the only amount that has been donated to the League in its first six months.   22.____

23. The magazine receives many letters commending Joan for the courage it took for her to apologize publicly in the interview.   23.____

24. Immediately after the interview appears, another one of Joan's performances is cancelled.   24.____

25. Due to a printers' strike, the article was not published until the following week.   25.____

Questions 26-30.

DIRECTIONS: Questions 25 through 30 are based on the following paragraph.

     The law-making body of Country X must decide what to do about the issue of recording television shows for home use. There is currently no law against recording shows directly from the TV as long as the DVDs are not used for commercial purposes. The increasing popularity of pay TV and satellite systems, combined with the increasing number of homes that own recording equipment, has caused a great deal of concern in some segments of the entertainment industry. Companies that own the rights to films, popular television shows, and sporting events feel that their copyright privileges are being violated, and they are seeking compensation or the banning of TV recording. Legislation has been introduced to make it illegal to record television programs for home use. Separate proposed legislation is also pending that would continue to allow recording of TV shows for home use, but would place a tax of 10% on each DVD that is purchased for home use. The income from that tax would then be proportionately distributed as royalties to those owning the rights to programs being aired. A weighted point system coupled with the averaging of several national viewing rating systems would be used to determine the royalties. There is a great deal of lobbying being done for both bills, as the manufacturers of DVDs and recording equipment are against the passage of the bills.

CONCLUSION: The legislature of Country X rejects both bills by a wide margin.

A. The statement proves the conclusion.
   B. The statement supports the conclusion but does not prove it.
   C. The statement disproves the conclusion.
   D. The statement weakens the conclusion.
   E. The statement is irrelevant to the conclusion.

26. Country X's Department of Taxation hires 500 new employees to handle the increased paperwork created by the new tax on DVDs. 26._____

27. A study conducted by the country's most prestigious accounting firm shows that the cost of implementing the proposed new DVD tax would be greater than the income expected from it. 27._____

28. It is estimated that 80% of all those working in the entertainment industry, excluding performers, own DVD recorders. 28._____

29. The head of Country X's law enforcement agency states that legislation banning the home recording of TV shows would be unenforceable. 29._____

30. Financial experts predict that unless a tax is placed on DVDs, several large companies in the entertainment industry will have to file for bankruptcy. 30._____

Questions 31-38.

DIRECTIONS: Questions 31 through 38 are variations on the type of question you just had. It is important that you read the question very carefully to determine exactly what is required.

31. In this question, select the choice that is MOST relevant to the conclusion. 31._____
    I. The Buffalo Bills football team is in second place in its division.
    II. The New England Patriots are in first place in the same division.
    III. There are two games left to play in the season, and the Bills will not play the Patriots again.
    IV. The New England Patriots won ten games and lost four games, and the Buffalo Bills have won eight games and lost six games.
    CONCLUSION: The Buffalo Bills win their division.
      A. The conclusion is proved by sentences I-IV.
      B. The conclusion is disproved by sentences I-IV.
      C. The facts are not sufficient to prove or disprove the conclusion.

32. In this question, select the choice that is MOST relevant to the conclusion.
    I. On the planet of Zeinon there are only two different eye colors and only two different hair colors.
    II. Half of those beings with purple hair have golden eyes.
    III. There are more inhabitants with purple hair than there are inhabitants with silver hair.
    IV. One-third of those with silver hair have green eyes.
    CONCLUSION: There are more golden-eyed beings on Zeinon than green-eyed ones.
    A. The conclusion is proved by sentences I-IV.
    B. The conclusion is disproved by sentences I-IV.
    C. The facts are not sufficient to prove or disprove the conclusion.

33. In this question, select the choice that is MOST relevant to the conclusion.
    John and Kevin are leaving Amaranth to go to school in Bethany. They've decided to rent a small truck to move their possessions. Joe's Truck Rental charges $100 plus 30¢ a mile. National Movers charges $50 more but gives free mileage for the first 100 miles. After the first 100 miles, they charge 25¢ a mile.
    CONCLUSION: John and Kevin rent their truck from National Movers because it is cheaper.
    A. The conclusion is proved by the facts in the above paragraph.
    B. The conclusion is disproved by the facts in the above paragraph.
    C. The facts are not sufficient to prove or disprove the conclusion.

34. For this question, select the choice that supports the information given in the passage.
    Municipalities in Country X are divided into villages, towns, and cities. A village has a population of 5,000 or less. The population of a town ranges from 5,001 to 15,000. In order to be incorporated as a city, the municipality must have a population over 15,000. If, after a village becomes a town, or a town becomes a city, the population drops below the minimum required (for example, the population of a city goes below 15,000), and stays below the minimum for more than ten years, it loses its current status, and drops to the next category. As soon as a municipality rises in population to the next category (village to town, for example), however, it is immediately reclassified to the next category.
    In the 2000 census, Plainfield had a population of 12,000. Between 2000 and 2010, Plainfield grew 10%, and between 2010 and 2020 Plainfield grew another 20%. The population of Springdale doubled from 2000 to 2010, and increased 25% from 2010 to 2020. The city of Smallville's population, 20,283, has not changed significantly in recent years. Granton had a population of 25,000 people in 1990, and has decreased 25% in each ten year period since then. Ellenville had a population of 4,283 in 1990, and grew 5% in each ten year period since 1990.

In 2020,
- A. Plainfield, Smallville, and Granton are cities.
- B. Smallville is a city, Granton is a town, and Ellenville is a village.
- C. Springdale, Granton, and Ellenville are towns.
- D. Plainfield and Smallville are cities, and Ellenville is a town.

35. For this question, select the choice that is MOST relevant to the conclusion.

    A study was done for a major food-distributing firm to determine if there is any difference in the kind of caffeine containing products used by people of different ages. A sample of one thousand people between the ages of twenty and fifty were drawn from selected areas in the country. They were divided equally into three groups.

    Those individuals who were 20-29 were designated Group A, those 30-39 were Group B, and those 40-50 were placed in Group C.

    It was found that on the average, Group A drank 1.8 cups of coffee, Group B 3.1, and Group C 2.5 cups of coffee daily. Group A drank 2.1 cups of tea, Group B drank 1.2, and Group C drank 2.6 cups of tea daily. Group A drank 3 1.8 ounces glasses of cola, Group B drank 1.9, and Group C drank 1.5 glasses of cola daily.

    CONCLUSION: According to the study, the average person in the 20-29 age group drinks less tea daily than the average person in the 40-50 age group, but drinks more coffee daily than the average person in the 30-39 age group drinks cola.
    - A. The conclusion is proved by the facts in the above paragraph.
    - B. The conclusion is disproved by the facts in the above paragraph.
    - C. The facts are not sufficient to prove or disprove the conclusion.

36. For this question, select the choice that is MOST relevant to the conclusion
    I. Mary is taller than Jane but shorter than Dale.
    II. Fred is taller than Mary but shorter than Steven.
    III. Dale is shorter than Steven but taller than Elizabeth.
    IV. Elizabeth is taller than Mary but not as tall as Fred.
    CONCLUSION: Dale is taller than Fred.
    - A. The conclusion is proved by sentences I-IV.
    - B. The conclusion is disproved by sentences I-IV.
    - C. The facts are not sufficient to prove or disprove the conclusion.

37. For this question, select the choice that is MOST relevant to the conclusion.
    I. Main Street is between Spring Street and Glenn Blvd.
    II. Hawley Avenue is one block south of Spring Street and three blocks north of Main Street.
    III. Glenn Street is five blocks south of Elm and four blocks south of Main.
    IV. All the streets mentioned are parallel to one another.
    CONCLUSION: Elm Street is between Hawley Avenue and Glenn Blvd.
    - A. The conclusion is proved by the facts in sentences I-IV.
    - B. The conclusion is disproved by the facts in sentences I-IV.
    - C. The facts are not sufficient to prove or disprove the conclusion.

38. For this question, select the choice that is MOST relevant to the conclusion.
    I. Train A leaves the town of Hampshire every day at 5:50 A.M. and arrives in New London at 6:42 A.M.
    II. Train A leaves New London at 7:00 A.M. and arrives in Kellogsville at 8:42 A.M.
    III. Train B leaves Kellogsville at 8:00 A.M. and arrives in Hampshire at 10:45 A.M.
    IV. Due to the need for repairs, there is just one railroad track between New London and Hampshire.
    CONCLUSION: It is impossible for Train A and Train B to follow these schedules without colliding.
    A. The conclusion is proved by the facts in sentences I-IV.
    B. The conclusion is disproved by the facts in sentences I-IV.
    C. The facts are not sufficient to prove or disprove the conclusion.

38.____

KEY (CORRECT ANSWERS)

1.	D	11.	C	21.	D	31.	C
2.	B	12.	C	22.	A	32.	A
3.	E	13.	D	23.	C	33.	C
4.	B	14.	B	24.	B	34.	B
5.	C	15.	E	25.	E	35.	B
6.	A	16.	B	26.	C	36.	C
7.	D	17.	A	27.	B	37.	A
8.	B	18.	B	28.	E	38.	B
9.	B	19.	D	29.	B		
10.	B	20.	E	30.	D		

SOLUTIONS TO QUESTIONS

1. The answer is D. This statement weakens the conclusion, but does not disprove it. If a new branch of the community college opened in September, it could possibly bring in new business for Mr. Bryant. Since it states in the conclusion that Mr. Bryant felt there would not be enough new business to support the additional stores, this would tend to disprove the conclusion. Choice C would not be correct because it's possible that he felt that the students would not have enough additional money to support his new venture, or would not be interested in his clothing styles. It's also possible that the majority of the students already live in the area, so that they wouldn't really be a new customer population. This type of question is tricky, and can initially be very confusing, so don't feel badly if you missed it. Most people need to practice with a few of these types of questions before they feel comfortable recognizing exactly what they're being asked to do.

2. The answer is B. It supports the conclusion because the closing of the factory would probably take money and customers out of the town, causing Mr. Bryant to lose some of his present business. It doesn't prove the conclusion, however, because we don't know how large the factory was. It's possible that only a small percentage of the population was employed there, or that they found other jobs.

3. The answer is E. The fact that the number of children per household dropped slightly nationwide in the decade is irrelevant. Statistics showing a drop nationwide doesn't mean that there was a drop in the number of children per household in Mr. Bryant's hometown. This is a tricky question, as choice B, supporting the conclusion but not proving it, may seem reasonable. If the number of children per household declined nationwide, then it may not seem unreasonable to feel that this would support Mr. Bryant's decision not to expand his business. However, we're preparing you for promotional exams, not "real life." One of the difficult things about taking exams is that sometimes you're forced to make a choice between two statements that both seem like they could be the possible answer. What you need to do in that case is choose the best choice. Becoming annoyed or frustrated with the question won't really help much. If there's a review of the exam, you can certainly appeal the question. There have been many cases where, after an appeal, two possible choices have been allowed as correct answers. We've included this question, however, to help you see what to do should you get a question like this. It's most important not to get rattled, and to select the BEST choice. In this case, the connection between the statistical information and Mr. Bryant's decision is pretty remote. If the question had said that the number of children in Mr. Bryant's <u>town</u> had decreased, then choice B would have been a more reasonable choice. It could also help in this situation to visualize the situation. Picture Mr. Bryant in his armchair reading that, nationwide, the average number of children per household has declined slightly. How likely would this be to influence his decision, especially since he sells men's and women's clothing? It would take a while for this decline in population to show up, and we're not even sure if it applies to Mr. Bryant's hometown. Don't feel badly if you missed this; it was tricky. The more of these you do, the more comfortable you'll feel.

4. The answer is B. If a new clothing boutique specializing in casual women's clothing were to open soon, this would lend support to Mr. Bryant's decision not to expand, but would not prove that he had actually made the decision to expand. A new women's clothing boutique would most likely be in competition with his existing business, thus making any possible expansion a riskier venture. We can't be sure from this, however, that he didn't go ahead and expand his business despite the increased competition. Choice A, proves the conclusion, would only be the answer if we could be absolutely sure from the statement that Mr. Bryant had actually not expanded his business.

5. The answer is C. This statement disproves the conclusion. In order for his sister to buy several items for her baby at Mr. Bryant's store, he would have to have changed his business to include children's clothing.

6. The answer is A. It definitely proves the conclusion. The passage states that Mr. Bryan's store had been in business since 1920. A pie baked in honor of his store's 100th anniversary would have to be presented sometime in 2020. The conclusion states that he made his decision not to expand on November 7, 2018. If, more than a year later Mrs. MacIntyre comments that his store has maintained the same look and feel over the years, it could not have been expanded, or otherwise significantly changed.

7. The answer is D. If Mr. Bryant's aunt lent him $50,000 in October, this would tend to weaken the conclusion, which took place in November. Because it was stated that Mr. Bryant would need to borrow money in order to expand his business, it would be logical to assume that if he borrowed money he had decided to expand his business, weakening the conclusion. The reason C, disproves the conclusion, is not the correct answer is because we can't be sure Mr. Bryant didn't borrow the money for another reason.

8. The answer is B. If Mr. Bryant's town is eligible for federal funds to encourage the location of new businesses in the central district, this would tend to support his decision not to expand his business. Funds to encourage new business would increase the likelihood of there being additional competition for Mr. Bryant's store to contend with. Since we can't say for sure that there would be direct competition from a new business, however, choice A would be incorrect. Note that this is also a tricky question. You might have thought that the new funds weakened the conclusion because it would mean that Mr. Bryant could easily get the money he needed. Mr. Bryant is expanding his present business, not creating a new business. Therefore, he is not eligible for the funding.

9. The answer is B. This is a very tricky question. It's stated that 59% of car occupants don't use seat belts. The legislature is considering the use of air bags because of safety issues. The advantage of air bags over seat belts is that they inflate upon impact, and don't require car occupants to do anything with them ahead of time. Since the population has strongly resisted using seat belts, the air bags could become even more important in saving lives. Since saving lives is the purpose of the proposed legislation, the information that a small percentage of people use seat belts could be helpful to the passage of the legislation. We can't be sure that this is reason enough for the legislature to vote for the legislation, however, so choice A in incorrect.

10. The answer is B, as the information that 5,900 lives could be saved would tend to support the conclusion. Saving that many lives through the use of air bags could be a very persuasive reason to vote for the legislation. Since we don't know for sure that it's enough of a compelling reason for the legislature to vote for the legislation, however, choice A could not be the answer.

11. The answer is C, disproves the conclusion. If the legislation had been passed as stated in the conclusion, there would be no reason to appoint someone head of an advisory committee six days later to analyze the "feasibility of the proposed legislation." The key word here is "proposed." If it has been proposed, it means it hasn't been passed. This contradicts the conclusion and, therefore, disproves it.

12. The answer is C, disproves the conclusion. If the legislation had passed, there would be no reason for supporters of the legislation to accuse the legislature of rejecting the legislation for political reasons. This question may have seemed so obvious that you might have thought there was a trick to it. Exams usually have a few obvious questions, which will trip you up if you begin reading too much into them.

13. The answer is D, as this would tend to disprove the conclusion. A projected dramatic rise in imported cars could be very harmful to the country's economy and could be a very good reason for some legislators to vote against the proposed legislation. It would be assuming too much to choose C, however, because we don't know if they actually did vote against it.

14. The answer is B. This information would tend to support the passage of the legislation. The estimate of the cost of the air bags is $800 less than the cost estimated by opponents, and it's stated that the protection would be more reliable than any other type of seat belt. Both of these would be good arguments in favor of passing the legislation. Since we don't know for sure, however, how persuasive they actually were, choice A would not be the correct choice.

15. The answer is E, as this is irrelevant information. It really doesn't matter whether auto sales in 2001 have increased slightly over the previous year. If the air bag legislation were to go into effect in 2004, that might make the information somehow more relevant. But the air bag legislation would not take effect until 2009, so the information is irrelevant, since it tells us nothing about the state of the auto industry then.

16. The answer is B, supports the conclusion. This is a tricky question. While at first it might seem to prove the conclusion, we can't be sure that the air bag legislation is responsible for the drop in automobile deaths. It's possible air bags came into popular use without the legislation, or with different legislation. There's no way we can be sure that it was the proposed legislation mandating the use of air bags that was responsible.

17. The answer is A. If, in June of 2009, the lobbyist received a bonus "for her work on the air bag legislation," we can be sure that the legislation passed. This proves the conclusion.

18. The answer is B. This is another tricky question. A three-fold stock increase would strongly suggest that the legislation had been passed, but it's possible that factors other than the air bag legislation caused the increase. Note that the stock is in "crash protection

equipment." Nowhere in the statement does it say air bags. Seat belts, motorcycle helmets, and collapsible bumpers are all crash protection equipment and could have contributed to the increase. This is just another reminder to read carefully because the questions are often designed to mislead you.

19. The answer is D. This would tend to weaken the conclusion because Joan is very fond of her mother and she would not want to upset her unnecessarily. It does not prove it, however, because if Joan strongly feels she is right, she probably wouldn't let her mother's opinion sway her. Choice E would also not be correct, because we cannot assume that Joan's mother's opinion is of so little importance to her as to be considered irrelevant.

20. The answer is E. The statement is irrelevant. We are told that Joan's income has doubled but we are not old why. The phrase "six months after the interview" can be misleading in that it leads us to assume that the increase and the interview are related. Her income could have doubled because she regained her popularity but it could also have come from stocks or some other business venture. Because we are not given any reason for her income doubling, it would be impossible to say whether or not this statement proves or disproves the conclusion. Choice E is the best choice of the five possible choices. One of the problems with promotional exams is that sometimes you need to select a choice you're not crazy about. In this case, "not having enough information to made a determination" would be the best choice. However, that's not an option, so you're forced to work with what you've got. On these exams it's sometimes like voting for President; you have to pick the "lesser of the two evils" or the least awful choice. In this case, the information is more irrelevant to the conclusion than it is anything else.

21. The answer is D, weakens the conclusion. We've been told that Joan's agent feels that she should apologize. If he is pleased with her interview, then it would tend to weaken the conclusion but not disprove it. We can't be sure that he hasn't had a change of heart, or that there weren't other parts of the interview he liked so much that they outweighed her unwillingness to apologize.

22. The answer is A. The conclusion states that Joan will donate $1 to the Cellulite Prevention League for every pound the actress loses. Joan's sister's financial report on the League's activities directly supports and proves the conclusion.

23. The answer is C, disproves the conclusion. If the magazine receives many letters commending Joan for her courage in apologizing, this directly contradicts the conclusion, which states that Joan didn't apologize.

24. The answer is B. It was stated in the passage that two of Joan's performances were cancelled after the controversy first occurred. The cancellation of another performance immediately after her interview was published would tend to support the conclusion that she refused to apologize. Because we can't be sure, however, that her performance wasn't cancelled for another reason, choice A would be incorrect.

25. The answer is E, as this information is irrelevant. Postponing the article an extra week does not affect Joan's decision or the public's reaction to it.

13 (#1)

26. The answer is C. If 500 new employees are hired to handle the "increased paperwork created by the new tax on DVDs," this would directly contradict the conclusion, which states that the legislature defeated both bills. (They should all be this easy.)

27. The answer is B. The results of the study would support the conclusion. If implementing the legislation was going to be so costly, it is likely that the legislature would vote against it. Choice A is not the answer, however, because we can't be sure that the legislature didn't pass it anyway.

28. The answer is E. It's irrelevant to the conclusion that 80% of all those working in the entertainment industry own DVD recorders. Sometimes if you're not sure about these, it can help a lot to try and visualize the situation. Why would someone voting on this legislation care about this fact? It doesn't seem to be the kind of information that would make any difference or impact upon the conclusion.

29. The answer is B. The head of the law enforcement agency's statement that the legislation would be unenforceable would support the conclusion. It's possible that many legislators would question why they should bother to pass legislation that would be impossible to enforce. Choice A would be incorrect, however, because we can't be sure that the legislation wasn't passed in spite of his statement.

30. The answer is D. This would tend to weaken the conclusion because the prospect of several large companies going bankrupt would seem to be a good argument in favor of the legislation. The possible loss of jobs and businesses would be a good reason for some people to vote for the legislation. We can't be sure, however, that this would be a competing enough reason to ensure passage of the legislation so choice C is incorrect.

This concludes our section on the "Validity of Conclusion" type of questions. We hope these weren't too horrible for you. It's important to keep in mind <u>exactly</u> what you've been given and <u>exactly</u> what they want you to do with it. It's also necessary to remember that you may have to choose between two possible answers. In that case, you must choose the one that seems the best. Sometimes you may think there is no good answer. You will probably be right, but you can't let that upset you. Just choose the one you dislike the least.

We want to repeat that it is unlikely that this exact format will appear on the exam. The skills required to answer these questions, however, are the same as those you'll need for the exam so we suggest that you review this section before taking the actual exam.

31. The answer is C. This next set of questions requires you to "switch gears" slightly, and get used to different formats. In this type of question, you have to decide whether the conclusion is proved by the facts give, disproved by the facts given, or neither because note enough information has been provided. Fortunately, unlike the previous questions, you don't have to decide whether particular facts support or don't support the conclusion. This type of question is more straight forward, but the reasoning behind it is the same. We are told that the Bills have won two games less than the Patriots, and that the Patriots are in first place and the Bills are in second place. We are also told that there are two games left to play, and that they won't play each other again. The conclusion states that the Bills won the division. Is there anything in the four statements that would prove this? We have

no idea what the outcome of the last two games of the season was. The Bills and Patriots could have ended up tied at the end of the season, or the Bills could have lost both or one of their last games while the Patriots did the same. There might even be another team tied for first or second place with the Bills or Patriots. Since we don't know for sure, Choice A is incorrect. Choice B is trickier. It might seem at first glance that the best the Bills could do would be to tie the Patriots if the Patriots lost their last two games and the Bills won their last two games. But it would be too much to assume that there is no procedure for a tiebreaker that wouldn't give the Bills the division championship. Since we don't know what the rules are in the event of a tie (for example, what if a tie was decided on the results of what happened when the two teams had played each other, or on the best record in the division, or on most points scored?), we can't say for sure that it would be impossible for the Bills to win their division. For this reason, choice C is the answer, as we don't have enough information to prove or disprove the conclusion. This question looked more difficult than it actually was. It's important to disregard any factors outside of the actual question, and to focus only on what you've been given. In this case, as on all of these types of questions, what you know or don't know about a subject is actually irrelevant. It's best to concentrate only on the actual facts given.

32. The answer is A. The conclusion is proved by the facts given.

    In this type of problem, it is usually best to pull as many facts as possible from the sentences and then put them into a simpler form. The phrasing and the order of exam questions are designed to be confusing so you need to restate things as clearly as possible by eliminating the extras.

    Sentence I tells us that there are only two possible colors for eyes and two for hair. Looking at the other sentences we learn that eyes are either green or gold and that hair is either silver or purple. If half the beings with purple hair have golden eyes, then the other half must have green eyes since it is the only other eye color. Likewise, if one-third of those with silver hair have green eyes, the other two-thirds must have golden eyes.

    This information makes it clear that there are more golden-eyed beings on Zeinon than green-eyed ones. It doesn't matter that we don't know exactly how many are actually living on the planet. The number of those with gold eyes (1/2 plus 2/3) will always be greater than the number of those with green eyes (1/2 plus 1/3), no matter what the actual figures might be. Sentence III is totally irrelevant because even if there were more silver-haired inhabitants it would not affect the conclusion.

33. The answer is C. The conclusion is neither proved nor disproved by the facts because we don't know how many miles Bethany is from Amoranth.

    With this type of question, if you're not sure how to approach it, you can always substitute in a range of "real numbers" to see what the result would be. If they were 200 miles apart, Joe's Truck Rental would be cheaper because they would charge a total of $160 while National Movers would charge $175.

    Joe's - $100 plus .30 x 200 (or $60) = $160
    National - $150 plus .25 x 100 (or $25) = $175

    If the towns were 600 miles apart, however, National Movers would be cheaper. The cost of renting from National would be $275 compared to the $280 charged by Joe's Trucking.

    Joe's - $100 plus .30 x 600 (or $180) = $280
    National - $150 plus .25 x 500 (or $125) = $275

15 (#1)

34. The answer is B. We've varied the format once more, but the reasoning is similar. This is a tedious question that is more like a math question, but we wanted to give you some practice with this type, just in case. You won't be able to do this question if you've forgotten how to do percents. Many exams require this knowledge, so if you feel you need a review we suggest you read Booklets 1, 2 or 3 in this series.

   The only way to attack this problem is to go through each choice until you find the one that is correct. Choice A states that Plainfield, Smallville, and Granton are cities. Let's begin with Plainfield. The passage states that in 1990 Plainfield had a population of 12,000, and that it grew 10% between 1990 and 2000, and another 20% between 2000 and 2010. Ten percent of 12,000 is 1200 (12,000 x .10 = 1200). Therefore, the population grew from 12,000 in 1990 to 12,000 + 1200 between 1990 and 2000. At the time of the 2000 Census, Plainfield's population was 13,200. It then grew another 20% between 2000 and 2010, so, 13,200 x .20 = 2640. 13,200 plus the additional increase of 2640 would make the population of Plainfield 15,840. This would qualify it as a city, since its population is over 15,000. Since a change upward in the population of a municipality is re-classified immediately, Plainfield would have become a city right away. So far, statement A is true. The passage states that Smallville's population has not changed significantly in the last twenty years. Since Smallville's population was 20,283, Smallville would still be a city. Granton had a population of 25,000 (what a coincidence that so any of these places have such nice, even numbers) in 1980. The population has decreased 25% in each ten year period since that time. So from 1980 to 1990, the population decreased 25%. 25,000 x .25 = 6,250. 25,000 minus 6,250 = 18,750. So the population of Granton in 1990 would have been 18,750. (Or, you could have saved a step and multiplied 25,000 by .75 to get 18,750.) The population from 1990 to 2000 decreased an additional 25%. So: 18,750 x .25 = 4,687.50. 18,750 minus 4,687.50 = 14,062.50. Or: 18,750 x .75 = 14,062.50. (Don't let the fact that a half of a person is involved confuse you; these are exam questions, not real life.) From 2000 to 2010 the population decreased an additional 25%. This would mean that Granton's population was below 15,000 for more than ten years, so it's status as a city would have changed to that of a town, which would make choice A incorrect.

   Choice B states that Smallville is a city and Granton is a town, which we know to be true from the information above. Choice B is correct so far. We next need to determine if Ellenville is a village. Ellenville had a population of 4,283 in 1980, and increased 5% in each ten year period since 1980. 4,283 x .05 = 214.15. 4,283 plus 214.15 = 4,497.15, so Ellenville's population from 1980 to 1990 increased to 4,497.15. (Or: 4,283 x 1.05 – 4,497.15.) From 1990 to 2000 Ellenville's population increased another 5%: 4,497.15 x .05 = 224.86. 4,497.15 plus 224.86 = 4,772.01 (or: 4,497.15 x 1.05 = 4,722.01.) From 2000 to 2010, Ellenville's population increased another 5%: 4,722.01 x .05 = 236.10. 4,722.01 plus 236.10 = 4,958.11. (Or: 4,722.01 x 1.05 = 4,958.11.).
   Ellenville's population is still under 5,000 in 2010, so it would continue to be classified as a village. Since all three statements in choice B are true, choice B must be the answer. However, we'll go through the other choices. Choice C states that Springdale is a town. The passage tells us that the population of Springdale doubled from 1990 to 2000, and increased 25% from 2000 to 2010. It doesn't give us any actual population figures, however, so it's impossible to know what the population of Springdale is, making choice C incorrect. Choice C also states that Granton is a town, which is true, and that Ellenville is

a town, which is false (from choice B we know it's a village). Choice D states that Plainfield and Smallville are cities, which is information we already know is true, and that Ellenville is a town. Since Ellenville is a village, choice D is also incorrect.

This was a lot of work for just one question and we doubt you'll get one like this on this section of the exam, but we included it just in case. On an exam, you can always put a check mark next to a question like this and come back to it later, if you feel you're pressed for time and cold spend your time more productively on other, less time-consuming problems.

35. The answer is B. This question requires very careful reading. It's best to break the conclusion down into smaller parts in order to solve the problem. The first half of the conclusion states that the average person in the 20-29 age group (Group A) drinks less tea daily than the average person in the 40-50 age group (Group C). The average person in Group A drinks 2.1 cups of tea daily, while the average person in Group C drinks 2.6 cups of tea daily. Since 2.1 is less than 2.6, the conclusion is correct so far. The second half of the conclusion states that the average person in Group A drinks more coffee daily than the average person in the 30-39 age group (Group B) drinks cola. The average person in Group A drinks 1.8 cups of coffee daily, while the average person in Group B drinks 1.9 glasses of cola. This disproves the conclusion, which states that the average person in Group A drinks more coffee daily than the average person in Group B drinks cola.

36. The answer is C. The easiest way to approach a problem that deals with the relationship between a number of different people or things is to set up a diagram. This type of problem is usually too confusing to do in your head. For this particular problem, the "diagram" could be a line, one end of which would be labeled tall and the other end labeled short. Then, taking one sentence at a time, place the people on the line to see where they fall in relation to one another.

The diagram of the first sentence would look like this:

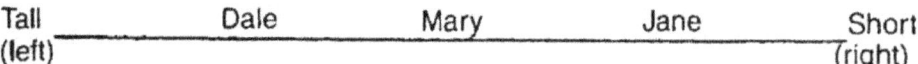

Mary is taller than Jane but shorter than Dale, so she would fall somewhere between the two of them. We have placed tall on the left and labeled it left just to make the explanation easier. You could just as easily have reversed the position.

The second sentence places Fred somewhere to the left of Mary because he is taller than she is. Steven would be to the left of Fred for the same reason. At this point we don't know whether Steven and Fred are taller or shorter than Dale. The new diagram would look like this:

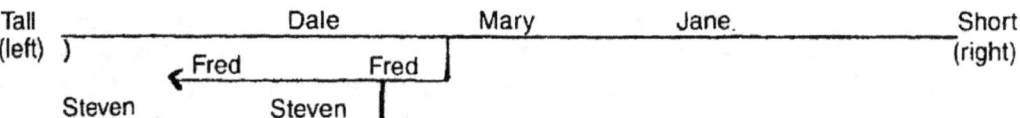

The third sentence introduces Elizabeth, presenting a new problem. Elizabeth can be anywhere to the right of Dale. Don't make the mistake of assuming she falls between Dale and Mary. At this point we don't know where she fits in relation to Mary, Jane, or even Fred.

We do get information about Steven, however. He is taller than Dale so he would be to the left of Dale. Since he is also taller than Fred (see sentence II), we know that Steven is the tallest person thus far. The diagram would now look like this:

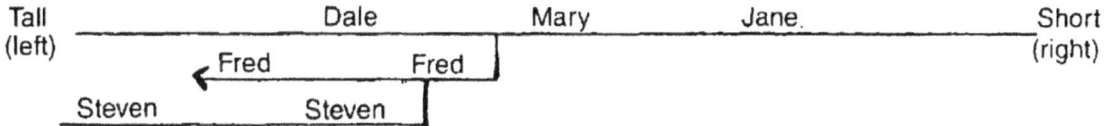

Fred's height is somewhere between Steven and Mary, Elizabeth's anywhere between Dale and the end of the line.

The fourth sentence tells us where Elizabeth stands, in relation to Fred and the others in the problem. The fact that she is taller than Mary means she is also taller than Jane. The final diagram would look like this:

Tall   Steven   Dale   Elizabeth   Mary   Jane   Short
(left) _____ (right)
                    Fred

We still don't know whether Dale or Fred is taller, however. Therefore, the conclusion that Dale is taller than Fred can't be proved. It also can't be disproved because we don't know for sure that he isn't. The answer has to be choice C, as the conclusion can't be proved or disproved.

37. The answer is A. This is another problem that is easiest for most people if they make a diagram. Sentence I states that Main Street is between Spring Street and Glenn Blvd. At this point we don't know if they are next to each other or if they are separated by a number of streets. Therefore, you should leave space between streets as you plot your first diagram.

The order of the streets could go either:

        Spring St.   or   Glenn Blvd.
        Main St.   Main St.
        Glenn Blvd.   Spring St.

Sentence II states that Hawley Street is one block south of Spring Street and 3 blocks north of Main Street. Because most people think in terms of north as above and south as below and because it was stated that Hawley is one block south of Spring Street and three blocks north of Main Street, the next diagram could look like this:

Spring
Hawley
———
———
Main
Glenn

The third sentence states that Glenn Street is five blocks south of Elm and four blocks south of Main. It could look like this:

Spring
Hawley

———
Elm
Main

———
———

Glenn

The conclusion states that Elm Street is between Hawley Avenue and Glenn Blvd. From the above diagram, we can see that this is the case.

38. The answer is B. For most people, the best way to do this problem is to draw a diagram, plotting the course of both trains. Sentence I states that Train A leaves Hampshire at 5:50 A.M. and reaches New London at 6:42. Your first diagram might look like this:

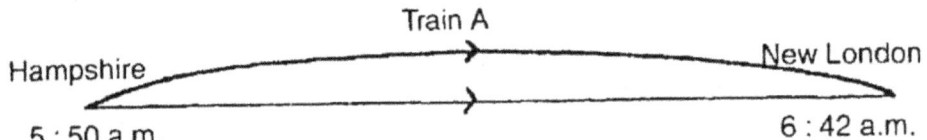

Sentence II states that the train leaves New London at 7:00 a.m. and arrives in Kellogsville at 8:42 a.m. The diagram might now look like this:

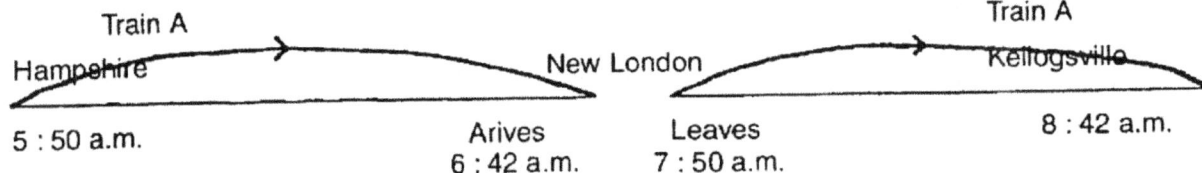

Sentence III gives us the rest of the information that must be included in the diagram. It introduces Train B, which moves in the opposite direction, leaving Kellogsville at 8:00 a.m. and arriving at Hampshire at 10:42 a.m. The final diagram might look like this:

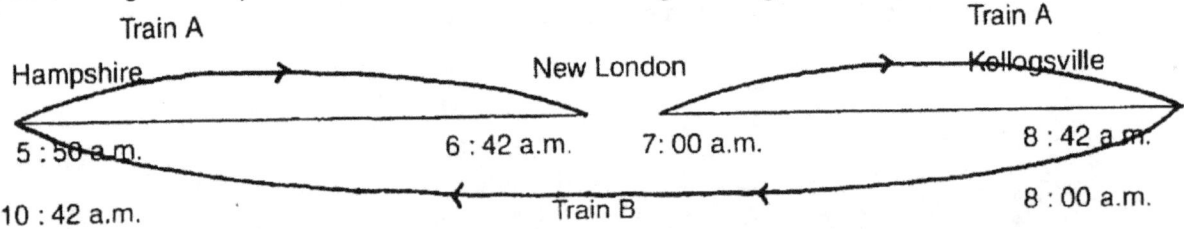

19 (#1)

As you can see from the diagram, the routes of the two trains will overlap somewhere between Kellogsville and New London. If you read sentence IV quickly and assumed that that was the section with only one track, you probably would have assumed that there would have had to be a collision. Sentence IV states, however, that there is only one railroad track between New London and Hampshire. That is the only section, then, where the two trains could collide. By the time Train B gets to that section, however, Train A will have passed it. The two trains will pass each other somewhere between New London and Kellogsville, not New London and Hampshire.

———

EVALUATING INFORMATION AND EVIDENCE
EXAMINATION SECTION
TEST 1

DIRECTIONS: Each question or incomplete statement is followed by several suggested answers or completions. Select the one that BEST answers the question or completes the statement. *PRINT THE LETTER OF THE CORRECT ANSWER IN THE SPACE AT THE RIGHT.*

Questions 1-9.

DIRECTIONS: Questions 1 through 9 measure your ability to (1) determine whether statements from witnesses say essentially the same thing and (2) determine the evidence needed to make it reasonably certain that a particular conclusion is true.

1. Which of the following pairs of statements say essentially the same thing in two different ways?
   I. If you get your feet wet, you will catch a cold.
      If you catch a cold, you must have gotten your feet wet.
   II. If I am nominated, I will run for office.
      I will run for office only if I am nominated.
   The CORRECT answer is:
   A. I only   B. I and II   C. II only   D. Neither I nor II

1._____

2. Which of the following pairs of statements say essentially the same thing in two different ways?
   I. The enzyme Rhopsin cannot be present if the bacterium Trilox is absent.
      Rhopsin and Trilox always appear together.
   II. A member of PENSA has an IQ of at least 175.
      A person with an IQ of less than 175 is not a member of PENSA
   The CORRECT answer is;
   A. I only   B. I and II   C. II only   D. Neither I nor II

2._____

3. Which of the following pairs of statements say essentially the same thing in two different ways?
   I. None of Finer High School's sophomores will be going to the prom.
      No student at Finer High School who is going to the prom is a sophomore.
   II. If you have 20/20 vision, you may carry a firearm.
      You may not carry a firearm unless you have 20/20 vision.
   The CORRECT answer is:
   A. I only   B. I and II   C. II only   D. Neither I nor II

3._____

4. Which of the following pairs of statements say essentially the same thing in two different ways?
   I. If the family doesn't pay the ransom, they will never see their son again.
      It is necessary for the family to pay the ransom in order for them to see their son again.
   II. If it is raining, I am carrying an umbrella.
       If I am carrying an umbrella, it is raining.
   The CORRECT answer is:
   A. I only   B. I and II   C. II only   D. Neither I nor II

4._____

5. Summary of Evidence Collected to Date:
   In the county's maternity wards, over the past year, only one baby was born who did not share a birthday with any other baby.
   Prematurely Drawn Conclusion: At least one baby was born on the same day as another baby in the county's maternity wards.
   Which of the following pieces of evidence, if any, would make it reasonably certain that the conclusion drawn is true?
   A. More than 365 babies were born in the county's maternity wards over the past year.
   B. No pairs of twins were born over the past year in the county's maternity wards.
   C. More than one baby was born in the county's maternity wards over the past year.
   D. None of the above

5._____

6. Summary of Evidence Collected to Date:
   Every claims adjustor for MetroLife drives only a Ford sedan when on the job.
   Prematurely Drawn Conclusion: A person who works for MetroLife and drives a Ford sedan is a claims adjustor.
   Which of the following pieces of evidence, if any, would make it reasonably certain that the conclusion drawn is true?
   A. Most people who work for MetroLife are claims adjustors.
   B. Some people who work for MetroLife are not claims adjustors.
   C. Most people who work for MetroLife drive Ford sedans
   D. None of the above

6._____

7. Summary of Evidence Collected to Date:
   Mason will speak to Zisk if Zisk will speak to Ronaldson.
   Prematurely Drawn Conclusion: Jones will not speak to Zisk if Zisk will speak to Ronaldson.
   Which of the following pieces of evidence, if any, would make it reasonably certain that the conclusion drawn is true?
   A. If Zisk will speak to Mason, then Ronaldson will not speak to Jones.
   B. If Mason will speak to Zisk, then Jones will not speak to Zisk.
   C. If Ronaldson will speak to Jones, then Jones will speak to Ronaldson.
   D. None of the above

7._____

8. Summary of Evidence Collected to Date:
No blue lights on the machine are indicators for the belt drive status.
Prematurely Drawn Conclusion: Some of the lights on the lower panel are not indicators for the belt drive status.
Which of the following pieces of evidence, if any, would make it reasonably certain that the conclusion drawn is true?
   A. No lights on the machine's lower panel are blue.
   B. An indicator light for the machine's belt drive status is either green or red.
   C. Some lights on the machine's lower panel are blue.
   D. None of the above

8._____

9. Summary of Evidence Collected to Date:
Of the four Sweeney sisters, two are married, three have brown eyes, and three are doctors.
Prematurely Drawn Conclusion: Two of the Sweeney sisters are brown-eyed, married doctors.
Which of the following pieces of evidence, if any, would make it reasonably certain that the conclusion is true?
   A. The sister who does not have brown eyes is married.
   B. The sister who does not have brown eyes is not a doctor, and one who is not married is not a doctor.
   C. Every Sweeney sister with brown eyes is a doctor.
   D. None of the above

9._____

Questions 10-14.

DIRECTIONS: Questions 10 through 14 refer to Map #5 and measure your ability to orient yourself within a given section of town, neighborhood or particular area. Each of the questions describes a starting point and a destination. Assume that you are driving a car in the area shown on the map accompanying the questions. Use the map as a basis for the shortest way to get from one point to another without breaking the law.

On the map, a street marked by arrows, or by arrows and the words "One Way," indicates one-way travel and should be assumed to be one-way for the entire length, even when there are breaks or jogs in the street. EXCEPTION: A street that does not have the same name over the full length.

4 (#1)

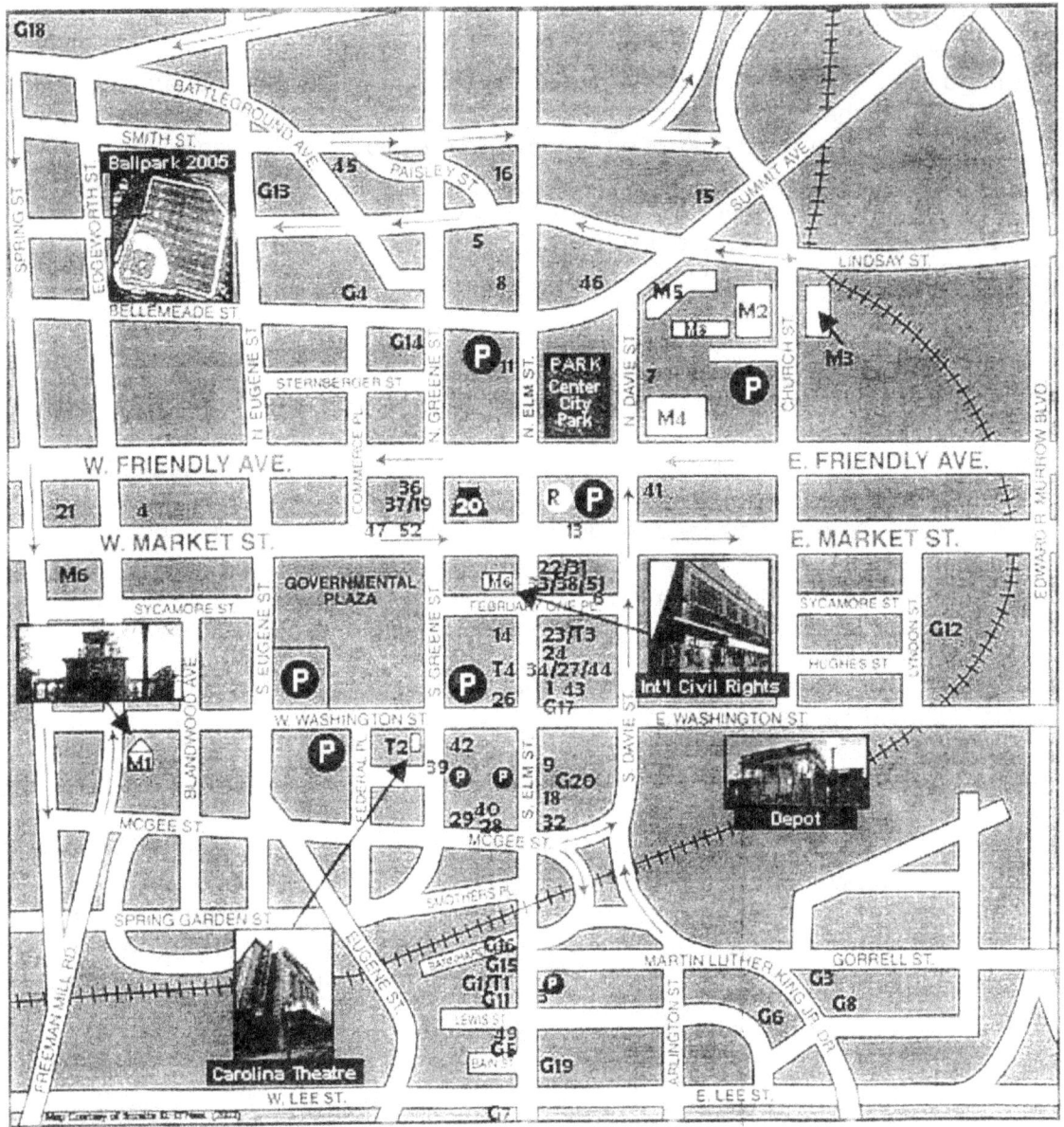

Map #5

10. The SHORTEST legal way from the depot to Center City Park is
    A. north on Church, west on Market, north on Elm
    B. east on Washington, north on Edward R. Murrow Blvd., west on Friendly Ave.
    C. west on Washington, north on Greene, east on Market, north on Davie
    D. north on Church, west on Friendly Ave.

10._____

11. The SHORTEST legal way from the Governmental Plaza to the Ballpark is   11.____
    A. west on Market, north on Edgeworth
    B. west on Market, north on Eugene
    C. north on Greene, west on Lindsay
    D. north on Commerce Place, west on Bellemeade

12. The SHORTEST legal way from the International Civil Rights Building to the   12.____
    building marked "M3" on the map is
    A. east on February One Place, north on Davie, east on Friendly Ave., north on Church
    B. south on Elm, west on Washington, north on Greene, east on Market, north on Church
    C. north on Elm, east on Market, north on Church
    D. north on Elm, east on Lindsay, south on Church

13. The SHORTEST legal way from the Ballpark to the Carolina Theatre is   13.____
    A. east on Lindsay, south on Greene
    B. south on Edgeworth, east on Friendly Ave., south on Greene
    C. east on Bellemeade, south on Elm, west on Washington

14. A car traveling north or south on Church Street may NOT go   14.____
    A. west onto Friendly Ave.   B. west onto Lindsay
    C. east onto Market   D. west onto Smith

Questions 15-19.

DIRECTIONS: Questions 15 through 19 refer to Figure #3, on the following page, and measure your ability to understand written descriptions of events. Each question presents a description of an accident or event and asks you which of the following five drawings in Figure #3 BEST represents it.
In the drawings, the following symbols are used:
Moving vehicle ⌂   Non-moving vehicle ♦
Pedestrian or bicyclist •
The path and direction of travel of a vehicle or pedestrian is indicated by a solid line.
The path and direction of travel of each vehicle or pedestrian directly involved in a collision from the point of impact is indicated by a dotted line.

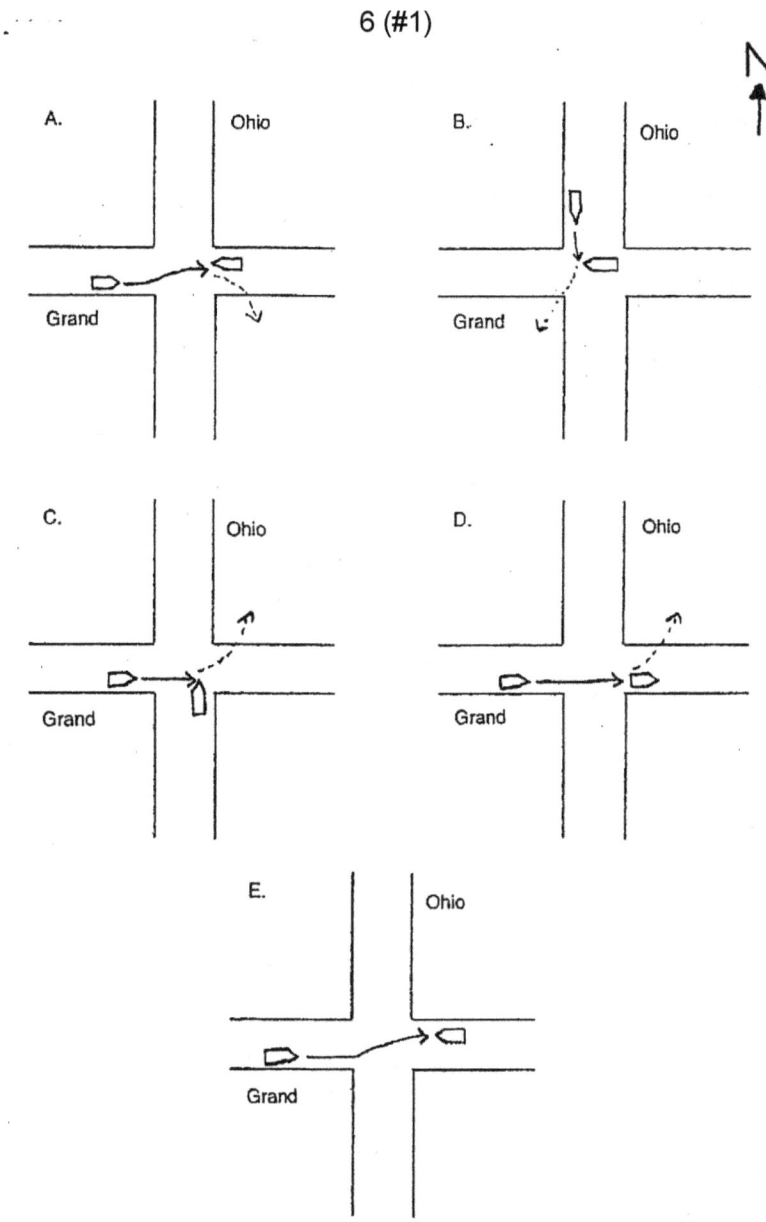

In the space at the right, print the letter of the drawing that BEST fit the descriptions written below.

15. A driver headed south on Ohio runs a red light and strikes the front of a car headed west on Grand. He glances off and leaves the roadway at the southwest corner of Grand and Ohio.

15.____

16. A driver heading east on Grand drifts into the oncoming lane as it travels through the intersection of Grand and Ohio, and strikes an oncoming car head-on

16.____

17. A driver heading east on Grand veers into the oncoming lane, sideswipes a westbound car and overcorrects as he swerves back into his lane. He leaves the roadway near the southeast corner of Grand and Ohio.

17.____

18. A driver heading east on Grand strikes the front of a car that is traveling north on Ohio and has run a red light. After striking the front of the northbound car, the driver veers left and leaves the roadway at the northeast corner of Grand and Ohio.

18.____

19. A driver heading east on Grand is traveling above the speed limit and clips the rear end of another eastbound car. The driver then veers to the left and leaves the roadway at the northeast corner of Grand and Ohio.

19.____

Questions 20-22.

DIRECTIONS: In Questions 20 through 22, choose the word or phrase CLOSEST in meaning to the word or phrase printed in capital letters.

20. PETITION
    A. appeal   B. law   C. oath   D. opposition

20.____

21. MALPRACTICE
    A. commission   B. mayhem   C. error   D. misconduct

21.____

22. EXONERATE
    A. incriminate   B. accuse   C. lengthen   D. acquit

22.____

Questions 23-25.

DIRECTIONS: Questions 23 through 25 measure your ability to do fieldwork-related arithmetic. Each question presents a separate arithmetic problem for you to solve.

23. Officers Lane and Bryant visited another city as part of an investigation. Because each is from a different precinct, they agree to split all expenses. With her credit card, Lane paid $70 for food and $150 for lodging. Bryant wrote checks for gas ($50) and entertainment ($40).
    How much does Bryant owe Lane?
    A. $65   B. $90   C. $155   D. $210

23.____

24. In a remote mountain pass, two search-and-rescue teams, one from Silverton and one from Durango, combine to look for a family that disappeared in a recent snowstorm. The combined team is composed of 20 members.
    Which of the following statements could NOT be true?
    A. The Durango team has a dozen members.
    B. The Silverton team has only one member.
    C. The Durango team has two more members than the Silverton team.
    D. The Silverton team has one more member than the Durango team.

24.____

25. Three people in the department share a vehicle for a period of one year. The average number of miles traveled per month by each person is 150.
How many miles will be added to the car's odometer at the end of the year?   25.____
   A. 1,800   B. 2,400   C. 3,600   D. 5,400

KEY (CORRECT ANSWERS)

1. D
2. C
3. A
4. A
5. A

6. A
7. B
8. C
9. B
10. D

11. D
12. C
13. D
14. D
15. B

16. E
17. A
18. C
19. D
20. A

21. D
22. D
23. A
24. D
25. D

SOLUTIONS TO QUESTIONS 1-9

P implies Q = original statement

Not Q implies not P = contrapositive of the original statement. A statement and its contrapositive are logically equivalent.

Q implies P = converse of the original statement

Not P implies not Q = inverse of the original statement. The converse and inverse of an original statement are logically equivalent.

P implies Q = Not P or Q.

1. The CORRECT answer is D.
   In items I and II, each statement is the converses of the other. A converse of a statement is not equivalent to its original statement.

2. The CORRECT answer is C.
   In item I, the first statement is equivalent to "If Trilox is absent, then Rhopsin is also absent." But this does NOT imply that if Trilox is present, so too must Rhopsin be present. In item II, each statement is the contrapositive of the other. Thus, they are equivalent.

3. The CORRECT answer is A.
   In item I, the first sentence tells us that if a student is a sophomore, he/she will not go the prom. The second statement is equivalent to "If a student does attend the prom, he/she is not a sophomore." This is the contrapositive of the first statement, (so it is equivalent to it).

4. The CORRECT answer is A.
   In item I, the second statement can be written as "If the family sees their son again, then they must have paid the ransom." This is the contrapositive of the first statement. In item II, these statements are converses of each other; thus, they are not equivalent.

5. The CORRECT answer is A.
   If more than 365 babies were born in the county in one year, then at least two babies must share the same birthday.

6. The CORRECT answer is A.
   Given that most people who work for MetroLife are claims adjustors, plus the fact that all claims adjustors drive only a Ford sedan, it is a reasonable conclusion that any person who drives a Ford sedan and works for MetroLife is a claims adjustor.

7. The CORRECT answer is B.
   Jones will not speak to Zisk if Zisk will speak to Ronaldson, which will happen if Mason will speak to Zisk.

8. The CORRECT answer is C.
We are given that blue lights are never an indicator for the drive belt status. If some of the lights on the lower panel of the machine are blue, then it is reasonable to conclude that some of the lights on the lower panel are not indicators for the drive belt status.

9. The CORRECT answer is B.
There is only one sister that does not have brown eyes and only one sister that is not a doctor, and if the information in answer B is correct, then we learn that the same sister is a non-doctor without brown eyes. We also learn that this same non-doctor is not married. Since this all describes the same sister, we can conclude that two of the other sisters must be married doctors with brown eyes.

TEST 2

DIRECTIONS: Each question or incomplete statement is followed by several suggested answers or completions. Select the one that BEST answers the question or completes the statement. *PRINT THE LETTER OF THE CORRECT ANSWER IN THE SPACE AT THE RIGHT.*

Questions 1-9.

DIRECTIONS: Questions 1 through 9 measure your ability to (1) determine whether statements from witnesses say essentially the same thing and (2) determine the evidence needed to make it reasonably certain that a particular conclusion is true.
To do well on this part of the test, you do NOT have to have a working knowledge of police procedures and techniques. Nor do you have to have any more familiarity with criminals and criminal behavior than that acquired from reading newspapers, listening to radio or watching TV. To do well in this part, you must read and reason carefully.

1. Which of the following pairs of statements say essentially the same thing in two different ways?   1.____
   I. If there is life on Mars, we should fund NASA.
      Either there is life on Mars, or we should not fund NASA.
   II. All Eagle Scouts are teenage boys.
       All teenage boy are Eagle Scouts.
   The CORRECT answer is:
      A. I only   B. I and II   C. II only   D. Neither I nor II

2. Which of the following pairs of statements say essentially the same thing in two different ways?   2.____
   I. If that notebook is missing its front cover, it definitely belongs to Carter.
      Carter's notebook is the only one missing its front cover.
   II. If it's hot, the pool is open.
       The pool is open if it's hot.
   The CORRECT answer is:
      A. I only   B. I and II   C. II only   D. Neither I nor II

3. Which of the following pairs of statements say essentially the same thing in two different ways?   3.____
   I. Nobody who works at the mill is without benefits.
      Everyone who works at the mill has benefits.
   II. We will fund the program only if at least 100 people sign the petition.
       Either we will fund the program or at least 100 people will sign the petition.
   The CORRECT answer is:
      A. I only   B. I and II   C. II only   D. Neither I nor II

4. Which of the following pairs of statements say essentially the same thing in two different ways?
   I. If the new parts arrive, Mr. Luther's request has been answered.
   Mr. Luther requested new parts to arrive.
   II. The machine's test cycle will not run unless the operation cycle is not running.
   The machine's test cycle must be running in order for the operation cycle to run.
   The CORRECT answer is:
   A. I only   B. I and II   C. II only   D. Neither I nor II

5. Summary of Evidence Collected to Date:
   I. To become a member of the East Side Crips, a kid must be either "jumped in" or steal a squad car without getting caught.
   II. Sid, a kid on the East Side, was caught stealing a squad car.
   Prematurely Drawn Conclusion: Sid did not become a member of the East Side Crips.
   Which of the following pieces of evidence, if any, would make it reasonably certain that the conclusion drawn is true?
   A. "Jumping in" is not allowed in prison.
   B. Sid was not "jumped in."
   C. Sid's stealing the squad car had nothing to do with wanting to join the East Side Crips.
   D. None of the above

6. Summary of Evidence Collected to Date:
   I. Jones, a Precinct 8 officer, has more arrests than Smith.
   II. Smith and Watson have exactly the same number of arrests.
   Prematurely Drawn Conclusion: Watson is not a Precinct 8 officer.
   Which of the following pieces of evidence, if any, would make it reasonably certain that the conclusion drawn is true?
   A. All the officers in Precinct 8 have more arrests than Watson.
   B. All the officers in Precinct 8 have fewer arrests than Watson.
   C. Watson has fewer arrests than Jones.
   D. None of the above

7. Summary of Evidence Collected to Date:
   I. Twenty one-dollar bills are divided among Frances, Kerry, and Brian.
   II. If Kerry gives her dollar bills to Frances, then Frances will have more money than Brian.
   Prematurely Drawn Conclusion: Frances has twelve dollars.
   Which of the following pieces of evidence, if any, would make it reasonably certain that the conclusion drawn is true?
   A. If Brian gives his dollars to Kerry, then Kerry will have more money than Frances.
   B. Brian has two dollars.
   C. If Kerry gives her dollars to Brian, Brian will still have less money than Frances.
   D. None of the above

8. Summary of Evidence Collected to Date:
   I. The street sweepers will be here at noon today.
   II. Residents on the west side of the street should move their cars before noon.
   Prematurely Drawn Conclusion: Today is Wednesday.
   Which of the following pieces of evidence, if any, would make it reasonably certain that the conclusion drawn is true?
   A. The street sweepers never sweep the east side of the street on Wednesday.
   B. The street sweepers arrive at noon every other day.
   C. There is no parking allowed on the west side of the street on Wednesday.
   D. None of the above

8.____

9. Summary of Evidence Collected to Date:
   The only time the warning light comes on is when there is a power surge.
   Prematurely Drawn Conclusion: The warning light does not come on if the air conditioner is not running.
   Which of the following pieces of evidence, if any, would make it reasonably certain that the conclusion drawn is true?
   A. The air conditioner does not turn on if the warning light is on.
   B. Sometimes a power surge is caused by the dishwasher.
   C. There is only a power surge when the air conditioner turns on.
   D. None of the above

9.____

Questions 10-14.

DIRECTIONS: Questions 10 through 14 refer to Map #3 and measure your ability to orient yourself within a given section of town, neighborhood or particular area. Each of the questions describes a starting point and a destination. Assume that you are driving a car in the area shown on the map accompanying the questions. Use the map as a basis for the shortest way to get from one point to another without breaking the law.
On the map, a street marked by arrows, or by arrows and the words "One Way," indicates one-way travel and should be assumed to be one-way for the entire length, even when there are breaks or jogs in the street. EXCEPTION: A street that does not have the same name over the full length.

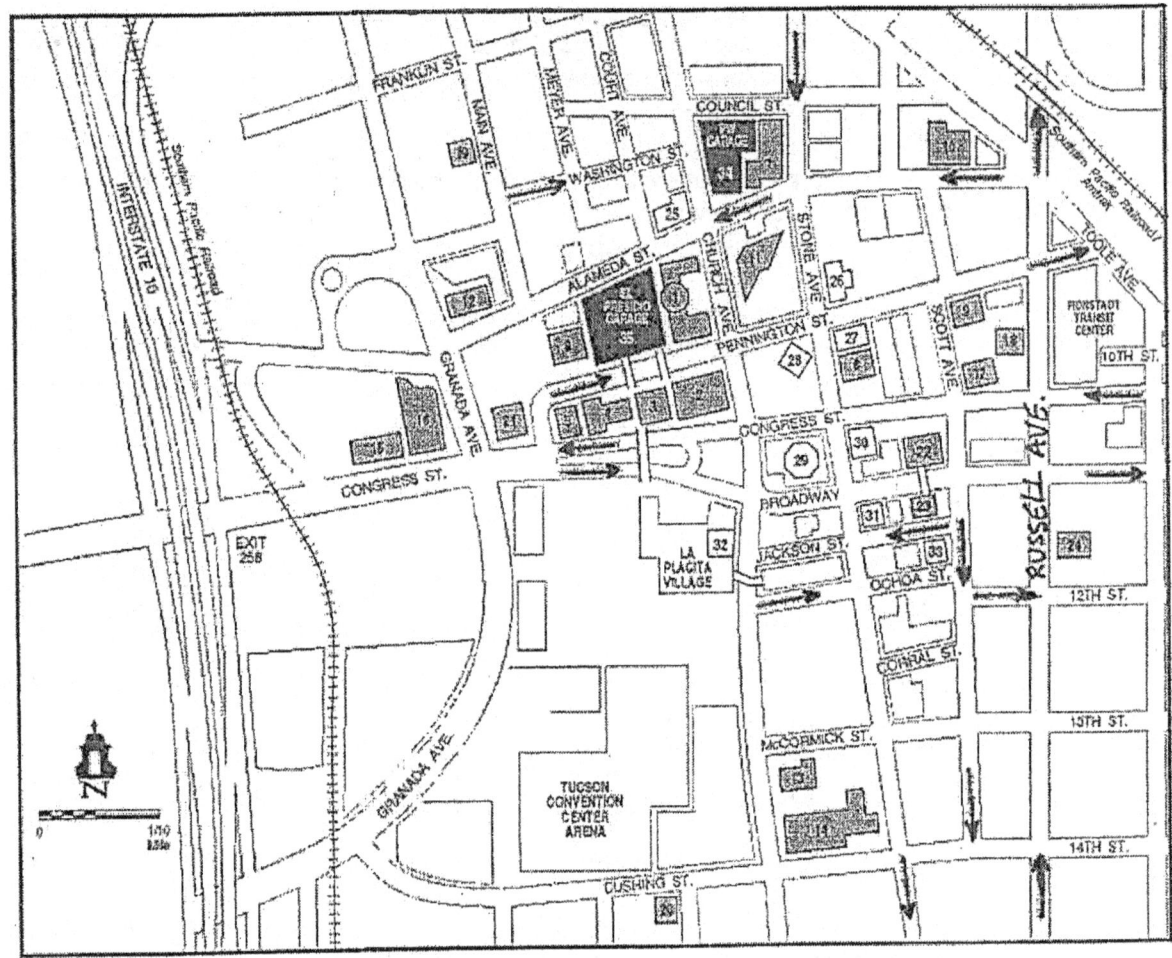

PIMA COUNTY
1. Old Courthouse
2. Superior Court Building
3. Administration Building
4. Health and Welfare Building
5. Mechanical Building
6. Legal Services Building
7. County/City Public Works Center

CITY OF TUCSON
8. City Hall
9. City Hall Annex
10. Alameda Plaza City Court Building
11. Public Library – Main Branch
12. Tucson Water Building
13. Fire Department Headquarters
14. Police Department Building

10. The SHORTEST legal way from the Public Library to the Alameda Plaza City Court Building is
   A. north on Stone Ave., east of Alameda
   B. south on Stone Ave., east on Congress, north on Russell Ave., west on Alameda
   C. south on Stone Ave., east on Pennington, north on Russell Ave., west on Alameda
   D. south on Church Ave., east on Pennington, north on Russell Ave., west on Alameda

10.____

5 (#2)

11. The SHORTEST legal way from City Hall to the Police Department is 11.____
    A. east on Congress, south on Scott Ave., west on 14th
    B. east on Pennington, south on Stone Ave.
    C. east on Congress, south on Stone Ave.
    D. east on Pennington, south on Church Ave.

12. The SHORTEST legal way from the Tucson Water Building to the Legal Service 12.____
    Building is
    A. south on Granada Ave., east on Congress, north to east on Pennington, south on Stone Ave.
    B. east on Alameda, south on Church Ave., east on Pennington, south on Stone Ave.
    C. north on Granada Ave., east on Washington, south on Church Ave., east on Pennington, south on Stone Ave.
    D. south on Granada Ave., east on Cushing, north on Stone Ave.

13. The SHORTEST legal way from the Tucson Convention Center Arena to the 13.____
    City Hall Annex is
    A. west on Cushing, north on Granada Ave., east on Congress east on Broadway
    B. east on Cushing, north on Church Ave., east on Pennington
    C. east on Cushing, north on Russel Ave., west on Pennington
    D. east on Cushing, north on Stone Ave., east on Pennington

14. The SHORTEST legal way from Ronstadt Transit Center to the Fire Department 14.____
    is
    A. west on Pennington, south on Stone Ave., west on McCormick
    B. west on Congress, south on Russell Ave., west on 13th
    C. west on Congress, south on Church Ave.
    D. west on Pennington, south on Church Ave.

Questions 15-19.

DIRECTIONS: Questions 15 through 19 refer to Figure #3, on the following page, and measure your ability to understand written descriptions of events. Each question presents a description of an accident or event and asks you which of the following five drawings in Figure #3 BEST represents it.
In the drawings, the following symbols are used:
Moving vehicle ⌂   Non-moving vehicle ▮
Pedestrian or bicyclist •
The path and direction of travel of a vehicle or pedestrian is indicated by a solid line.
The path and direction of travel of each vehicle or pedestrian directly involved in a collision from the point of impact is indicated by a dotted line.

In the space at the right, print the letter of the drawing that BEST fit the descriptions written below.

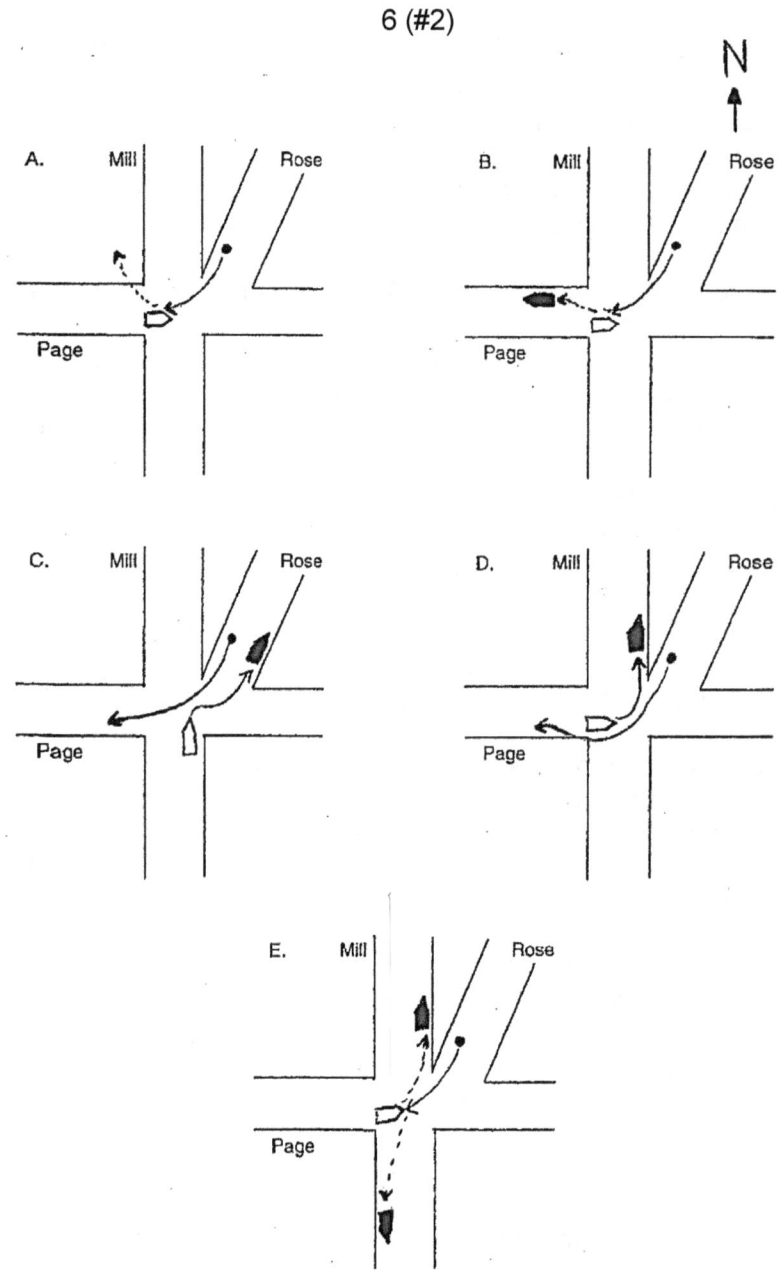

15. A bicyclist heading southwest on Rose travels into the intersection, sideswipes a car that is heading east on Page, and veers right, leaving the roadway at the northwest corner of Page and Mill.

    15.____

16. A driver traveling north on Mill swerves right to avoid a bicyclist that is traveling southwest on Rose. The driver strikes the rear end of a car parked on Rose. The bicyclist continues through the intersection and travels west on Page.

    16.____

17. A bicyclist heading southwest on Rose travels into the intersection, sideswipes a car that is heading east on Page, and veers right, striking the rear end of a car parked in the westbound lane on Page.

    17.____

18. A driver traveling east on Page swerves left to avoid a bicyclist that is traveling southwest on Rose. The driver strikes the rear end of a car parked on Mill. The bicyclist continues through the intersection and travels west on Page.

18.____

19. A bicyclist heading southwest on Rose enters the intersection and sideswipes a car that is swerving left to avoid her. The bicyclist veers left and collides with a car parked in the southbound lane on Mill. The driver of the car veers left and collides with a car parked in the northbound lane on Mill.

19.____

Questions 20-22.

DIRECTIONS: In Questions 20 through 22, choose the word or phrase CLOSEST in meaning to the word or phrase printed in capital letters.

20. WAIVE
    A. cease   B. surrender   C. prevent   D. die

20.____

21. DEPOSITION
    A. settlement   B. deterioration   C. testimony   D. character

21.____

22. IMMUNITY
    A. exposure   B. accusation   C. protection   D. exchange

22.____

Questions 23-25.

DIRECTIONS: Questions 23 through 25 measure your ability to do fieldwork-related arithmetic. Each question presents a separate arithmetic problem for you to solve.

23. Dean, a claims investigator, is reading a 445-page case record in his spare time at work. He has already read 157 pages.
    If Dean reads 24 pages a day, he should finish reading the rest of the record in ____ days.
    A. 7   B. 12   C. 19   D. 24

23.____

24. The Fire Department owns four cars. The Department of Sanitation owns twice as many cars as the Fire Department. The Department of Parks and Recreation owns one fewer car than the Department of Sanitation. The Department of Parks and Recreation is buying new tires for each of its cars. Each tire costs $100.
    How much is the Department of Parks and Recreation going to spend on tires?
    A. $400   B. $2,800   C. $3,200   D. $4,900

24.____

25. A dance hall is about 5,000 square feet. The local ordinance does not allow more than 50 people per every 100 square feet of commercial space.
    The maximum capacity of the hall is
    A. 500   B. 2,500   C. 5,000   D. 25,000

25.____

KEY (CORRECT ANSWERS)

1.	D	11.	D
2.	B	12.	A
3.	A	13.	B
4.	D	14.	C
5.	B	15.	A
6.	D	16.	C
7.	D	17.	B
8.	A	18.	D
9.	C	19.	E
10.	C	20.	B

21.	C
22.	C
23.	B
24.	B
25.	B

SOLUTIONS TO QUESTIONS 1-9

P implies Q = original statement

Not Q implies not P = contrapositive of the original statement. A statement and its contrapositive are logically equivalent.

Q implies P = converse of the original statement

Not P implies not Q = inverse of the original statement. The converse and inverse of an original statement are logically equivalent.

P implies Q = Not P or Q.

1. The CORRECT answer is D.
   For item I, the second statement should be "Either there is no life on Mars or we should fund NASA" in order to be logically equivalent to the first statement. For item II, the statements are converses of each other; thus, they are not equivalent.

2. The CORRECT answer is B.
   In item I, this is an example of P implies Q and Q implies P. In this case, P = the notebook is missing its cover and Q = the notebook belongs to Carter. In item II, the ordering of the words is changed, but the If P then Q is exactly the same. P = it is hot and Q = the pool is open.

3. The CORRECT answer is A.
   For item I, if nobody is without benefits, then everybody has benefits. For item II, the second equivalent statement should be "either we will not fund the program or at least 100 people will sign the petition."

4. The CORRECT answer is D.
   For item I, the first statement is an implication, whereas the second statement mentions only one part of the implication (new parts are requested) and says nothing about the other part. For item II, the first statement is equivalent to "if the operating cycle is not running, then the test cycle will run." The second statement is equivalent to "if the operating cycle is running, then the test cycle will run." So, these statements in item II are not equivalent.

5. The CORRECT answer is B.
   Since Sid did not steal a car and avoid getting caught, the only other way he could become a Crips member would be "jumped in." Choice B tells us that Sid was not "jumped in," so we conclude that he did not become a member of the Crips.

6. The CORRECT answer is D.
   Since Smith and Watson have the same number of arrests, Watson must have fewer arrests than Jones. This means that each of choices A and B is impossible. Choice C would also not reveal whether or not Watson is a Precinct 8 officer.

10 (#2)

7. The CORRECT answer is D.
Exact dollar amounts still cannot be ascertained by using any of the other choices.

8. The CORRECT answer is A.
The street sweepers never sweep on the east side of the street on Wednesday; however, they will be here at noon today. This implies that they will sweep on the west side of the street. Since the residents should move their cars before noon, we can conclude that today is Wednesday.

9. The CORRECT answer is C.
We start with W implies P, where W = warning light comes on and P = power surge. Choice C would read as P implies A, where A = air conditioning is running. Combining these statements leads to W implies A. The conclusion can be read as: Not A implies Not W, which is equivalent to W implies A.

EXAMINATION SECTION
TEST 1

DIRECTIONS: Each question or incomplete statement is followed by several suggested answers or completions. Select the one that BEST answers the question or completes the statement. *PRINT THE LETTER OF THE CORRECT ANSWER IN THE SPACE AT THE RIGHT.*

Questions 1-9.

DIRECTIONS: Questions 1 through 9 measure your ability to (1) determine whether statements from witnesses say essentially the same thing, and (2) determine the evidence need to make it reasonably certain that a particular conclusion is true.

1. Which of the following pairs of statements say essentially the same thing in two different ways?
   I. The only time the machine's red light is on is when the door is locked.
      If the machine's door is locked, the red light is on.
   II. Some gray-jacketed cables are connected to the blower.
      If a cable is connected to the blower, it must be gray-jacketed.
   The CORRECT answer is:
   A. I only   B. I and II   C. II only   D. Neither I nor II

   1.____

2. Which of the following pairs of statements say essentially the same thing in two different ways?
   I. If you live on Maple Street, your child is in the Valley District.
      If your child is in the Valley District, you must live on Maple Street.
   II. All the Smith children are brown-eyed.
      If a child is brown-eyed, it is not one of the Smith children.
   The CORRECT answer is:
   A. I only   B. I and II   C. II only   D. Neither I nor II

   2.____

3. Which of the following pairs of statements say essentially the same thing in two different ways?
   I. If it's Monday, Mrs. James will be here.
      Mrs. James is here every Monday.
   II. Most people in the Drama Club do not have stage fright, but everyone in the Drama Club wants to be noticed.
      Some people in the Drama Club have stage fright and want to be noticed.
   The CORRECT answer is:
   A. I only   B. I and II   C. II only   D. Neither I nor II

   3.____

4. Which of the following pairs of statements say essentially the same thing in two different ways?
   I. If you are older than 65, you will get a senior's discount.
   Either you will get a senior's discount, or you are not older than 65.
   II. Every cadet in Officer Johnson's class has passed the firearms safety course.
   No cadet that has failed the firearms safety course is in Officer Johnson's class.
   The CORRECT answer is:
   A. I only   B. I and II   C. II only   D. Neither I nor II

5. Summary of Evidence Collected to Date:
   Most people in the Greenlawn housing project do not have criminal records.
   Prematurely Drawn Conclusion:
   Some people in Greenlawn who have been crime victims have criminal records themselves.
   Which of the following pieces of evidence, if any, would make it *reasonably certain* that the conclusion drawn is TRUE?
   A. Some of those who live in the Greenlawn project have been arrested or convicted of "victimless" crimes.
   B. Most people in Greenlawn have been the victims of crime.
   C. Everyone in Greenlawn has been the victim of crime.
   D. None of the above

6. Summary of Evidence Collected to Date:
   Every drug dealer in the Oak Lawn neighborhood wears blue and carries a Glock.
   Prematurely Drawn Conclusion:
   A person in the Oak Lawn neighborhood who carries a Glock is a drug dealer.
   Which of the following pieces of evidence, if any, would make it *reasonably certain* that the conclusion drawn is TRUE?
   A. In the Oak Lawn neighborhood, only drug dealers wear blue.
   B. Drug dealers in Oak Lawn only carry Glocks when they're dealing drugs.
   C. In the Oak Lawn neighborhood, only drug dealers carry Glocks.
   D. None of the above

7. Summary of Evidence Collected to Date:
   I. Dr. Jones is older than Dr. Gupta.
   II. Dr. Gupta and Dr. Unruh were born on the same day.
   Prematurely Drawn Conclusion:
   Dr. Gupta does not work in the emergency room.
   Which of the following pieces of evidence, if any, would make it *reasonably certain* that the conclusion drawn is TRUE?
   A. Dr. Jones is older than Dr. Unruh.
   B. Dr. Jones works in the emergency room.
   C. Every doctor in the emergency room is older than Dr. Unruh.
   D. None of the above

8. Summary of Evidence Collected to Date:
   I. On the street, a "dose" of a certain drug contains four "drams."
   II. A person can trade three "rolls" of a drug for a "plunk."
   Prematurely Drawn Conclusion:
   A plunk is the most valuable amount of the drug on the street.
   Which of the following pieces of evidence, if any, would make it *reasonably certain* that the conclusion drawn is TRUE?
   A. A person can trade five doses for two rolls.
   B. A dram contains two rolls.
   C. A roll is larger than a dram.
   D. None of the above

9. Summary of Evidence Collected to Date:
   Sam is a good writer and editor.
   Prematurely Drawn Conclusion:
   Sam is qualified for the job.
   Which of the following pieces of evidence, if any, would make it *reasonably certain* that the conclusion drawn is TRUE?
   A. The job calls for good writing and editing skills.
   B. A person who is not a good editor could still apply for the job on the strength of his/her writing skills.
   C. If Sam applies for the job, he must be both a good writer and editor.
   D. None of the above

Questions 10-14.

DIRECTIONS: Questions 10 through 14 refer to Map #7 and measure your ability to orient yourself within a given section of town, neighborhood or particular area. Each of the questions describes a starting point and a destination. Assume that you are driving a car in the area shown on the map accompanying the questions. Use the map as a basis for the shortest way to get from one point to another without breaking the law.
On the map, a street marked by arrows, or by arrows and the words "One Way," indicates one-way travel, and should be assumed to be one-way for the entire length, even when there are breaks or jogs in the street. EXCEPTION: A street that does not have the same name over the full length.

Map #7.

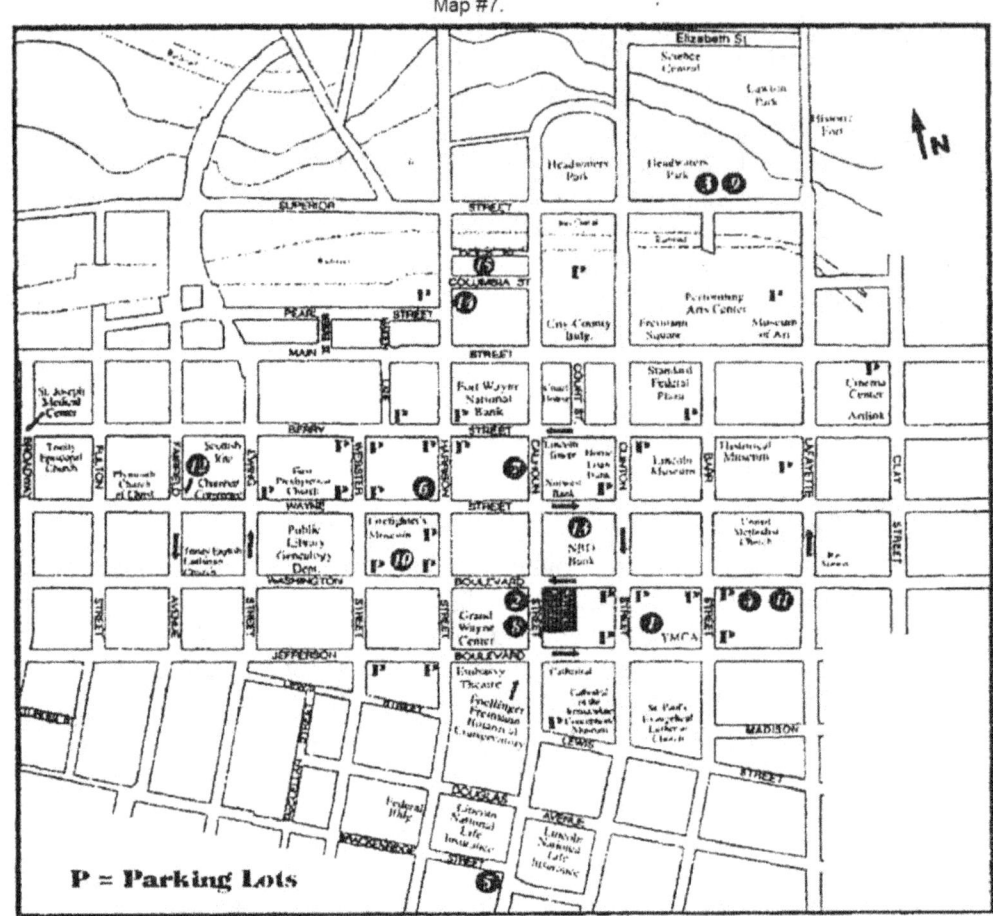

10. The SHORTEST legal way from Trinity Episcopal Church to Science Central is   10.____
    A. east on Berry, north on Clinton, east on Elizabeth
    B. east on Berry, north on Lafayette, west on Elizabeth
    C. north on Fulton, east on Main, north on Lafayette, west on Elizabeth
    D. north on Fulton, east on Main, north on Calhoun

11. The SHORTEST legal way from the Grand Wayne Center to the Museum of   11.____
    Art is
    A. north on Harrison, east on Superior, south on Lafayette
    B. east on Washington Blvd., north on Lafayette
    C. east on Jefferson Blvd., north on Clinton, east on Main
    D. east on Jefferson Blvd., north on Lafayette

12. The SHORTEST legal way from the Embassy Theatre too the City/County   12.____
    Building is
    A. west on Jefferson Blvd., north on Ewing, east on Main
    B. east on Jefferson Blvd., north on Lafayette, west on Main
    C. east on Jefferson Blvd., north on Clinton
    D. north on Harrison, east on Main

13. The SHORTEST legal way from the YMCA to the Firefighter's Museum is 13._____
    A. west on Jefferson Blvd., north on Webster
    B. north on Barr, west on Washington Blvd., north on Webster
    C. north on Barr, west on Wayne
    D. north on Barr, west on Berry, south on Webster

14. The SHORTEST legal way from the Historic Fort to Freimann Square is 14._____
    A. north on Lafayette, west on Elizabeth, south on Clinton
    B. north on Lafayette, west on Elizabeth, west/south on Calhoun, east on Main
    C. south on Lafayette, west on Main
    D. south on Lafayette, west on Superior, south on Clinton

Questions 15-19.

DIRECTIONS: Questions 15 through 19 refer to Figure #7, on the following page, and measure your ability to understand written descriptions of events. Each question presents a description of an accident or event and asks you which of the five drawings in Figure #7 BEST represents it.

In the drawings, the following symbols are used:

Moving Vehicle: ◯   Non-moving Vehicle: ▮

Pedestrian or Bicyclist: ●

The path and direction of travel of a vehicle or pedestrian is indicated by a solid line.

The path and direction of travel of each vehicle or pedestrian directly involved in a collision from the point of impact is indicated by a dotted line.

In the space at the right, print the letter of the drawing that BEST fits the descriptions written below:

15. A driver headed northeast on Cary strikes a car in the intersection and is 15._____
    diverted north, where he collides with the rear of a car that is traveling north on Park. The northbound car is knocked into the rear of another car that is traveling north ahead of it.

16. A driver headed northeast on Cary strikes a car in the intersection and is 16._____
    diverted north, where he collides head-on with a car stopped at a traffic light in the southbound lane on Park.

17. A driver headed northeast on Cary strikes a car in the intersection and is 17._____
    diverted east, where he collides head-on with a car stopped at a traffic light in the westbound lane on Roble.

18. A driver headed east on Roble collides with the left front of a car that is turning right from Knox onto Roble. The driver swerves right after the collision and collides head-on with another car headed north on Park.   18._____

19. A driver headed northeast on Cary strikes a car in the intersection and is diverted north, where he collides with the rear of a car parked on the northbound lane on Park.   19._____

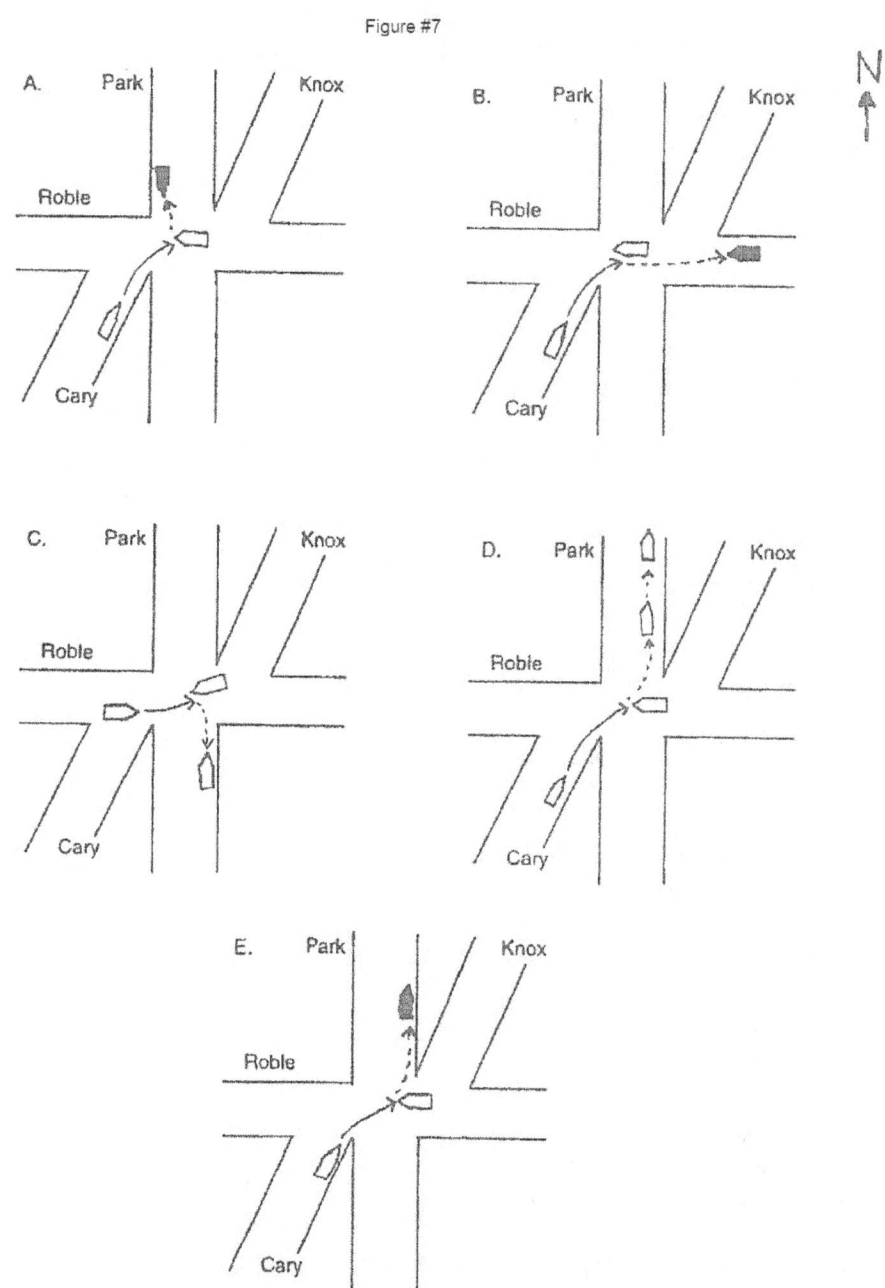

Figure #7

Questions 20-22.

DIRECTIONS: In Questions 20 through 22, choose the word or phrase CLOSEST in meaning to the word or phrase printed in capital letters.

20. JURISDICTION   20.____
    A. authority   B. decision   C. judgment   D. argument

21. PROXY   21.____
    A. neighbor   B. agent   C. enforcer   D. impostor

22. LARCENY   22.____
    A. theft   B. assault   C. deceit   D. gentleness

Questions 23-25.

DIRECTIONS: Questions 22 through 25 measure your ability to do fieldwork-related arithmetic. Each question presents a separate arithmetic problem for you to solve.

23. Mr. Long has 14 employees. He has four more male employees than female employees.   23.____
    How many female employees does he have?
    A. 4   B. 5   C. 9   D. 10

24. A box of latex gloves costs $18. A crate has 12 boxes, each of which contains 48 gloves.   24.____
    How much does a crate of latex gloves cost?
    A. $216   B. $328   C. $576   D. $864

25. In a single week, the Department of Parking collected 540 quarter, 623 dimes, and 146 nickels from its parking meters.   25.____
    What was the TOTAL revenue collected from the meters during the week?
    A. $135.00   B. $154.00   C. $204.60   D. $270.30

KEY (CORRECT ANSWERS)

1.	A		11.	D
2.	D		12.	D
3.	B		13.	B
4.	B		14.	A
5.	C		15.	D
6.	C		16.	A
7.	C		17.	B
8.	A		18.	C
9.	A		19.	E
10.	C		20.	A

21. B
22. A
23. B
24. A
25. C

SOLUTIONS (QUESTIONS 1-9)

P implies Q = original statement

Not Q implies not P = contrapositive of the original statement. A statement and its contrapositive are logically equivalent.

Q implies P = converse of the original statement.

Not P implies not Q = inverse of the original statement. The converse and inverse of an original statement are logically equivalent.

P implies Q = Not P or Q

1. CORRECT ANSWER: A
   For Item I, the equivalent of the first statement would be "If the red light is on, the door is locked." This is the converse of the second statement, so it is not equivalent to the first statement. For Item II, the first statement does not guarantee that all cables that are connected to the blower must be gray-jacketed. There may very well be other cables that are connected to the blower that are not gray-jacketed. Equally possible, some gray-jacketed cables are not necessarily connected to the blower.

2. CORRECT ANSWER: D
   For Item I, the second statement is the converse of the first statement, so it is not logically equivalent. For Item II, the equivalent of the first statement is "If a child is not brown-eyed, then it is not one of the Smith children." Thus, statement II as it stands is not equivalent to statement I.

3. CORRECT ANSWER: B
   For Item I, Mrs. James is here every Monday, so we conclude that if it is Monday, she is here. (She may be here on other days as well.) For Item II, we can conclude that there are some people in the Drama Club who do have stage fright. Since everyone in the Drama Club wants to be noticed, this would include those who have stage fright.

4. CORRECT ANSWER: B
   For Item I, these two statements represent "P implies Q" and "Not P or Q," where P = Older than 65 and Q = Get a senior discount. These are equivalent statements. For Item II, these statements are contrapositive of each other and so must be equivalent. (P = Cadet in Johnson's class and Q = Passes the safety course.)

5. CORRECT ANSWER: C
   If everyone in the housing project has been a victim of crime and most of these people do not have a criminal record, we can conclude that some of them do have a criminal record. Thus, we have the situation that some of the people who live in this housing project are both a victim of crime as well as a perpetrator of crime.

6. CORRECT ANSWER: C
This choice can be written as "In this neighborhood, if a person carries a Glock, he is a drug dealer." This would lead directly to the drawn conclusion.

7. CORRECT ANSWER: C
We know that every doctor in the emergency room is older than Dr. Unruh; it is not possible for Dr. Gupta to be working in the emergency room since he is the same age as Dr. Unruh.

8. CORRECT ANSWER: A
From statement I, a dose is worth more than a dram. If 5 doses is equal to 2 rolls, then a roll is worth more than a dose. So of these three, a roll is worth the most. Finally, statement II tells us that a plunk is worth more than a roll. This means that a plunk is worth the most among all four of these categories.

9. CORRECT ANSWER: A
Sam has the qualifications of being a good writer and editor, which is exactly what is needed for the job. Therefore, Sam is qualified for this job.

TEST 2

DIRECTIONS: Each question or incomplete statement is followed by several suggested answers or completions. Select the one that BEST answers the question or completes the statement. *PRINT THE LETTER OF THE CORRECT ANSWER IN THE SPACE AT THE RIGHT.*

Questions 1-9.

DIRECTIONS: Questions 1 through 9 measure your ability to (1) determine whether statements from witnesses say essentially the same thing, and (2) determine the evidence need to make it reasonably certain that a particular conclusion is true.

To do well on this part of the test, you do NOT have to have a working knowledge of police procedures and techniques. Nor do you have to have any more familiarity with criminals and criminal behavior than that acquired from reading newspapers, listening to radio or watching TV. To do well in this part, you must read and reason carefully.

1. Which of the following pairs of statements say essentially the same thing in two different ways?
   I. If the garbage is collected today, it is definitely Wednesday.
      The garbage is collected every Wednesday.
   II. Nobody has no answer to the question.
      Everybody has at least one answer to the question.
   The CORRECT answer is:
   A. I only   B. I and II   C. II only   D. Neither I nor II

2. Which of the following pairs of statements say essentially the same thing in two different ways?
   I. If it trains, the streets will be wet.
      If the streets are wet, it has rained.
   II. All of the Duluth Five are immune from prosecution.
      No member of the Duluth Five can be prosecuted.
   The CORRECT answer is:
   A. I only   B. I and II   C. II only   D. Neither I nor II

3. Which of the following pairs of statements say essentially the same thing in two different ways?
   I. Ms. Friar will accept her promotion if and only if she is offered a 10% raise.
      For Ms. Friar to accept her promotion, it is necessary that she be offered a 10% raise.
   II. If the hydraulic lines are flushed, it is definitely inspection day.
      The hydraulic lines are flushed only on inspection days.
   The CORRECT answer is:
   A. I only   B. I and II   C. II only   D. Neither I nor II

4. Which of the following pairs of statements say essentially the same thing in two different ways?
   I. If you are tall you will get onto the basketball team.
      Unless you are tall, you will not get onto the basketball team.
   II. That raven is black.
      If that bird is black, it's a raven.
   The CORRECT answer is:
   A. I only   B. I and II   C. II only   D. Neither I nor II

5. Summary of Evidence Collected to Date:
   Every member of the Rotary Club is retired.
   Prematurely Drawn Conclusion:
   At least some people in the planning commission are retired.
   Which of the following pieces of evidence, if any, would make it *reasonably certain* that the conclusion drawn is TRUE?
   A. Retirement is a condition for membership in the Rotary Club.
   B. Every member of the planning commission has been in the Rotary Club at one time.
   C. Every member of the Rotary Club is also on the planning commission.
   D. None of the above

6. Summary of Evidence Collected to Date:
   Some of the SWAT team snipers have poor aim.
   Prematurely Drawn Conclusion:
   The snipers on the SWAT team with the worst aim also have 20/20 vision.
   Which of the following pieces of evidence, if any, would make it *reasonably certain* that the conclusion drawn is TRUE?
   A. Some of the SWAT team snipers have 20/20 vision.
   B. Every sniper on the SWAT team has 20/20 vision.
   C. Some snipers on the SWAT team wear corrective lenses.
   D. None of the above

7. Summary of Evidence Collected to Date:
   The only time Garson hears voices is on a day when he doesn't take his medication.
   Prematurely Drawn Conclusion:
   On Fridays, Garson never hears voices.
   Which of the following pieces of evidence, if any, would make it *reasonably certain* that the conclusion drawn is TRUE?
   A. Garson is supposed to take his medication every day.
   B. Garson usually undergoes shock therapy on Fridays.
   C. Garson usually takes his medication and undergoes shock therapy on Fridays.
   D. None of the above

8. **Summary of Evidence Collected to Date:**
   Among the three maintenance workers, Frank, Lily and Jean, Frank is not the tallest.
   Prematurely Drawn Conclusion:
   Lily is the tallest.
   Which of the following pieces of evidence, if any, would make it *reasonably certain* that the conclusion drawn is TRUE?
   - A. Jean is not the tallest.
   - B. Frank is the shortest.
   - C. Jean is the shortest.
   - D. None of the above

8.____

9. **Summary of Evidence Collected to Date:**
   Doctor Lyons went to the cafeteria for lunch today and did not eat dessert.
   Prematurely Drawn Conclusion:
   The cafeteria did not serve dessert.
   Which of the following pieces of evidence, if any, would make it *reasonably certain* that the conclusion drawn is TRUE?
   - A. Dr. Lyons never eats dessert.
   - B. When the cafeteria serves dessert, Dr. Lyons always eats it.
   - C. The cafeteria rarely serves dessert when Dr. Lyons eats there.

9.____

Questions 10-14.

DIRECTIONS: Questions 10 through 14 refer to Map #8 and measure your ability to orient yourself within a given section of town, neighborhood or particular area. Each of the questions describes a starting point and a destination. Assume that you are driving a car in the area shown on the map accompanying the questions. Use the map as a basis for the shortest way to get from one point to another without breaking the law.
On the map, a street marked by arrows, or by arrows and the words "One Way," indicates one-way travel, and should be assumed to be one-way for the entire length, even when there are breaks or jogs in the street. EXCEPTION: A street that does not have the same name over the full length.

4 (#2)

Map #8

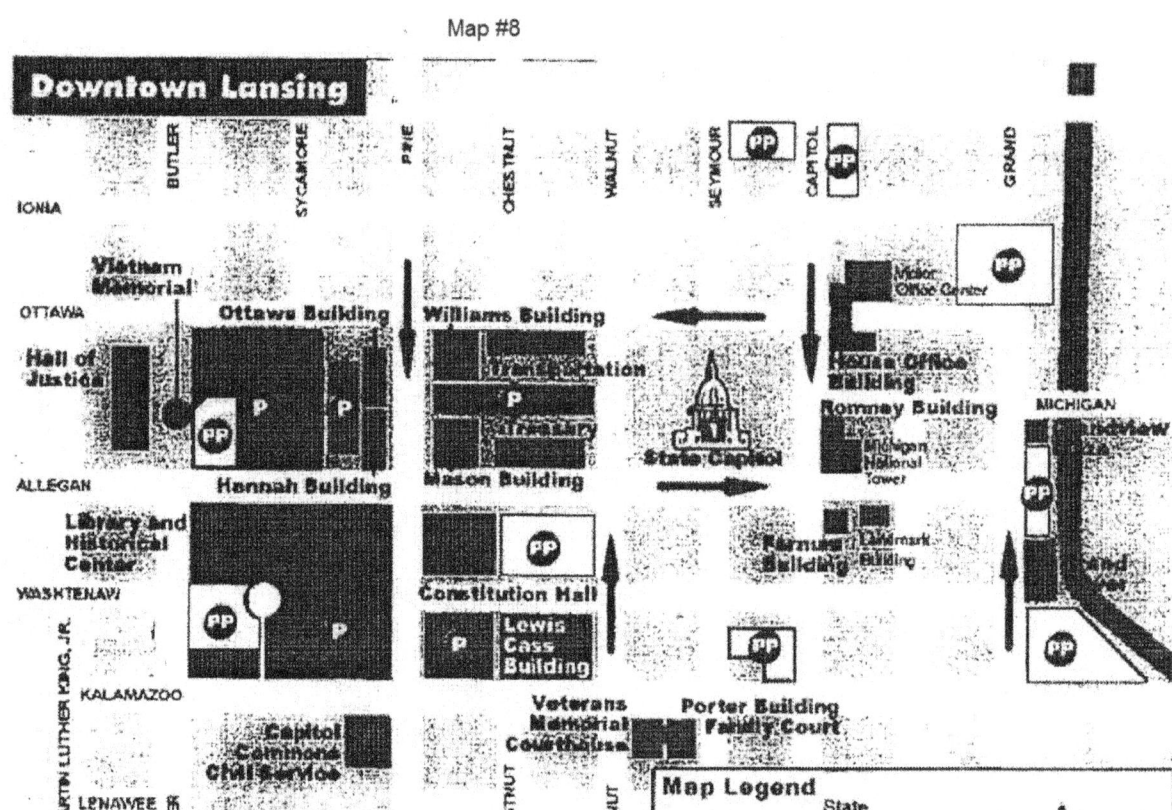

10. The SHORTEST legal way from the Library and Historical Center to Grandview Plaza is
    A. south on Butler, east on Kalamazoo, north on Grand
    B. east on Allegan, north on Grand
    C. north on Butler, east on Ionia, south on Grand
    D. north on Martin Luther King, Jr., east on Ottawa, south on Pine, east on Allegan, north on Grand

10.____

11. The SHORTEST legal way from the Victor Office Center to the Mason Building is
    A. west on Ottawa, south on Pine
    B. south on Capitol, west on Allegan, north on Pine
    C. south on Capitol, west on Washtenaw, north on Walnut, west on Allegan
    D. west on Ottawa, north on Seymour, west on Ionia, south on Pine

11.____

12. The SHORTESST legal way from the Treasury to the Hall of Justice is
    A. north on Walnut, west on Ottawa, south on Martin Luther King, Jr.
    B. west on Allegan
    C. east on Allegan, north on Grand, west on Ottawa, south on Martin Luther King. Jr.
    D. south on Walnut, west on Kalamazoo, north on Martin Luther King, Jr.

12.____

5 (#2)

13. The SHORTEST legal way from the Veterans Memorial Courthouse to the 13.____
    House Office Building is
    A. north on Walnut, east on Ottawa
    B. east on Kalamazoo, north on Capitol
    C. east on Kalamazoo, north on Grand, west on Ottawa
    D. north on Walnut, east on Allegan, north on Capitol

14. The SHORTEST legal way from Grand Tower to Constitution Hall is 14.____
    A. west on Washtenaw
    B. north on Grand, west on Allegan, south on Pine
    C. north on Grand, west on Ottaway, south on Pine
    D. south on Grand, west on Kalamazoo, north on Pine

Questions 15-19.

DIRECTIONS: Questions 15 through 19 refer to Figure #8, on the following page, and measure your ability to understand written descriptions of events. Each question presents a description of an accident or event and asks you which of the five drawings in Figure #8 BEST represents it.

In the drawings, the following symbols are used:

Moving Vehicle: ⌂   Non-moving Vehicle: ▮

Pedestrian or Bicyclist: ●

The path and direction of travel of a vehicle or pedestrian is indicated by a solid line.

The path and direction of travel of each vehicle or pedestrian directly involved in a collision from the point of impact is indicated by a dotted line.

In the space at the right, print the letter of the drawing that BEST fits the descriptions written below:

15. A driver headed west on Holly runs a red light and turns left. He sideswipes 15.____
    a car headed south in the intersection, and then flees south on Bay. The
    southbound car is diverted into the rear end of a car parked in the southbound
    lane on Bay.

16. A driver headed east on Holly runs a red light. Another driver headed south 16.____
    through the intersection slams on her brakes just in time to avoid a serious
    collision. The eastbound driver glances off the front of the southbound car and
    continues east, where he collides with a car parked in the eastbound lane on
    Holly.

17. A driver headed east on Holly runs a red light. She strikes the left front of a 17.____
    westbound car that is turning left from Holly onto Bay, and then veers left and
    strikes the rear end of a car parked in the northbound lane on Bay.

18. A driver headed north on Bay strikes the right front of a car heading south in the intersection of Bay and Holly. After the collision, the driver veers left and collides with the rear end of a car parked in the westbound lane of Holly. The southbound car veers left and collides with the rear end of a car in the eastbound lane on Holly.

18.____

19. A driver headed north on Bay strikes the left front of a car heading south in the intersection of Bay and Holly. After the collision, the driver continues north and collides with the rear end of a car parked in the northbound lane. The southbound car continues south and collides with the rear end of a car in the southbound lane.

19.____

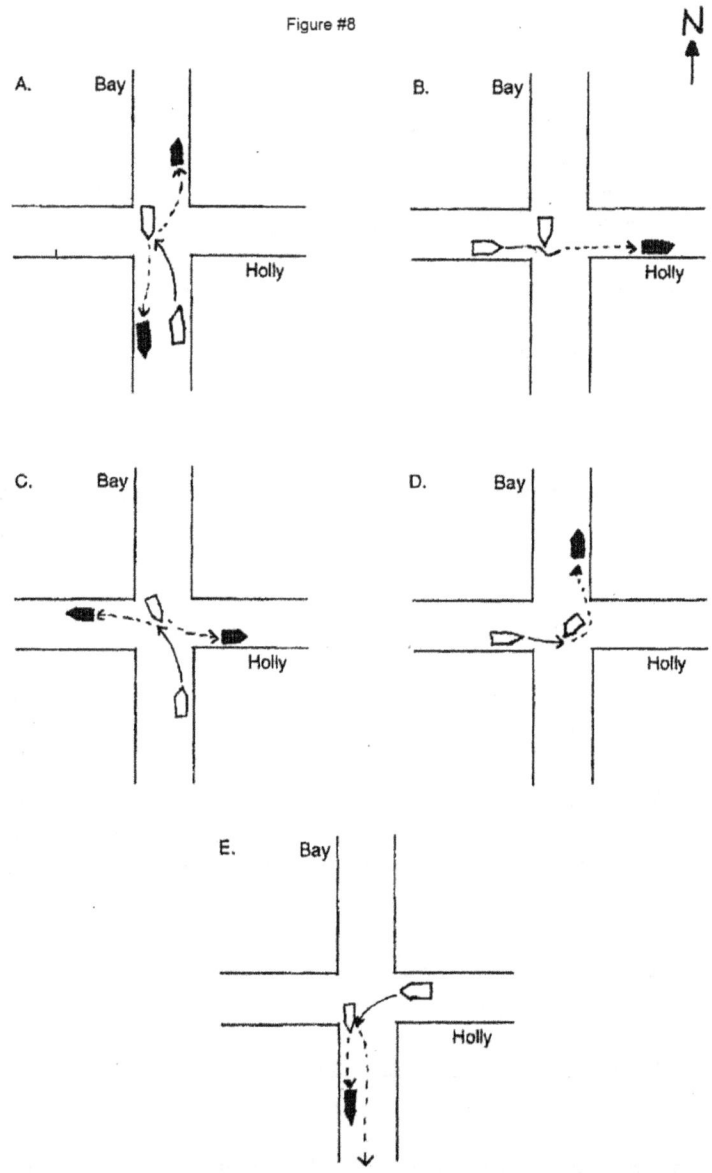

Figure #8

Questions 20-22.

DIRECTIONS: In Questions 20 through 22, choose the word or phrase CLOSEST in meaning to the word or phrase printed in capital letters.

20. LIABLE 20.____
    A. sensitive   B. dishonest   C. responsible   D. valid

21. CLAIM 21.____
    A. debt   B. period   C. denial   D. banishment

22. ADMISSIBLE 22.____
    A. false   B. conclusive   C. acceptable   D. indsputable

Questions 23-25.

DIRECTIONS: Questions 22 through 25 measure your ability to do fieldwork-related arithmetic. Each question presents a separate arithmetic problem for you to solve.

23. Three departments divide an $800 payment. Department 1 takes $270, and Department 2 takes $150 more than Department 3. 23.____
    How much does Department 2 take?
    A. $150   B. $190   C. $340   D. $490

24. Detective Smalley cleared 100 murder cases in five years. Each year he cleared six more than he cleared in the previous year. 24.____
    How many cases did he clear during the first year?
    A. 6   B. 8   C. 12   D. 18

25. The purchasing agent bought three binders for $2 each, four reams of copier paper for $3 each and five packs of black pens for $7 each. 25.____
    How much did the agent spend?
    A. $12.00   B. $25.20   C. $53.00   D. $72.00

KEY (CORRECT ANSWERS)

1.	B	11.	A
2.	C	12.	A
3.	B	13.	C
4.	D	14.	A
5.	C	15.	E
6.	B	16.	B
7.	D	17.	D
8.	A	18.	C
9.	B	19.	A
10.	B	20.	C

21. A
22. C
23. C
24. B
25. C

9 (#2)

SOLUTIONS (QUESTIONS 1-9)

P implies Q = original statement

Not Q implies not P = contrapositive of the original statement. A statement and its contrapositive are logically equivalent.

Q implies P = converse of the original statement.

Not P implies not Q = inverse of the original statement. The converse and inverse of an original statement are logically equivalent.

P implies Q = Not P or Q

1. CORRECT ANSWER: B
   For Item I, we can conclude that it is Wednesday if and only if the garbage is collected. For Item II, the phrase "nobody has no" is equivalent to everybody has at least one."

2. CORRECT ANSWER: C
   For Item I, each statement is the converse of the other. Thus, they are not equivalent. For Item II, each statement says that each member of the Duluth Five is immune from prosecution.

3. CORRECT ANSWER: B
   For Item I, accepting a promotion is a necessary and sufficient condition for receiving a 10% raise. For Item II, we have the P implies Q condition, where P = hydraulic lines are flushed and Q = it is an inspection day.

4. CORRECT ANSWER: D
   For Item I, each statement is the converse of the other (so they are not equivalent). For Item II, the first statement simply states that a particular raven is black. The second statement says that all black birds are ravens. They are not equivalent.

5. CORRECT ANSWER: C
   The two scenarios are (a) a Rotary Club member is a subset of the set of all retirees, which is a subset of all planning commission member or (b) a Rotary Club member is a subset of all planning commission members, which is a subset of all retirees.

6. CORRECT ANSWER: B
   We know that some SWAT sniper members have poor aim. If we also know that all snipers on the SWAT team also have 20/20 vision, then we conclude that any sniper (including those with the worst aim) must have 20/20 vision.

7. CORRECT ANSWER: D
   The only way that Garson will not hear voices is if he takes his medication. The premature conclusion can only be correct if he takes his medication every Friday. None of choices A, B, or C mentions this specifically.

8. CORRECT ANSWER: A
If Frank is not the tallest and Jean is not the tallest, then the conclusion that Lily is the tallest is correct. This is a reasonable conclusion, unless all three are the same height (very unlikely).

9. CORRECT ANSWER: B
We are given that Dr. Lyons went to the cafeteria for lunch and that he did not have dessert. If Dr. Lyons always eats dessert when it is served in the cafeteria, we can conclude that the cafeteria did not serve dessert.

EXAMINATION SECTION
TEST 1

DIRECTIONS: Each question or incomplete statement is followed by several suggested answers or completions. Select the one that BEST answers the question or completes the statement. *PRINT THE LETTER OF THE CORRECT ANSWER IN THE SPACE AT THE RIGHT.*

1. Agent Jenner's team took on 25 cases last year and solved 17. The ratio of unsolved cases to the number of solved cases is

   A. 17:25
   B. 8:25
   C. 17:8
   D. 8:17

2. If x is an odd number, then $x + 1$ is

   A. an even number.
   B. an odd number.
   C. divisible by x
   D. a prime number

3. Which of the following statements is logically equivalent to the one below?
   "If you work for Excorp, you are a millionaire."

   A. If you do not work for Excorp, you are not a millionaire.
   B. If you do not work for Excorp, you may be a millionaire.
   C. If you are not a millionaire, you do not work for Excorp.
   D. If you are a millionaire, you work for Excorp.

4. Of the following, which is the largest fraction?

   A. 7/8
   B. 4/5
   C. 3/4
   D. 7/9

5. A hexagon has _____ sides.

   A. 5
   B. 6
   C. 7
   D. 8

6. A rectangle is 5 inches wide and 2 inches tall. The perimeter of the rectangle is _____ inches.

   A. 7
   B. 10
   C. 14
   D. 20

7. Which of the following must contain only right angles?
    I. square
    II. rectangle
    III. parallelogram
    IV. right triangle

    A. I only
    B. I and II
    C. I, II and III
    D. I, II, III and IV

8. In the annual promotion examinations,
    1. Marcus scored higher than Franklin.
    2. Taggart scored higher than Rosewood.
    3. Rosewood scored higher than Franklin.
    4. Yarnell scored higher than Taggart.

    Which of the following pieces of information would allow all five agents to be ranked in the order of their performance on the examination?

    A. Rosewood scored higher than Marcus.
    B. Yarnell had the highest score.
    C. Marcus, scored higher than Taggart.
    D. Yarnell scored higher than Marcus.

9. Carter closed 4 cases last month. Bloom closed 3 times as many-cases as Carter. Which of these will show the total number of cases closed by Bloom?

    A. The product of 4 and 3.
    B. The quotient of 4 and 3.
    C. The difference between 12 and 4.
    D. The quotient of 12 and 3.

10. $45/9 = 12 - y$
    $y =$

    A. 6   B. 7   C. 8   D. 9

11. Agent Langley recently started work on her new job. She worked 20% more hours in her third week than she did in the second week. She worked 30% more hours during her second week than her first, and she worked 10% less during her first week than her regularly scheduled weekly hours. If Agent Langley worked 46 hours in her third week on the job, approximately what are her regularly scheduled weekly work hours?

    A. 33   B. 38   C. 40   D. 48

12. In the Niagara office, there are x men and y women. The ratio of the number of men to the total number of people in the Niagara office would be expressed

    A. $(x - y):x$ B. $x:y$ C. $x:(x+y)$ D. $(x+y):x$

13. How many, faces does a triangular prism have? 13.____

    A. 3   B. 4   C. 5   D. 6

14. The Maloneys, whose house was assessed at $100,000, paid $3000 in property taxes last year. If the Joneses paid the same rate, how much property tax did they pay on their house, assessed at $155,000? 14.____

    A. $3333   B. $4200   C. $4650   D. $5640

15. Warren invested $6,000 in AmNex stock a year ago. Today the value of Warren's investment has risen to $7,200. If Warren had invested $15,000 a year ago instead of $6000, what would his investment be worth today? 15.____

    A. $16,400 B. $18,000 C. $22,500 D. $33,000

16. The best estimate of the capacity of an ordinary drinking glass is 16.____

    A. 3 liters   B. 30 cups
    C. 300 milliliters   D. 30 fluid ounces

17. The fraction 3/5, expressed as a percent, is 17.____

    A. 30%   B. 35%   C. 60%   D. 80%

18. What is the missing number in the following sequence? 28, 31,37,?, 58 18.____

    A. 43   B. 46   C. 48   D. 49

19. Bob, Tom, Gary, and Claire all work in Alexandria. One is an administrative assistant, one a supervisor, one a detective, and one a special agent. 19.____
    1. Bob and Gary have lunch with the special agent.
    2. Claire and Tom carpool with the detective.
    3. Gary works in the same building as the administrative assistant and the detective.

    Given the information above, the detective

    A. must be Bob
    B. must be Claire
    C. must be Gary
    D. cannot be determined from the given information

20. 20 / 0.8 = 20.____

    A. 16   B. 24   C. 25   D. 27

21. A pyramid has a square base. How many edges does the pyramid have? 21.____

    A. 4   B. 6   C. 8   D. 10

22. The menu at Al's Restaurant offers 5 entrees, 4 sides, and 3 desserts. If a meal consists of an entree, a side, and a dessert, how many possible meals can be chosen from Al's menu?

    A. 25   B. 30   C. 60   D. 90

23. Agent Turco is marking off a perimeter in the shape of a regular polygon and plans to enclose it with orange tape. Which of the following pieces of information can be used to determine the total length of tape Agent Turco will need?
    I. The length of one side of the perimeter to be cordoned off
    II. The number of sides on the perimeter
    III. The distance from the center of the cordoned-off area to one side of the perimeter
    IV. The area enclosed by the perimeter

    A. I only
    B. I and II
    C. II and III
    D. I, II and IV

24. A victim's purse contains only nickels and dimes. The ratio of nickels to dimes is 3: 4. There are 28 coins in all. What is the value of the dimes?

    A. $0.80   B. $1.60   C. $2.10   D. $2.40

25. Agent Brooks is examining a crime scene. Given the marks on the road, she concludes that a tire, on the truck that left tracks at the scene, traveled 82 inches in one full rotation. The approximate diameter of the tire that left the track is _____ inches.

    A. 13   B. 26   C. 32   D. 41

26. 2/4 ? 2/3
    In order to denote the relationship between the two numbers above, which of the following mathematical symbols belongs between the two numbers above

    A. =   B. <   C. ≥   D. >

27. Aaron is twice as old as Bob. Five years ago, Aaron was 3 times as old as Bob. How old is Bob now?

    A. 8   B. 10   C. 15   D. 20

28. Detective Sturgis is directing a search over a rectangular grid that has sides of lengths x and y. He wants to cover the rectangle by using the smallest number of identical square search zones possible. The zones are to be placed adjacent to each other and are not to be exceed the area of the rectangle. The side length of each zone would be represented by the

    A. largest number that can divide both x and y
    B. smallest number that is divisible by both x and y
    C. difference between x and y
    D. remainder of $x \div y$

29. At 3:00, the hands of a round analog clock are at a _____° angle to each other 29._____

   A. 45
   B. 90
   C. 180
   D. 240

30. The county planning commission must decide how to use a 240-acre parcel of land. The commission sets aside 24 acres for watershed protection and an additional 88 acres for recreation. How many acres of land are set aside for watershed protection and recreation? 30._____

   A. 64
   B. 88
   C. 112
   D. 128

31. Which of the following always has four sides that are each equal in measure? 31._____
   I. square
   II. rectangle
   III. parallelogram
   IV. rhombus

   A. I only
   B. I and II
   C. I and IV
   D. I, II and III

32. Mr. Alexis is younger than 50 years of age. His age is a multiple of 3, 5, and 6. Mr. Alexis's age 32._____

   A. is 15
   B. is 30
   C. is 40
   D. can't be determined from the given information

33. On Friday morning the temperature was 78°F. By noon it had gone up 5°F, and by sundown it had gone down another 2°F. What was the temperature at sundown? 33._____

   A. 71°F
   B. 75°F
   C. 81°F
   D. 83°F

34. Of the following, the best estimate of the weight of a commercial delivery truck is 34._____

   A. 300 ounces
   B. 3000 grams
   C. 3000 pounds
   D. 300 tons

35. Each day that Scranton is late, he earns 5 demerits. Scranton has been late on each of the last 8 days. How many demerits did Scranton earn during that period?

   A. 15
   B. 20
   C. 40
   D. 85

36. Smith, Taylor and Long solved a total of 56 cases during the last year. Smith solved 4 more cases than Taylor, and Long solved twice as many cases as Taylor. Which of the following is a reasonable conclusion?

   A. Taylor solved exactly half the total cases.
   B. Smith and long solved an equal number of cases.
   C. Long solved the most cases.
   D. Smith solved the least number of cases.

37. Rectangle Q is 6 inches wide and 4 inches tall. Rectangle R is 5 inches wide and 3 inches tall. The perimeter of rectangle Q is _____ inches longer than the perimeter of rectangle R.

   A. 1
   B. 2
   C. 3
   D. 4

38. Agent Stuckey cordons off a crime scene, outlining a square whose area is about 125 square yards. Which of the following measures, in yards, would be closest to the length of one side of this square?

   A. 9.5
   B. 10
   C. 11
   D. 13

39. A binar is worth four sepetas. You can trade 3 hirseths for a jelet. You can trade 5 binars for 2 hirseths.
    Which is most valuable?

   A. Binar
   B. Sepeta
   C. Jelet
   D. It cannot be determined from the information given

40. Harkin and Laws are in business together. They have agreed to split the profits in a ratio of 60% to 40%. The total profits are $80,000. The largest share of the profits equals.

   A. $36,000
   B. $40,000
   C. $48,000
   D. $60,000

41. In the five-story Cl]aremont Building, each floor is occupied by the offices of a professional.
    1. Ms. Garrity's story is above Mr. Ishmael's.
    2. Ms. Johnson's story is between Ms. Garrity's and Dr. Hortense's.
    3. Ms. Penelope's story is between Dr. Hortense's and Mr. Ishmael's.
    4. Ms. Johnson is on the fourth story.

    Who occupies the second story?

    A. Ms. Penelope
    B. Ms. Garrity
    C. Mr. Ishmael
    D. It cannot be determined from the given information.

42. Agent Grimley can complete an average of 18 pages of paperwork during his 30-minute lunch break. He has 380 pages of paperwork outstanding. How many hours will it take him to complete this amount?

    A. 9
    B. 11
    C. 13
    D. 15

43. Which of the following fractions is the smallest?

    A. 7/32
    B. 7/8
    C. 9/16
    D. 3/4

44. Which of the following figures has only one pair of parallel lines?

    A. Trapezoid
    B. Hexagon
    C. Parallelogram
    D. Rhombus

45. The only time Henry and June patrol together is on an evening when Henry is assigned to the 12th precinct. Henry is assigned to the 12th precinct on Tuesdays and Thursdays. Based only on the information above, which of the following must be true?

    A. Henry and June usually patrol on Thursday.
    B. Henry and June would not be patrolling together if Henry were not assigned to the 12th precinct.
    C. Henry and June never patrol on Friday or Saturday.
    D. Henry and June patrol at least eight times a month.

46. When 123,456 is divided by 12, the remainder is

    A. 0
    B. 18
    C. 144
    D. 10,288

47. Agent Speer uses his cell phone to interview a potential witness. The first minute of the call costs $1.23, and each additional minute costs 89 cents. The total cost of the call is $15.47. If x is used to represent the total of minutes talked, which of the following equations can be used to solve the problem?

    A. 1.23 + 0.89(x-1)= 15.47
    B. (1.23 + 0.89)(x-1)= 15.47
    C. (1.23 + 0.89)x= 15.47
    D. 1.23 + 0.89=15.47

48. Ms. Stanislaus is paid on commission. She receives 6% of the total real estate sales that are conducted by her office. Last year, Ms. Stanislaus made $420,000. How much real estate did her office sell?

    A. $2.52 million
    B. $6.6 million
    C. $7 million
    D. $8.3 million

49. An agent interviews 26 people in an apartment building. She discovers that 14 knew the victim; 10 knew the suspect; and 5 were at home when the crime was committed. Four knew both the victim and the suspect; three knew the victim and were at home when the crime was committed; and one knew the suspect and was at home when the crime was committed. None of the 26 people knows both the victim and the suspect, and was at home when the crime was committed.
    How many of the people interviewed know neither the victim nor the suspect, and were not at home when the crime was committed?

    A. 3
    B. 5
    C. 8
    D. The answer cannot be determined from the given information.

50. Mrs. Nesbit drove 150 miles in 2 hours and 30 minutes. Which of the following formulas will give Mrs. Nesbit's average speed in miles per hour?

    A. 150 multiplied by 2.5
    B. 150 multiplied by 150
    C. 150 divided by 2.5
    D. 150 divided by 2.3

KEY (CORRECT ANSWERS)

1. D	11. A	21. C	31. C	41. A
2. A	12. C	22. C	32. B	42. B
3. C	13. C	23. B	33. C	43. A
4. A	14. C	24. B	34. C	44. A
5. B	15. B	25. B	35. C	45. C
6. C	16. C	26. B	36. C	46. A
7. B	17. C	27. B	37. D	47. A
8. A	18. B	28. A	38. C	48. C
9. A	19. A	29. B	39. C	49. B
10. B	20. C	30. C	40. C	50. C

TEST 2

DIRECTIONS: Each question or incomplete statement is followed by several suggested answers or completions. Select the one that BEST answers the question or completes the statement. *PRINT THE LETTER OF THE CORRECT ANSWER IN THE SPACE AT THE RIGHT.*

1. What is the missing number in the following series of numbers? 1, 4, 9, ?, 25   1.____

   A. 12
   B. 15
   C. 16
   D. 18

2. During the course of her investigations, Agent Stearns drove these distances in one week: 102.4, 187.6, 89.4, and 206.0 miles.   2.____
   To calculate how many gallons of gas Agent Stearns consumed during this week, it is necessary to know the

   A. cost per gallon of gasoline
   B. number of trips made by Agent Stearns during the week
   C. average number of miles per gallon of gasoline for Agent Stearns' car
   D. average speed, in miles per hour, driven by Agent Stearns during these trips

3. Which of these is NOT equal to 2.87?   3.____

   A. 2.87 ÷ 0.1
   B. 7.2 - 4.33
   C. 287%
   D. 0.0287 x 100

4. The best estimate of 281 x 324 is   4.____

   A. 900
   B. 9,000
   C. 90,000
   D. 900,000

5. In the annual promotion examinations,   5.____
   1. Marcus scored higher than Franklin.
   2. Taggart scored higher than Rosewood.
   3. Rosewood scored higher than Franklin.
   4. Yarnell scored higher than Taggart.

   Based only on the information above, which of the following must be true?

   A. Franklin had the lowest score.
   B. Rosewood scored higher than Yarnell.
   C. Taggart scored higher than Marcus.
   D. Taggart had the highest score.

6. Gerald patrols from 2:45 pm to 5:15 pm each day. How long does he patrol each day?   6.____

   A. 1 hour and 45 minutes   B. 2 hours and 30 minutes
   C. 3 hours and 15 minutes   D. 3 hours and 30 minutes

186

7. On the first day of the year, the Granada Division opened 4 cases. After 9 days, they had opened 36 cases. After 15 days, they had opened 60 cases. At this rate, how many cases will the Granada Division have opened after 21 days?

    A. 66
    B. 84
    C. 111
    D. 120

7._____

8. Of the 400 people who work at Galatea Inc., 90 work in administrative or supervisory positions and 230 work in production. Exactly 20 people occupy positions that are classified as both production and administrative/ supervisory in nature. What is the probability that an employee of Galatea is in a position that is classified as *neither* administrative/ supervisory or production?

    A. 1/4
    B. 1/14
    C. 3/20
    D. 3/4

8._____

9. An officer is trying to arrange four men in a lineup. Each man is wearing a different colored shirt. The man in the blue shirt—the main suspect—cannot be placed on either end of the row because he begins to shout disruptively. He insists on being placed immediately next to the man in the white shirt. How many different ways can the officer arrange the men in the lineup?

    A. 1
    B. 2
    C. 4
    D. 6

9._____

10. 8/16 ? 16/32
    In order to denote the relationship between the two numbers above, which of the following mathematical symbols belongs between the two numbers above?

    A. =
    B. <
    C. ≥
    D. #

10._____

11. 30 Alkan employees walk to work; 90 take public transportation; 30 ride their bicycles; and 150 drive or carpool. What percentage of these employees ride their bicycles to work?

    A. 5
    B. 10
    C. 25
    D. 30

11._____

12. The comptroller of the Hudson office plans to buy 3 dozen forms for each person in the office. 28 people work in the office. If the forms cost $4.80 per package, what other information is needed to calculate the amount the comptroller will need to spend on forms?   12._____

    A. The number of tasks that will require forms.
    B. The number of forms per package.
    C. The number of forms in a dozen.
    D. The number of people who will use the forms.

13. How many edges does a cube have?   13._____

    A. 6
    B. 8
    C. 10
    D. 12

14. To be eligible for membership in the Black Berets, a person must be able to either swim underwater for at least a minute, or complete the Iron Man triathlon in less than eleven hours. Jennifer has run the Iron Man several times and her best time was 12:45:42. Which of the following statements must be true?   14._____

    A. No member of the Black Berets is capable of running the Iron Man triathlon in less than eleven hours.
    B. Jenniter can become a member of the Black Berets by swimming underwater for at least one minute.
    C. Some members of the Black Berets have never swum underwater for more than a minute.
    D. Jennifer cannot become a member of the Black Berets.

15. Hearns has a roll of crime scene tape 12 yards long. He needs 40 feet of tape to close off the crime scene. To find out if he has enough tape, Hearns should first   15._____

    A. multiply 40 by 3
    B. multiply 40 by 12
    C. multiply 12 by 12
    D. multiply 12 by 3

16. On Sunday, Frank builds a deck for his family in the back yard. He plans to use 30 redwood boards, and will need 12 screws for each board. To be safe, Frank buys 30 more screws than he needs. How many screws did he buy?   16._____

    A. 300
    B. 360
    C. 390
    D. 400

17. Of the following fractions, which is smallest?   17._____

    A. 8/15
    B. 5/6
    C. 11/20
    D. 7/12

18. 4% of 650 is   18.____
    A. 24
    B. 26
    C. 72
    D. 260

19. There are two sets of numbers, A and B. Each number in set A is related in the same way   19.____
    to the number below it in B:
    A: 1, 3, 5
    B: 6, 18, 30
    If the number in A is 9, one way to find out its corresponding number in set B is to

    A. add 9 and 2
    B. subtract 2 from 9
    C. add 9 and 6
    D. multiply 9 by 6

20. A random canvass on Boxelder Street shows that 42 out of 80 people have parked ille-   20.____
    gally in the past month. If 2,000 people live in the Boxelder neighborhood, what is the
    best prediction of the total number who will park illegally in a month?

    A. 120
    B. 280
    C. 420
    D. 1000

21. An employer administers random drug screenings to 40 out of every 100 employees. Of   21.____
    those employees screened, one out of every 20 tests positive for some kind of controlled
    substance. Based on the testing process described above, which of the following is true?

    A. Every batch of 100 employees will have about two employees who have a con-
       trolled substance in their systems.
    B. To achieve a representative sample, the employer should test a larger number of
       employees.
    C. About 2 percent of the employees screened test positive for a controlled substance
    D. About 5 percent of the employees screened test positive for a controlled substance

22. 4 tickets to the Murphy Follies cost $9.00. How much will a dozen tickets cost?   22.____

    A. $16.00
    B. $27.00
    C. $36.00
    D. $42.50

23. Officials estimate that of 320,000 people who attended the parade left behind 40 tons of   23.____
    garbage. A ton equals 2000 pounds. How many pounds of garbage did each person
    leave behind at the parade?

    A. 1/4
    B. 1/2
    C. 1 1/4
    D. 2 1/3

24. Agents Harris and Nieman discover a cardboard box filled with an illicit substance The box is 60 inches long, 18 inches wide, and 24 inches high. What is the approximate volume of the substance, in cubic feet?

   A. 7.5   B. 15   C. 19   D. 24

25. Agent Lopez does not work if Agent Hingis is not working.
    Given the above conclusion, which of the following would also be true?
    I. Agent Hingis may work when Agent Lopez is not working.
    II. Agent Lopez and Agent Hingis may work at the same time.
    III. Agent Lopez may work when Agent Hingis does not.

    A. I only   B. II only   C. II and III   D. I and II
    E. I and III

26. Of the following, which is the largest?

    A. 1/4   B. 3/5   C. 9/20   D. 1/2

27. Larry, Moe and Curly each have some coins in a pants pocket.
    1. Larry has three quarters and two dimes.
    2. Moe has two dimes and a nickel.
    3. Curly has three nickels and a penny.
    To be guaranteed of receiving at least one coin of each denomination, and without looking at any of the coins before accepting them, you must

    A. take four coins each from Larry and Curly
    B. take all five of Larry's coins, all four of Moe's, and three of Curly's
    C. take three coins from Larry, two from Moe, and three from Curly
    D. take four coins from Larry, two from Moe, and two from Curly

28. Greeley drove 1500 miles in 25 hours, and Earnhart drove 900 miles in 15 hours. Greeley's average speed was

    A. equal to Earnhart's average speed.
    B. 3 mph faster than Earnhart's.
    C. 5 mph faster than Earnhart's.
    D. 2 mph slower than Earnhart's.

29. *Agent Horner runs an eight-minute mile. At this average rate, how long will it take him to run a 26-mile marathon?*
    Which of the following problems can be solved using the same mathematical operations that would be used to solve the problem above?

    A. A clerk has to place a shipment of 480 cans on 22 shelves. If each shelf will contain the same number of cans, how many cans will the clerk place on each shelf?
    B. The average laptop computer weighs 3.4 pounds. What would be the weight of a shipment of 1500 laptop computers?
    C. Agent Dickey ran 26 miles in 320 minutes. On average, how long did it take her to run a mile?
    D. A bag of sand weighs 80 pounds. How many sandbags can be made from 5 tons of sand?

30. Together, two items of evidence, *x* and *y,* weigh one pound. If item * weighs 11 ounces, item *y* weighs

    A. 5 ounces
    B. 9 ounces
    C. 13 ounces
    D. 1.2 pounds

31. Agent Farkus interviews 30 people at the airport. 16 speak French; 16 speak Spanish, and 11 speak English. 5 speak both French and English, and of these, only 3 speak Spanish as well. 5 speak only English, and 8 speak only Spanish. How many of the 30 speak only French?

    A. 3
    B. 7
    C. 9
    D. The answer cannot be determined from the given information.

32. A crime was committed in a classroom that contained 2 teachers, 3 aides, 4 girls and 5 boys. Assuming that one of these committed the crime, what is the probability that the crime was committed by either an aide or a girl?

    A. 1/14
    B. 3/14
    C. 7/14
    D. 9/14

33. Which of the following has two pairs of opposite sides that are parallel?
    I. square
    II. rectangle
    III. rhombus
    IV. parallelogram

    A. I only
    B. I and II
    C. I, II and IV
    D. I, II, III and IV

34. Throughout the day, a preset traffic light functions as follows: it is red for 30 seconds, yellow for 15 seconds, and green for 45 seconds. What is the chance that the light is green at any given moment?

    A. 30%
    B. 45%
    C. 50%
    D. 65%

35. After an employee embezzled 20% of its Sunday donations, St Leo's Church had $2000 left. The original amount of the donations was

    A. $500
    B. $1500
    C. $2500
    D. $3000

36. Michaels estimates that he spends a third of his travel budget on gasoline and a quarter of it on meals. If his travel budget is $300 for the month, how much is left over for other expenses?   36._____

    A. $114.29
    B. $125.00
    C. $144.00
    D. $175.50

37. 56/7 = x - 5   37._____
    x =

    A. 13
    B. 14
    C. 15
    D. 16

38. What is the missing number in the following sequence? 79,67,55,43, ?   38._____

    A. 34
    B. 32
    C. 31
    D. 30

39. Officer Hardy confiscated 8 cases of beer from the party. There are 24 cans in a case. How many cans of beer did Officer Hardy confiscate?   39._____

    A. 160
    B. 172
    C. 184
    D. 192

40. Which of the following numbers is a multiple of 12 and a factor of 2400?   40._____

    A. 48
    B. 36
    C. 8
    D. 3

41. According to the state bureau of crime statistics, the number of burglary victims was 184% larger this year than it was in the previous year. In other words, the number of burglary victims   41._____

    A. almost tripled
    B. almost doubled
    C. almost quadrupled
    D. more than tripled

42. 7 is _____ % of 140.

    A. .5
    B. 1.5
    C. 5
    D. 12

43. 4 + x/6 = 6
    x=

    A. 2
    B. 12
    C. 16
    D. 10

44. A store is advertising a sale in which all merchandise is priced at 30% off the original price. If an item from the store originally cost x dollars, who much will it cost during the sale?

    A. 3x
    B. x - .3
    C. 1.3 x
    D. .7x

45. What is the rule for the following sequence of numbers? 18 , 25 ,32 , 39 ,46

    A. Each number in the sequence is 7 more than the previous number.
    B. Each number in the sequence is 8 more than the previous number.
    C. Each number in the sequence is 11 more than the previous number.
    D. Each number in the sequence is 13 more than the previous number.

46. Two numbers relate to each other in the ratio 3:5. Added together, the numbers equal 80. The smallest of the two numbers is

    A. 15
    B. 25
    C. 30
    D. 50

47. Which of the following statements is logically equivalent to the one below?
    "The *Agassiz* will launch if it does not rain."

    A. If it does not rain, the Agassiz will not launch.
    B. If the Agassiz did not launch, it did not rain.
    C. If it rains, the Agassiz may launch.
    D. If it rains, the Agassiz will not launch.

48. Which two consecutive, positive whole numbers have a product equal to 1122?

    A. 36 and 37
    B. 33 and 34
    C. 22 and 51
    D. 11 and 102

49. Increasing a number by 4 1/2% is equivalent to multiplying it by 49.___

    A. .045
    B. .45
    C. 1.045
    D. 1.45

50. Gerald's wage of $ 10 per hour is increased by 5%. If Gerald now works 8 hours, what will he be paid? 50.___

    A. $82.50
    B. $84.00
    C. $85.00
    D. $88.50

KEY (CORRECT ANSWERS)

1. C	11. B	21. D	31. B	41. A
2. C	12. B	22. B	32. C	42. C
3. A	13. D	23. A	33. D	43. B
4. C	14. B	24. B	34. C	44. D
5. A	15. D	25. D	35. C	45. A
6. B	16. C	26. B	36. B	46. C
7. B	17. A	27. A	37. A	47. D
8. A	18. B	28. A	38. C	48. B
9. C	19. D	29. B	39. D	49. C
10. A	20. D	30. A	40. A	50. B

INTERPRETING STATISTICAL DATA GRAPHS, CHARTS AND TABLES
EXAMINATION SECTION
TEST 1

DIRECTIONS: Each question or incomplete statement is followed by several suggested answers or completions. Select the one that BEST answers the question or completes the statement. *PRINT THE LETTER OF THE CORRECT ANSWER IN THE SPACE AT THE RIGHT.*

Questions 1-4.

DIRECTIONS: Questions 1 through 4 are to be answered SOLELY on the basis of the following table.

STOLEN AND RECOVERED PROPERTY IN COMMUNITY X
2018-2019

Type of Property	Value of Property Stolen 2018	Value of Property Stolen 2019	Value of Property Recovered 2018	Value of Property Recovered 2019
Currency	$264,925	$204,534	$10,579	$13,527
Jewelry	165,317	106,885	20,913	20,756
Furs	10,007	24,028	105	1,620
Clothing	62,265	49,219	4,322 7	15,821
Automobiles	740,719	606,062	36,701	558,442
Miscellaneous	356,901	351,064	62,077	103,117
TOTAL	$1,600,134	$1,341,792	$834,697	$713,283

1. Of the following types of property, the one which shows the HIGHEST ratio of *value of property recovered* to *value of property stolen* is

   A. clothing for 2018
   B. currency for 2018
   C. jewelry for 2019
   D. miscellaneous for 2019

   1.____

2. Of the types of property which show a decrease from 2018 to 2019 in the value of property stolen, the one which shows the GREATEST percentage decrease in the value of the property recovered is

   A. automobiles
   B. currency
   C. furs
   D. jewelry

   2.____

3. According to the above table, the total value of currency and jewelry stolen in 2019, as compared to 2018, decreased APPROXIMATELY by

   A. 3%   B. 20%   C. 28%   D. 38%

   3.____

195

4. According to the above table, the TOTAL value of all types of property recovered was 4._____
   A. a slightly lower percentage of the value of property stolen for 2018 than for 2019
   B. less for the year 2018 than the value of any individual type of property recovered for the year 2019
   C. approximately 60% of the value of all property stolen in 2018 and approximately 70% in 2019
   D. greater for the year 2019 than the value of any individual type of property recovered for the year 2018

KEY (CORRECT ANSWERS)

1. D
2. A
3. C
4. A

TEST 2

Questions 1-6.

DIRECTIONS: Questions 1 through 6 are to be answered SOLELY on the basis of the information supplied in the chart below.

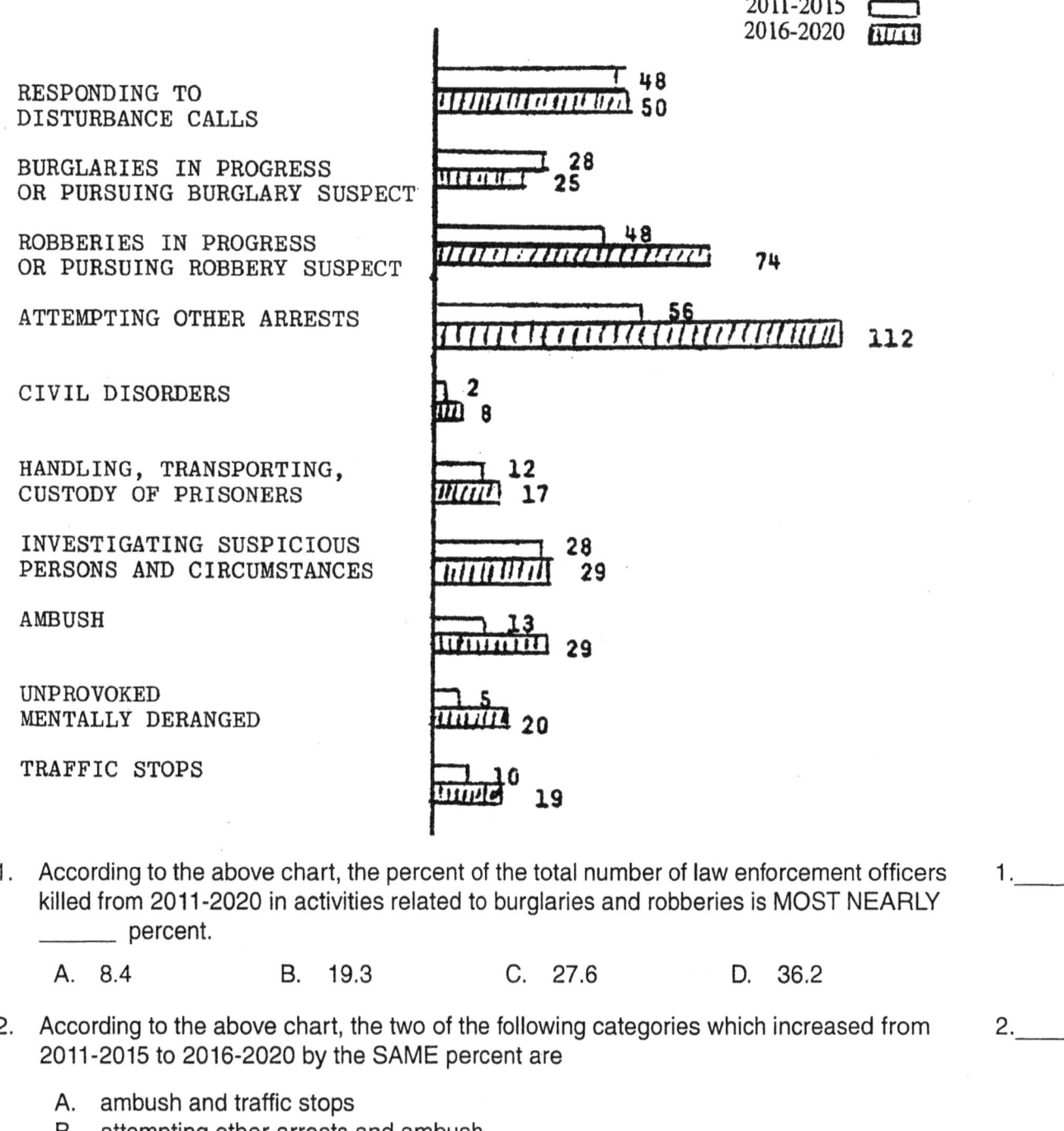

LAW ENFORCEMENT OFFICERS KILLED
(By Type of Activity)
2011-2020

2011-2015
2016-2020

RESPONDING TO DISTURBANCE CALLS — 48 / 50
BURGLARIES IN PROGRESS OR PURSUING BURGLARY SUSPECT — 28 / 25
ROBBERIES IN PROGRESS OR PURSUING ROBBERY SUSPECT — 48 / 74
ATTEMPTING OTHER ARRESTS — 56 / 112
CIVIL DISORDERS — 2 / 8
HANDLING, TRANSPORTING, CUSTODY OF PRISONERS — 12 / 17
INVESTIGATING SUSPICIOUS PERSONS AND CIRCUMSTANCES — 28 / 29
AMBUSH — 13 / 29
UNPROVOKED MENTALLY DERANGED — 5 / 20
TRAFFIC STOPS — 10 / 19

1. According to the above chart, the percent of the total number of law enforcement officers killed from 2011-2020 in activities related to burglaries and robberies is MOST NEARLY _____ percent.

   A. 8.4   B. 19.3   C. 27.6   D. 36.2

2. According to the above chart, the two of the following categories which increased from 2011-2015 to 2016-2020 by the SAME percent are

   A. ambush and traffic stops
   B. attempting other arrests and ambush

197

2 (#2)

C. civil disorders and unprovoked mentally deranged
D. response to disturbance calls and investigating suspicious persons and circumstances

3. According to the above chart, the percentage increase in law enforcement officers killed from the 2011-2015 period to the 2016-2020 period is MOST NEARLY _____ percent.

   A. 34   B. 53   C. 65   D. 100

3._____

4. According to the above chart, in which one of the following activities did the number of law enforcement officers killed increase by 100 percent?

   A. Ambush
   B. Attempting other arrests
   C. Robberies in progress or pursuing robbery suspect
   D. Traffic stops

4._____

5. According to the above chart, the two of the following activities during which the total number of law enforcement officers killed from 2011 to 2020 was the SAME are

   A. burglaries in progress or pursuing burglary suspect and investigating suspicious persons and circumstances
   B. handling, transporting, custody of prisoners and traffic stops
   C. investigating suspicious persons and circumstances and ambush
   D. responding to disturbance calls and robberies in progress or pursuing robbery suspect

5._____

6. According to the categories in the above chart, the one of the following statements which can be made about law enforcement officers killed from 2011 to 2015 is that

   A. the number of law enforcement officers killed during civil disorders equals one-sixth of the number killed responding to disturbance calls
   B. the number of law enforcement officers killed during robberies in progress or pursuing robbery suspect equals 25 percent of the number killed while handling or transporting prisoners
   C. the number of law enforcement officers killed during traffic stops equals one-half the number killed for unprovoked reasons or by the mentally deranged
   D. twice as many law enforcement officers were killed attempting other arrests as were killed during burglaries in progress or pursuing burglary suspect

6._____

KEY (CORRECT ANSWERS)

1. C
2. C
3. B
4. B
5. B
6. D

TEST 3

Questions 1-6.

DIRECTIONS: Questions 1 through 6 are to be answered SOLELY on the basis of the graph below.

YEARLY INCIDENCE OF MAJOR CRIMES FOR COMMUNITY Z
2017-2019

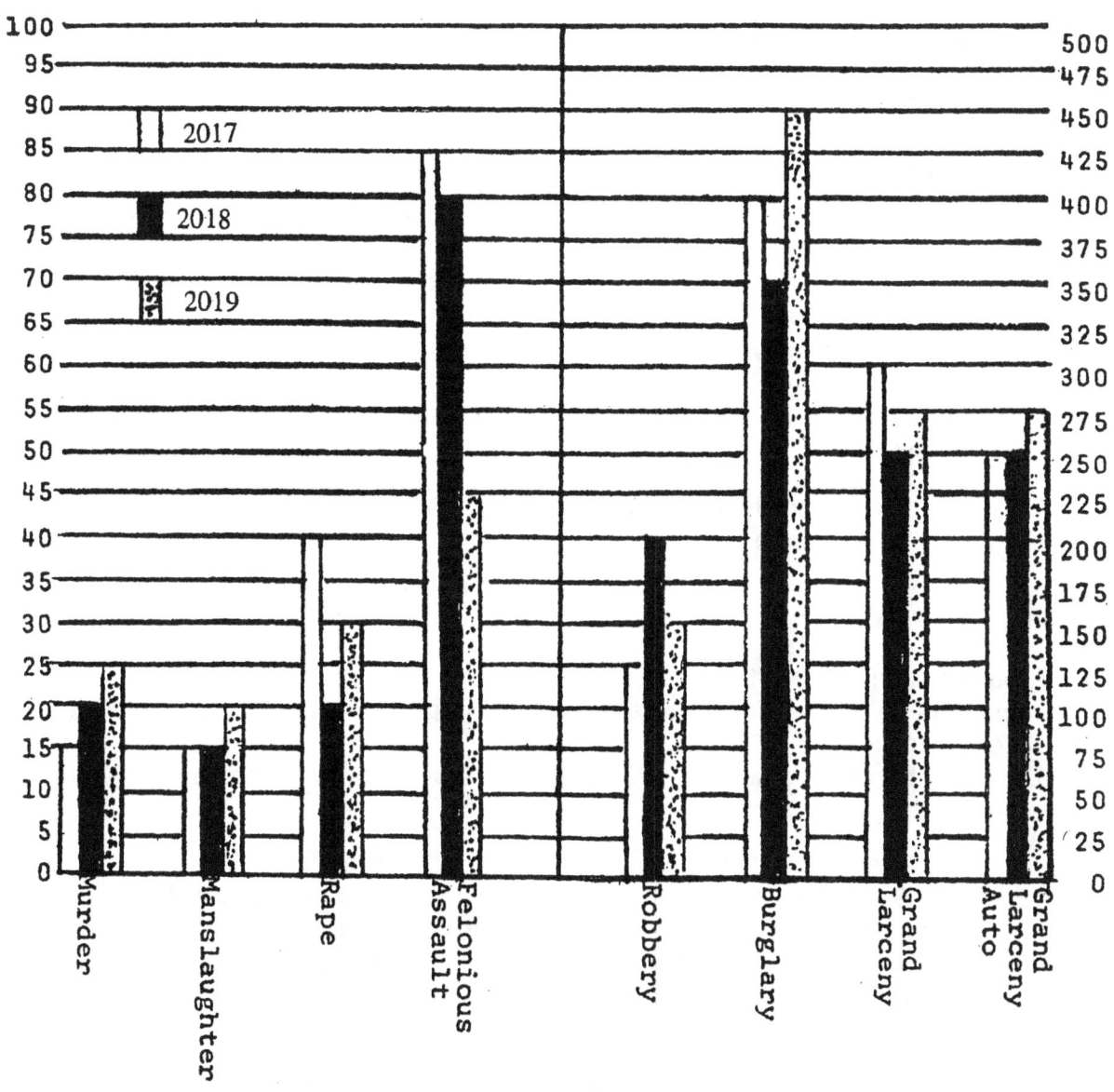

1. Of the following crimes, the one for which the 2019 figure was GREATER than the average of the previous two years was

   A. grand larceny
   B. manslaughter
   C. rape
   D. robbery

   1._____

2. If the incidence of burglary in 2020 were to increase over 2019 by the same number as it increased in 2019 over 2018, then the average for this crime for the four-year period from 2017 through 2020 would be MOST NEARLY

   A. 100   B. 400   C. 415   D. 440

   2._____

3. The above graph indicates that the percentage INCREASE in grand larceny auto over the previous year was

   A. greater in 2019 than in 2018
   B. greater in 2018 than in 2019
   C. greater in 2019 than in 2017
   D. the same in both 2018 and 2019

   3._____

4. The one of the following which cannot be determined because there is not enough information in the above graph to do so is the

   A. percentage of *Crimes Against Property* for the three-year period which were committed in 2017
   B. percentage of *Crimes Against the Person* for the three-year period which were murders committed in 2018
   C. percentage of *Major Crimes* for the three-year period which were committed in the first six months of 2018
   D. major crimes which were following a pattern of continuing yearly increases for the three-year period

   4._____

5. According to this graph, the ratio of *Crimes Against Property* to *Crimes Against the Person* for 2019, as compared to the ratio for 2018, is

   A. increasing
   B. decreasing
   C. about the same
   D. cannot be determined

   5._____

6. Assume that it is desired to present information from the above graph to the public in a form most likely to gain their cooperation in a special police effort to reduce the incidence of grand larceny auto.
   The one of the following which is MOST likely to result in such cooperation is a public statement that

   A. in 2019, approximately .75 of an automobile was stolen every day
   B. in 2019, one automobile was stolen, on the average, about, 32 hours hours
   C. the number of automobiles stolen per year will increase from year to year
   D. there were more crimes of grand larceny auto than crimes of robbery committed during the past three years

   6._____

KEY (CORRECT ANSWERS)

1. B	4. C
2. D	5. A
3. B	6. B

TEST 4

Questions 1-7.

DIRECTIONS: Questions 1 through 7 are to be answered SOLELY on the basis of the information contained in the following tables and chart.

TABLE 1

Number of Murders by Region, United States: 2014 and 2015

Region	Year	
	2014	2015
Northeastern States	2,521	2,849
North Central States	3,427	3,697
Southern States	6,577	7,055
Western States	2,062	2,211

Number in each case for given year and region represents total number (100%) of murders in that region for that year.

TABLE 2

Murder by Circumstance, U.S. - 2015
(Percent distribution by category)

Region	Total	Spouse Killing spouse	Parent Killing child	Other family killings	Romantic triangle and lovers' quarrels	Other arguments	Known Felony type	Suspected felony type
Northeastern States	100.0	9.6	3.7	6.1	7.9	38.4	25.4	8.9
North Central States	100.0	11.3	3.0	8.9	5.0	39.5	22.4	9.9
Southern States	100.0	13.8	2.2	8.8	8.4	46.0	13.9	6.9
Western States	100.0	12.5	4.9	7.0	6.4	32.2	28.0	9.0

CHART 1
Murder by Type of Weapon Used, U.S. - 2015
(Percent Distribution)

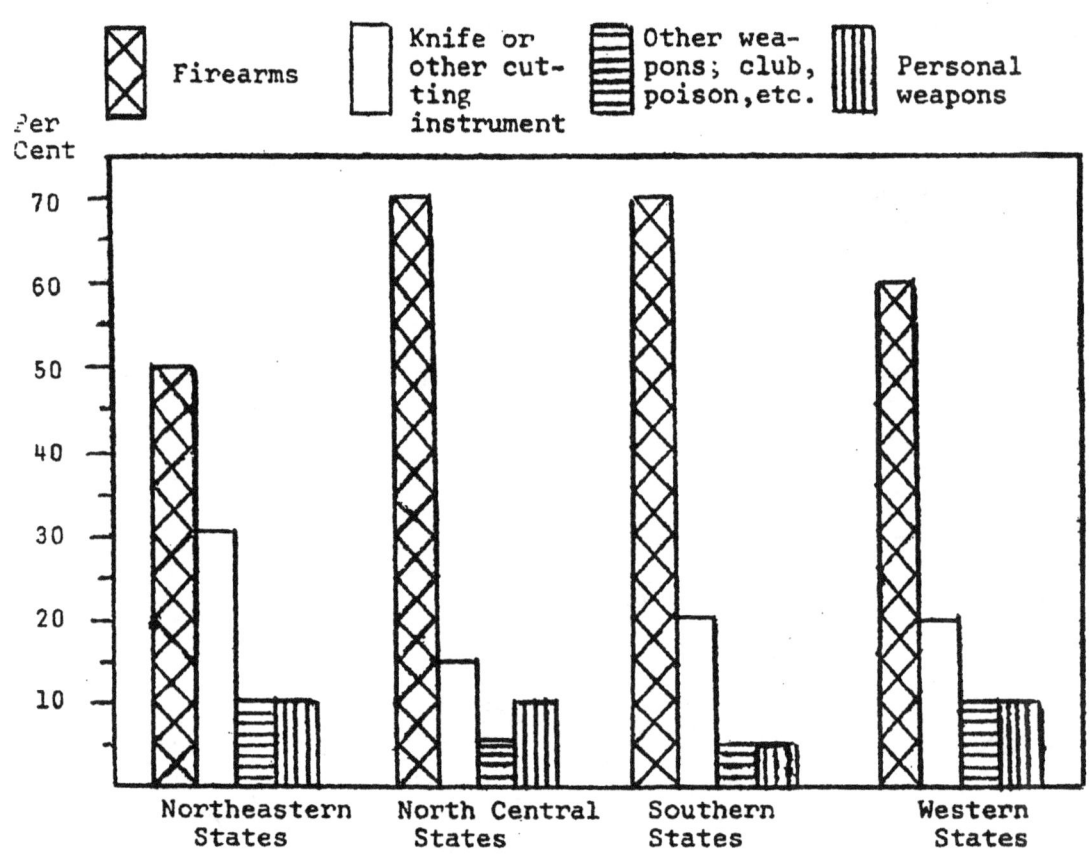

1. The number of persons murdered by firearms in the Western States in 2015 was MOST NEARLY

   A. 220   B. 445   C. 1235   D. 1325

2. In 2015, the number of murders in the category *Parent killing child* was GREATEST in the _____ States.

   A. Northeastern   B. North Central
   C. Southern   D. Western

3. The difference between the number of persons murdered with firearms and the number of persons murdered with other weapons (club, poison, etc.) in the North Central States in 2015 is MOST NEARLY

   A. 2200   B. 2400   C. 2600   D. 2800

4. In 2014, the ratio of the number of murders in the Western States to the total number of murders in the U.S. was MOST NEARLY

   A. 1 to 4   B. 1 to 5   C. 1 to 7   D. 1 to 9

5. The total number of murders in the U.S. in the category of *Romantic triangles and lovers' quarrels* in 2015 was MOST NEARLY

   A. 850   B. 950   C. 1050   D. 1150

6. Which of the following represents the GREATEST number of murders in 2015? Persons murdered by

   A. firearms in the Western States
   B. knives or other cutting instruments in the Southern States
   C. knives or other cutting instruments and persons murdered by other weapons (club, poison, etc.) in the Northeastern States
   D. knives or other cutting instruments, persons murdered by other weapons (club, poison, etc.) and persons murdered by personal weapons in the North Central States

7. From 2014 to 2015, the total number of murders increased by the GREATEST percentage in the _____ States.

   A. Northeastern   B. North Central
   C. Southern   D. Western

KEY (CORRECT ANSWERS)

1. D
2. C
3. B
4. C
5. D
6. B
7. A

TEST 5

Questions 1-5.

DIRECTIONS: Questions 1 through 5 are to be answered SOLELY on the basis of the following.

DISTRIBUTION OF CITIZENS' RESPONSES TO STATEMENTS
CONCERNING SHERIFFS' ARRESTS
(Number of citizens responding = 1171)

	CATEGORIES				
	(A) Strongly Agree	(B) Agree	(C) Disagree	(D) Strongly Disagree	(E) Don't Know
I. Sheriffs act improperly in arresting defendants, even when these persons are rude and ill-mannered	12%	37%	36%	9%	6%
II. Sheriffs frequently use more force than necessary when making arrests	9%	19%	46%	19%	7%
III. Any defendant who insults or physically abuses a sheriff has no complaint if he is sternly handled in return	13%	44%	32%	7%	4%

1. The total percentage of responses to Statement III OTHER THAN *Strongly Agree* and *Disagree* is

    A. 45%   B. 46%   C. 55%   D. 59%

2. The number of *Disagree* responses to Statement II is MOST NEARLY

    A. 71   B. 114   C. 539   D. 820

3. Assume that for Statement II the (B) percentage of responses were doubled and the (A) percentage increased one and a half times.
If the (D) and (E) percentages remained the same, the (C) percentage would then MOST NEARLY be

   A. 23% B. 26% C. 39% D. 52%

4. The total number of *Don't Know* responses is MOST NEARLY

   A. 17
   B. 188
   C. 200
   D. a figure which cannot be determined from the table

5. If the percentage of Disagree responses to Statement III were 35% less, the resulting percentage would MOST NEARLY be

   A. 11% B. 14% C. 15% D. 21%

KEY (CORRECT ANSWERS)

1. C
2. C
3. A
4. C
5. D

TEST 6

Questions 1-3.

DIRECTIONS: Questions 1 through 3 are to be answered SOLELY on the basis of the statistical report given below.

The following is a statistical report of the activities of the bureau during the current year as compared with the previous year.

	Current Year	Previous Year
Memoranda of law prepared	68	83
Legal matters forwarded to Corporation Counsel	122	144
Letters requesting legal information	756	807
Letters requesting departmental records	139	111
Matters for publication	17	26
Court appearances of members of bureau	4,678	4,621
Conferences	94	103
Lectures at Police Academy	30	33
Reports on proposed legislation	194	255
Deciphering of codes	79	27
Expert testimony	31	16
Notices to court witnesses	55	81
Briefs prepared	22	18
Court papers prepared	258	

1. According to the report, the percentage of bills prepared and sponsored by the Legal Bureau which were passed by the State Legislature and sent to the Governor for approval was APPROXIMATELY

    A. 3.1%
    B. 2.6%
    C. .5%
    D. not capable of determination from the data given

2. According to the statistical report, the activity showing the GREATEST percentage of *decrease* in the current year as compared with the previous year was

    A. matters for publication
    B. reports on proposed legislation

206

C. notices to court witnesses
  D. memoranda of law prepared

3. According to the statistical report, the activity showing the GREATEST percentage of *increase* in the current year as compared with the previous year was

   A. court appearances of members of the bureau
   B. giving expert testimony
   C. deciphering of codes
   D. letters requesting departmental records

KEY (CORRECT ANSWERS)

1. D
2. A
3. C

TEST 7

Questions 1-5.

DIRECTIONS: Questions 1 through 5 are to be answered SOLELY on the basis of the information contained in Tables I and II that appear below and on the following page.

TABLE I
NUMBER OF ARRESTS FOR VARIOUS CRIMES AND DISPOSITION

OFFENSES	TOTAL ARRESTED	INVESTIGATED AND RELEASED	HELD FOR PROSECUTION	GUILTY AS CHARGED	GUILTY OF LESSER OFFENSES	DISPOSITION OTHER THAN CONVICTION
Murder	48	10	38	12	9	17
Rape	41	10	31	8	3	20
Aggravated assault	241	106	135	36	32	67
Robbery	351	177	174	98	35	41
Burglary	890	371	519	322	88	109
Larceny	1,665	466 78	1,199	929	58	212
Auto theft	464		386	278	46	62
TOTAL	3,700	1,218	2,482	1,683	271	528

TABLE II

ARRESTS FOR LARCENY - PERCENTAGE OF SUCH ARRESTS BY AGE AND SEX

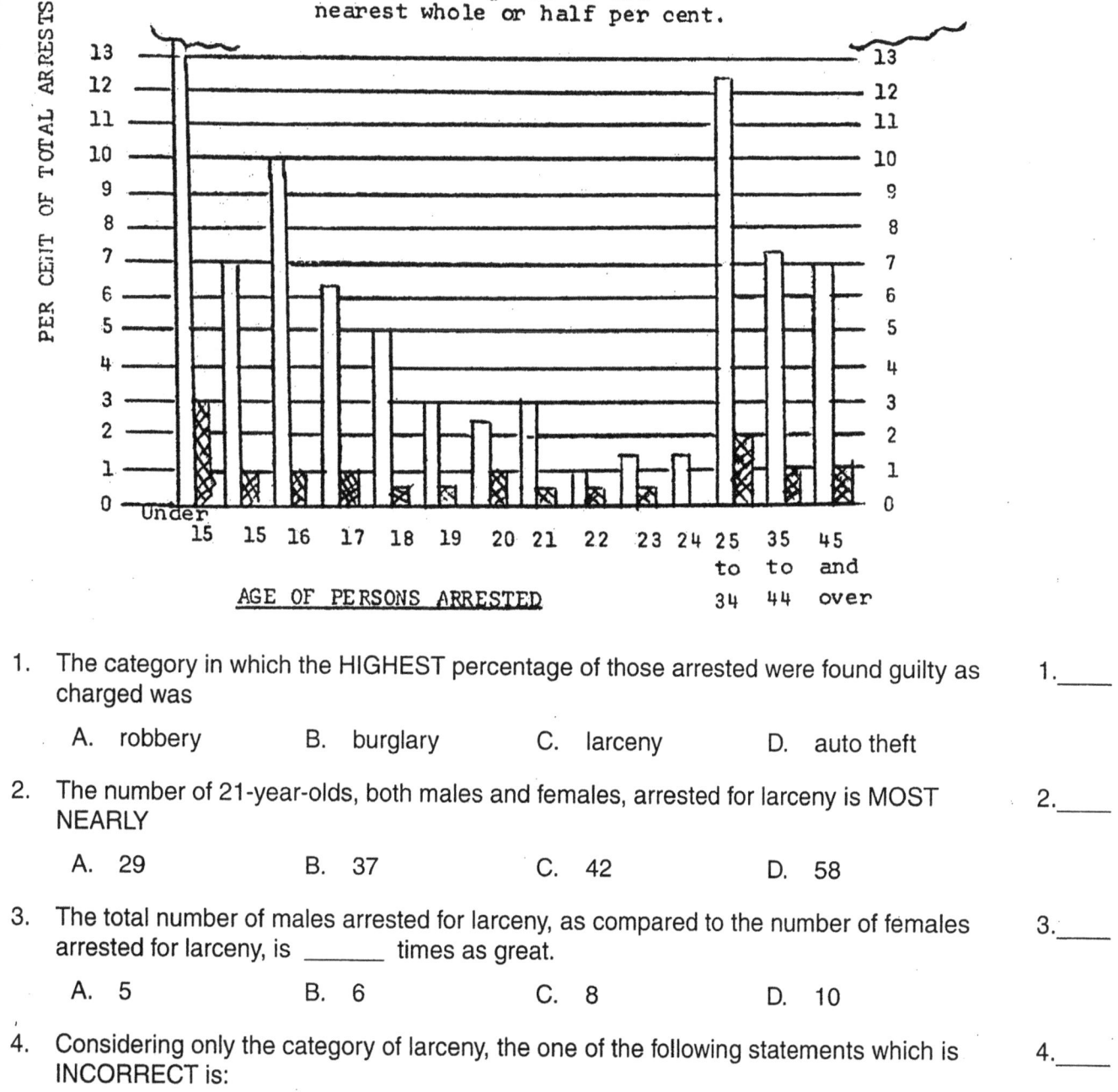

1. The category in which the HIGHEST percentage of those arrested were found guilty as charged was

    A. robbery　　B. burglary　　C. larceny　　D. auto theft

2. The number of 21-year-olds, both males and females, arrested for larceny is MOST NEARLY

    A. 29　　B. 37　　C. 42　　D. 58

3. The total number of males arrested for larceny, as compared to the number of females arrested for larceny, is _____ times as great.

    A. 5　　B. 6　　C. 8　　D. 10

4. Considering only the category of larceny, the one of the following statements which is INCORRECT is:

    A. The percentage of 25-year-old males arrested cannot be determined
    B. Twice as many 16-year-old males were arrested as 18-year-old males

C. The percentage of 16-year-old males arrested was twice as high as the percentage of 18-year-old males
D. Persons 19 years of age and younger accounted for exactly half of the total arrests for larceny

5. The one of the following which is the MOST accurate statement with respect to the disposition of arrests in each category is that in

   A. no category was the number investigated and released greater than half the number arrested
   B. no category was the number investigated and released less than one-fifth of those arrested
   C. only two categories was the number found guilty of lesser offense greater than one-tenth of those arrested
   D. only one category was the number found guilty as charged less than one-fourth of those arrested

KEY (CORRECT ANSWERS)

1. D
2. D
3. B
4. D
5. C

TEST 8

Questions 1-5.

DIRECTIONS: Questions 1 through 5 are to be answered SOLELY on the basis of the table below.

VALUE OF PROPERTY STOLEN - 2017 AND 2018
LARCENY

Category	2017		2018	
	Number of Offenses	Value of Stolen Property	Number of Offense	Value of Stolen Property
Pocket-picking	20	$1,950	10	$ 950
Purse-snatching	175	5,750	20	12,500
Shoplifting	155	7,950	225	17,350
Automobile thefts	1,040	127,050	860	108,000
Thefts of auto accessories	1,135	34,950	970	24,400
Bicycle thefts	355	8,250	240	6,350
All other thefts	1,375	187,150	1,300	153,150

1. Of the total number of larcenies reported for 2017, automobile thefts accounted for MOST NEARLY

    A. 5% B. 15% C. 25% D. 50%

2. The LARGEST percentage decrease in the value of the stolen property from 2017 to 2018 was in the category of

    A. pocket-picking
    B. automobile thefts
    C. thefts of automobile accessories
    D. bicycle thefts

3. In 2018, the average amount of each theft was LOWEST for the category of

    A. pocket-picking
    B. purse-snatching
    C. shoplifting
    D. thefts of auto accessories

4. The category which had the LARGEST numerical reduction in the number of offenses from 2017 to 2018 was

    A. pocket-picking
    B. automobile thefts
    C. thefts of auto accessories
    D. bicycle thefts

5. When the categories are ranked for each year according to the number of offenses committed in each category (largest number to rank first), the number of categories which will have the SAME rank in 2017 as in 2018 is

A. 3   B. 4   C. 5   D. 6

KEY (CORRECT ANSWERS)

1. C
2. A
3. D
4. B
5. C

TEST 9

Questions 1-5.

DIRECTIONS: Questions 1 through 5 are to be answered SOLELY on the basis of the graphs below.

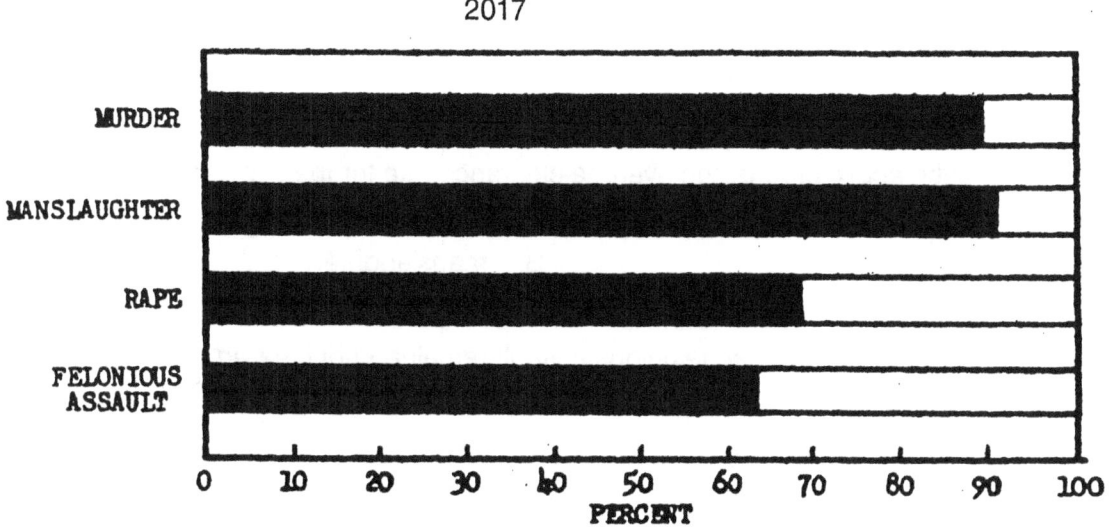

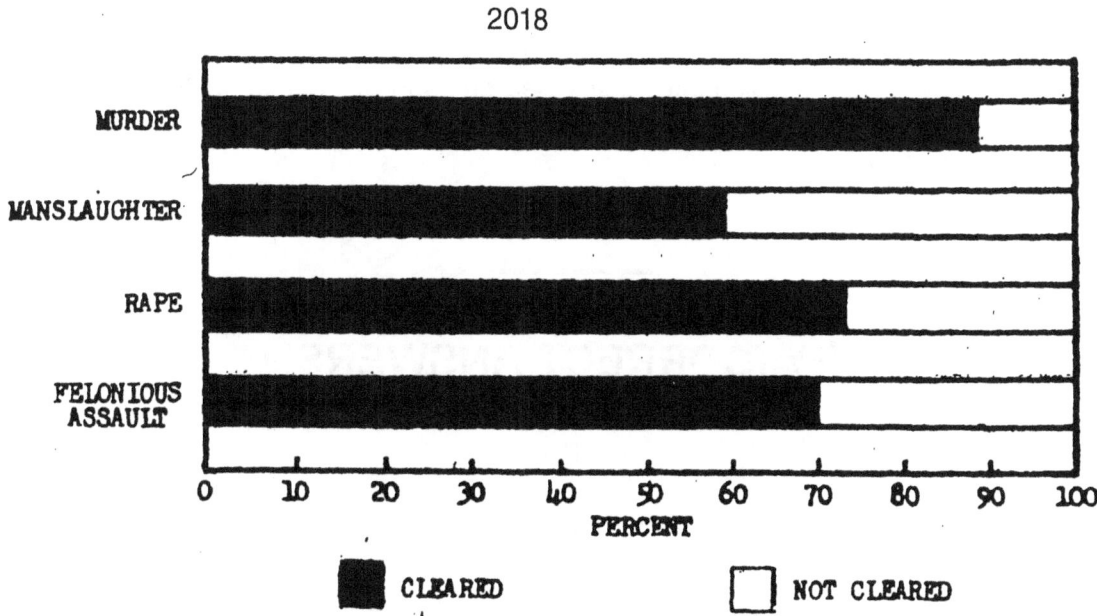

NOTE: The clearance rate is defined as the percentage of reported cases which were closed by the police through arrests or other means.

1. According to the above graphs, the AVERAGE clearance rate for all four crimes for 2018   1.____

   A. was greater than in 2017
   B. was less than in 2017

C. was the same as in 2017
D. cannot properly be compared to the 2017 figures

2. According to the above graphs, the crimes which did NOT show an increasing clearance rate from 2017 to 2018 were

   A. manslaughter and murder
   B. rape and felonious assault
   C. manslaughter and felonious assault
   D. rape and murder

2.____

3. According to the above graphs, the average clearance rate for the two-year period 2017-2018 was SMALLEST for the crime of

   A. murder
   C. rape
   B. manslaughter
   D. felonious assault

3.____

4. If, in 2018, 63 cases of reported felonious assault remained *not cleared,* then the total number of felonious assault cases reported that year was MOST NEARLY

   A. 90   B. 150   C. 210   D. 900

4.____

5. In comparing the graphs for 2017 and 2018, it would be MOST accurate to state that

   A. it is not possible to compare the total number of crimes cleared in 2017 with the total number cleared in 2018
   B. the total number of crimes reported in 2017 is greater than the number in 2018
   C. there were fewer manslaughter cases cleared during 2017 than in 2018
   D. there were more rape cases cleared during 2018 than manslaughter cases cleared in the same year

5.____

KEY (CORRECT ANSWERS)

1. B
2. A
3. D
4. C
5. A

TEST 10

Questions 1-5.

DIRECTIONS: Questions 1 through 5 are to be answered SOLELY on the basis of the following chart.

	FATAL HIGHWAY ACCIDENTS					
	Drivers Over 18 Years of Age			Drivers 18 Years of Age And Under		
2018	Auto	Other Vehicles	Total	Auto	Other Vehicles	Total
January	43	0	43	4	0	4
February	52	0	52	10	0	10
March	36	0	36	8	0	8
April	50	0	50	17	0	17
May	40	2	42	5	0	5
June	26	0	26	8	0	8
July	29	0	29	6	0	6
August	29	1	30	3	0	3
September	36	0	36	4	0	4
October	45	1	46	2	1	3
November	54	1	55	3	0	3
December	66	1	67	3	0	6
TOTALS	506	6	512	76	1	77

1. The average number of fatal auto accidents per month during 2018 involving drivers older than eighteen was MOST NEARLY

    A. 42   B. 43   C. 44   D. 45

2. The TOTAL number of fatal highway accidents during 2018 was

    A. 506   B. 512   C. 582   D. 589

3. The month during which the LOWEST number of fatal highway accidents occurred was

    A. March   B. June   C. July   D. August

4. Of the total number of fatal highway accidents during 2018 involving drivers older than eighteen, the percentage of accidents which took place during December is MOST NEARLY

   A. 10   B. 13   C. 16   D. 19

   4.____

5. The GREATEST percentage drop in fatal highway accidents occurred from

   A. February to March
   B. April to May
   C. June to July
   D. July to Augus

   5.____

KEY (CORRECT ANSWERS)

1. A
2. D
3. D
4. B
5. B